Labyrinths of Language

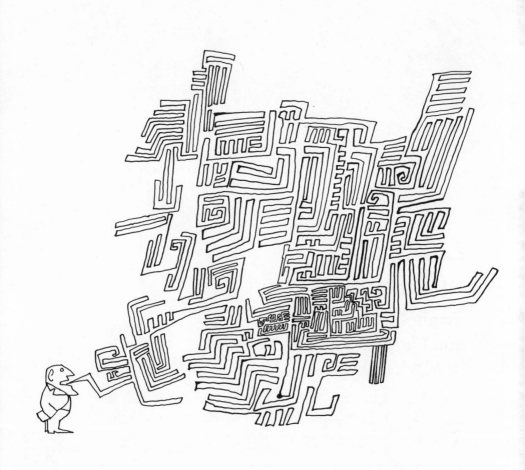

Labyrinths
of Language

Symbolic Landscape
and Narrative Design
in Modern Fiction

Wendy B. Faris

The Johns Hopkins University Press

BALTIMORE AND LONDON

©1988 The Johns Hopkins University Press
Printed in the United States of America

The Johns Hopkins University Press,
701 West 40th Street, Baltimore, Maryland 21211
The Johns Hopkins Press Ltd., London

The paper used in this publication meets the minimum requirements of American National Standard for Information Sciences—Permanence of Paper for Printed Library Materials, ANSI Z39.48-1984.

The frontispiece is from *Labyrinths,* © 1960 Saul Steinberg. Used by permission of the Wendy Weil Agency.

The poem "The Labyrinth" is from Jorge Luis Borges, *Selected Poems: 1923–1967.* Edited by Norman Thomas di Giovanni. Copyright 1968 by Emecé Editores S.A. and Norman Thomas di Giovanni. Reprinted by arrangement with Delacorte Press/Seymour Lawrence.

The poem "Labyrinth" is from Jorge Luis Borges, *In Praise of Darkness.* Translated by Norman Thomas di Giovanni. Copyright © 1969, 1970, 1971, 1972, 1973, 1974 by Emecé Editores S.A. and Norman Thomas di Giovanni. Reprinted by permission of the publisher, E. P. Dutton, a division of NAL Penguin Inc.

Library of Congress Cataloging-in-Publication Data

Faris, Wendy B.
  Labyrinths of language : symbolic landscape and narrative design
in modern fiction / Wendy B. Faris.
    p. cm.
  Bibliography: p.
  Includes index.
  ISBN 0-8018-3676-x (alk. paper)
    1. Fiction—20th century—History and criticism.   2. Labyrinths in
literature.   3. Symbolism in literature.   4. Narration (Rhetoric)
I. Title.
PN3503.F37 1988
809'.915—dc19   88-3026
                                                                            CIP

To the monster

Contents

Acknowledgments

MANY THANKS FOR ASSISTANCE OF ALL KINDS TO Bobby, Nancy, and Robert Bush, Bernard Benstock, Jean Bruneau, Mary Ann Caws, Avrom Fleishman, Roberto González Echevarría, Albert Guerard, Herbert Lindenberger, Judith McDowell, Octavio Paz, Richard Ratzan, Wendy Steiner, Robert Torrance, Victor Vitanza, Lynn Worsham, and several anonymous readers. Special thanks to Professor Harry Levin, who encouraged me right from the start, and to Steven Walker, Janet Walker, and Lois Zamora, who read the manuscript and gave me many helpful suggestions. Special, special thanks to Dave Faris for his guiding mind and sharp eye. I am also grateful to the National Endowment for the Humanities, which awarded me a fellowship to finish this book and to the Fulbright Commission under whose auspices I began it long ago in Paris.

Labyrinths of Language

1 / Introduction: Why Labyrinths?

Beware the dreadful Minotaur
That dwells within the Maze.
The monster feasts on human gore
And bones of those he slays;
Then softly through the labyrinth creep
And rouse him not to strife.
Take one short peep, prepare to leap
And run to save your life!

This English ballad projects the fear associated with the ancient myth of the labyrinth into the context of a children's game.[1] The unexpected conjunction helps to explain the persistence of the labyrinth as a compelling and versatile literary image.[2] The labyrinth pattern suggests play and terror; it expresses both our control over our environment and our bewilderment within it; it represents orderly disorder, the systematic creation of a mystery more powerful than the creator, who may subsequently become lost in it. Because the labyrinth encompasses these opposing forces—order and confusion, reason and passion, playfulness and fear—it can symbolize their combination in a work of art as well as their presence in the exterior world.

1

The labyrinth as it informs recent literature constantly reveals its cultural roots. The nature of the image causes it (in Bachelard's terms) to create echoes backwards in time.[3] According to Georges Matoré, an "image often retains, in its profoundest depths, the traces of its original values, and we could apply to it what we have said elsewhere of the word: the image remembers. It is at once potential and nostalgia."[4] To study such an image thus represents an alertness "to the historical sedimentation of the language which we use."[5] Therefore, in the following discussions I will often register such linguistic sedimentation by evoking past resonances of the labyrinth as they resonate in modern texts. In the case of the labyrinth, both nostalgia and potential derive substantial nourishment from nonliterary traditions; the literary figure of the labyrinth develops in close conjunction with its counterparts in the visual arts, so that it often mediates conceptually between symbolic and iconic modes of representation.

Most importantly, the spatial modeling of several twentieth-century fictions verbally activates in specifically labyrinthine prose the iconic potential of the ancient visual sign; in doing this, those fictions implicitly propose the labyrinth as a model for the complex processes of living, writing, and reading in the modern urban world. This means that Stendhal's image of the mirror carried along the roadway as a description of realistic fiction has found a significant counterpart in the image of the labyrinth as an analogue for modern and contemporary narrative.[6] Indeed, even though the recent fictions I will analyze here propose the labyrinthine model of narrative structure more explicitly than ever before, thereby suggesting that it constitutes a distinctive sign of writing, reading, and thinking in our era, at the same time they implicitly extend its referential dimension, presenting it as a paradigm for all literary discourse. For the most part, I will leave that extension for others to explore, although in focusing on the specifically modern aspects of the labyrinth, I will keep these broader metafictional implications in mind. That recent critical discourse frequently adopts the labyrinth as a metaphor for fiction confirms but does not explain its importance as a persistent figure of modern thought. Peter Brooks, for example, in his study of plotting recognizes the capacity of the labyrinth to symbolize all storytelling, suggesting that Borges's "garden of forking paths" can "stand as a final paradigm of plot."[7] After recognizing the appropriateness of the metaphor, it is still profitable to ask, *Why a labyrinth?* Why not a forest, a sea, a prism? It is this question of why especially a labyrinth that I hope to answer here. And as I have suggested, it seems the question of why often entails the question of whence.

Verbal Ambiguities

The development of the labyrinth from visual icon to verbal image is especially important in a study of its literary manifestations, for in removing the clear definition of an actual labyrinthine path, it allows several ambiguities to coexist.[8] The most important of these is the capacity of the labyrinth as a literary symbol to draw on two different visual manifestations of the pattern: unicursal and multicursal. The explorer may follow a single winding path to its conclusion, or he may encounter branching paths, in which case he must usually retrace his steps if he chooses wrongly. The earliest designs of labyrinths that we would recognize as such — on Cretan coins — and their continuations in Christian mosaic pavements in churches were generally unicursal. In his study of labyrinths, Paolo Santarcangeli argues that the multicursal labyrinth is of relatively recent origin. It is only during the Baroque period, according to Santarcangeli, that "we observe the beginning of bifurcations in the development of the labyrinthine design. To the impeded pilgrim two roads are simultaneously presented: one right and one wrong: he must choose."[9] As of the Baroque period, then, man can make a mistake that forces him to retrace his steps. This innovation is a logical development of the ancient myth and the idea of confusion long associated with the labyrinth, even in its early unicursal manifestations. The multicursal labyrinth seems to represent man's post-Renaissance belief in his ability and his obligation to choose his way of life, and the consequent fears attendant on choice. In a unicursal labyrinth, the explorer's powers of endurance are tested; in a multicursal one, his ingenuity comes into play as well. The traveler in the unicursal labyrinth feels himself subject to a power beyond his own; in the multicursal labyrinth he also suffers the responsibility of choice. Thus the possibilities of multicursal and unicursal paths that the verbal image of the labyrinth inherits from its visual manifestations sketch a landscape that includes both alternatives and entrapments, and creates an aura of simultaneous confusion and compulsion.[10] So just as the minotaur at its center is a hybrid being, the labyrinth, as a sign of language itself and of writing, embodies the sense in which we control and yet are controlled by language, in which we write and are written.

Another spatial variation in the visual image of the labyrinth that will be important in its verbal manifestations is that a labyrinth may be imagined either with or without a center. A center in a labyrinth implies a place of rest, an end to the confusion experienced in the paths of the labyrinth, or at least temporary respite from it. The center may contain a variety of experiences for the explorer, perhaps the most common being the adversary or the illumination—the bull or the temple, or else the mirror or the monster—the self or the other. As Michel Foucault has said with respect to the works of Raymond Roussel, "at the most enigmatic moment, when all paths stop and when one is at the point of being lost, or at the absolute beginning, when one is on the threshold of something else, the labyrinth suddenly again offers the *same:* its last puzzle, the trap hidden in the center—it is a mirror behind which the identical is located."[11]

A third ambiguity in the design of the labyrinth appears in the classical figures of Theseus and Daedalus, and concerns modes of perception. As Philip West has formulated it, the labyrinth may be experienced diachronically, through time, or synchronically, all at once—in other terms, from within or from above its space, by an explorer or a designer, a hero or a divinity, an ordinary man or an artist.[12] Theseus undergoes a trial in the labyrinth and thus sees it part by part, from within; Daedalus constructs it and thus sees it whole, from above. From the very beginning, this duality makes the labyrinth an appropriate sign of the artist and his audience—in literary texts, of the writer and the reader. Already in classical times, however, the stances of Theseus and Daedalus show a tendency to merge, for in several versions of the myth, Daedalus is described as becoming lost in his own creation, changed from synchronic planner to diachronic explorer.[13] This idea is present in Ovid's description of the labyrinth:

Just as the watery Maeander plays in the Phrygian fields, flows back and forth in doubtful course and, turning back on itself, beholds its own waves coming on their way, and sends its uncertain waters now towards their course and now towards the open sea; so Daedalus made those innumerable winding passages, and was himself scarce able to find his way back to the place of entry, so deceptive was the enclosure he had built.[14]

Even the river to which Ovid compares the labyrinth, like Daedalus, seems perplexed by its own design when it is imagined as "turning back on itself," surprised to behold the way its own waters move. That a man designs a structure in which he, the architect, may become lost, constitutes an especially ingenious act: reason deliberately manufactures bewilderment; it undermines its own enterprise, and in a sense transcends its own limitations. This fate of an architect entrapped in his own deceptive enclosure is thus an ironic tribute to the complex and introverted form of his creation, but it is also an implicit warning about the dangers of artistry, and prefigures the metatextual pull of the labyrinth image in later literature.

The Theseus/Daedalus dichotomy in spatial perception is the reason for yet another perplexing ambiguity of the labyrinth design — the discrepancy between the confusion that the labyrinth has come to symbolize and the formality of patterning that the image commonly evokes. This dichotomy becomes particularly clear during the medieval period when the church adapts the labyrinth to its doctrines, the era of the "labyrinthe moralisé," so to speak.[15] Christian interpretations explicitly develop the difference between the Thesean explorer and the Daedalian architect as an analogy for the different positions of man and God with reference to the universe. Sacred architecture mirrors the universe; stars on vaults represent heaven and mosaic labyrinths on floors picture the entangling layers of worldly sin surrounding man or the many perplexities of life in the world, where darkness will overtake anyone who strays from the narrow path. God perceives the order in the design; Thesean man needs the Ariadne's thread of grace to achieve unification with divine power at the sacred center of the design, often identified as the church.

Paradoxically, these Christian labyrinths contribute to the secularization of the pattern that continues in modern culture, and lead us to another ambiguity. They do this in two ways. First, for the church, the labyrinth symbolized not a special rite, but man's everyday life. Second, the potential for decorative variations on the design, exploited by church architects to produce attractive pavements, carried over into Renaissance garden mazes. The sacred convolutions of penance change into the secular intricacies of play.[16] Renaissance hedge mazes were often imagined to contain bowers of love at their centers; in them the play involved is amorous play, and so these labyrinths of love associate desire with decoding: to reach your object of desire, you must solve the puzzle. Such erotic resonances continue in the titles of complicated love stories like Boccaccio's and Cervantes's plays, both called *The Labyrinth of Love,* and we can see why. Besides obvious allusions to existing hedge mazes where lovers played and erred (in the senses of both "wandered" and "sinned"), the labyrinth is appropriate in dramatizations of love's entanglements because entry into a labyrinth, as into a love affair, represents voluntary disorientation; one chooses to enter the realm of the erotic just as one chooses to explore the maze at Hampton Court, but once inside, one is no longer entirely in control. The ambiguity here, then, closely related to the previous one, is between choice and chance, control and bewilderment.

One last ambiguity concerns the sexual dynamics of the labyrinth. Because the contours of early labyrinthine ritual spaces (tombs, temples, or palaces) are thought to have been designed to duplicate symbolically the form of sacred labyrinthine caves, the labyrinth belongs to the traditionally feminine domain of the earth mother, an association, according to W. F. Jackson Knight, developed out of "simple superstitions concerned with the motherhood of earth and with the return of the dead to her."[17] In many myths and rituals, the entrance to a labyrinth is often guarded by a woman, a clear classical reference to this tradition (besides Ariadne's string) being the Sibyll at Cumae, who guards the entrance to the underworld in *The Aeneid* with the aid of doors that have the Cretan labyrinth portrayed on them. These resonances persist in visual and verbal symbols; for Mircea Eliade, for example, "to penetrate a labyrinth or a cave was equivalent to a mystical return to the mother."[18] On the other hand, the association of the labyrinth with Daedalus, the meticulous artisan, suggests that it also belongs on occasion to the complementary domain of the sky father. Indeed, the labyrinth, like the Cretan culture with which it is consistently identified, seems to represent a form that mediates between the feminine and the masculine, between matriarchal and patriarchal systems of power.

In this context, the view of the labyrinth as great mother, with its implication that the young culture hero must make his way out of her devouring matrix in order to mature and to activate the divine gift of his supernatural father, suggests the possibility of a complementary reinterpretation from an avowedly feminist viewpoint.[19] We might name it after Pasiphae, the unacknowledged originator of the labyrinth, as the labyrinth can be seen to represent the secret powers of desire. The question we might ask in such a reinterpretation is, what is the nature of our divine gift and from where do we get it? If the gift is desire rather than culture, then the entrapment or channeling (or repression) of that desire may originate in the figures of Daedalus and Minos, in the patriarchal powers, who enclose the disruptive result of that desire in an increasingly formalized structure (beneath or within the palace of the king) and who, as it is female and dangerous to orderly rule, describe it as bestial. Recall that the daring feat of engendering the minotaur, which in most versions of the myth motivated the construction of the labyrinth, resulted from the passion of Pasiphae for the divine white bull that Minos had cherished too much to sacrifice.[20] In this light, Ariadne with her thread can be seen as a transitional figure, much like the goddesses in the *Odyssey,* between matriarchy and patriarchy, both deity and daughter, the earth mother's priestess and the father's child. From one viewpoint, then, it is the fertile, all-conceiving realm of undifferentiated wholeness, of female desire, the world before the word, even, that the labyrinth represents, even as it represses it, and which the texts I will discuss struggle (against their old fathers, old artificers) to reembody in its original labyrinthine form.

Finally, before considering reinscriptions of the labyrinth in modern texts, I would like to situate the image with respect to two primary spaces, spaces which it will often symbolize in literature. These are the house and the forest, dwelling place and path, center and periphery, place of rest or stasis and place of adventure or movement. Although the labyrinth is principally a structure of voyage or adventure, it may also suggest a protected place, even a dwelling. It thus encompasses the two elemental spaces of forest and house, which are of course related in the domain of magic by the idea of journeying: as Knight makes clear in the case of Troy and other ancient towns protected by convoluted walls, a labyrinthine house or city protects its inhabitants by hiding them in a defensive labyrinth of walls—by causing the enemy to take a journey. A labyrinthine house confronts intruders with characteristics of the forest, and in the same way that intruders may be trapped outside its walls, its inhabitants may be trapped inside, as well as protected. Gaston Bachelard notes the ambivalence in such a protective structure: the house is "not only a hiding place but also a prison cell." Furthermore, continues Bachelard, a related ambiguity characterizes the most labyrinthine part of a house, the cellar: "The underground life of an Edgar Poe naturally reveals the ambivalence of house and tomb."[21]

Angus Fletcher associates the labyrinth with the forest, and opposes both symbols in Spenserian and later English romantic verse to the image of the temple: "In essence, the temple is the image of gratified desire, and the labyrinth the image of terror and panic, . . . a general condition of unmapped disorder."[22] Labyrinthine imagery and action thus give the appearance of pathless wandering. I would argue, however, that the labyrinth often implies visual order. Indeed, it is just this sense of created paths that differentiates the labyrinth as a symbol from the forest. Similarly, the idea that "the image of the temple is strictly formalized, to frame the highest degree of order," and that "the idea of a labyrinth leads in the opposite direction," while it may describe Spenser's use of the images, is not always applicable to the wider context I am exploring here. The labyrinth also usually implies the existence of a center, as Eliade says, a "sacred zone," a temple, in fact.[23] The image of the labyrinth gains in poetic force because it permits a glimpse of sacred space through the profane space that surrounds it. Thus, as Paolo Santarcangeli points out, "the labyrinth is double: its corridors evoke the tortures of hell but they also lead to the space of enlightenment."[24] It embodies the idea that, like Dante the Pilgrim, we must go through darkness to reach light.

In this last case as in the others, spatial categories conflate. Often the wanderer in the labyrinth is also its creator, the prisoner of the labyrinth is also the liberated spirit, the potential victim also the potential victor. The path is at once the means and the end, the voyage and the destination. And like a text, a labyrinth is a half-closed, half-open space, which both reveals and hides, invites entry and prevents easy penetration; like any puzzle, it incites and delays its own solution.

The ambiguities in the image of the labyrinth I have outlined briefly here persist in modern uses of the pattern, though in many different forms. While they cause a certain amount of interference in the study of the labyrinth as verbal sign in literary texts, causing its referents to shift constantly (even within a given work), they also contribute to the flexibility in that sign, a flexibility that helps to explain its continuing fascination for modern writers.[25]

Modern Literary Labyrinths

This charting of the persistence of a particular literary figure illustrates the way in which we can observe that, in the words of Roland Barthes, "it is language which speaks, not the author; to write is, through a prerequisite impersonality . . . to reach that point where only language acts, 'performs,' and not 'me.'" Through the texts I discuss here, I show how the verbal sign of the labyrinth "performs" in its various manifestations within modern and contemporary literary discourse. Recognition of the antiquity and the dispersion of the labyrinth image as it appears in modern fiction illustrates particularly well Barthes's idea that "the text is a tissue of quotations drawn from the innumerable centres of culture."[26]

In ancient architecture and myth as in early church design and Christian doctrine the labyrinth oscillates between visual icon and verbal symbol. Recently, as I have suggested, a number of modern novels seem to exploit (as far as is possible) the labyrinth's iconic verbal properties as well as its symbolic resonances, so that in them the shape of rhetoric, we might say, corresponds imaginatively to the grammar of cities.[27] In an iconic mode of representation the physical qualities of the sign correspond to those of its referent. An iconic embodiment of the labyrinth, then, duplicates the form of the labyrinth in the structural design of the text; the placement of words, sentences, and ideas, and consequently the reader's progressive perception of them, traces a labyrinthine shape. In a symbolic mode, the correlation of sign and referent is arbitrary, conventional; the correspondence operates in the realm of ideas rather than in the domain of sensory forms, so that the word *labyrinth* or the description of a labyrinthine structure serves as a symbol for a forest, a city, a mind, or a text. James Joyce's *Ulysses,* Michel Butor's *Passing Time,* and Alain Robbe-Grillet's *In the Labyrinth* are examples of that first mode, the iconic. Since Joyce's stream-of-consciousness narration in *Ulysses* constitutes the most significant, seminal, and widely applicable reactivation of the labyrinth in the twentieth century, I begin my discussion with it. Building on Joyce's innovations, Butor and Robbe-Grillet develop more specifically the labyrinthine structure of the literary text as it exists in urban time and space in their novels.

These works by Joyce, Butor, and Robbe-Grillet demonstrate the modernist and postmodernist metamorphosis of the labyrinth design into narrative structure, into the process and product of writing itself; in them, in addition to encountering the labyrinths *in* the texts, we confront the labyrinths *of* the texts. Many of the stories of Jorge Luis Borges also propose this idea, evoking man's varied labyrinthine worlds of art, both actual and imaginary. To determine just how the formal design of a novel is analogous to the pattern of a labyrinth is very difficult. (We are always dealing with various levels of analogy here, since in no case that I know of has a writer "really" constructed a text in the recognizable shape of a labyrinth—though I doubt the event is far off.) As we will see, particularly with regard to *Ulysses,* in the domain of discourse the analogy can apply to style—the texture of the prose—which the reader perceives diachronically, or, in more conceptual fashion, to overall narrative design, which the reader apprehends synchronically, after having completed a reading of the work.

The most radical innovation in the texts we will study, and others like them, is that they incorporate the element of choice—in labyrinthine terms, of bifurcations in a path.[28] Choices of interpretation have always existed for readers, but not choices of referent. This is one significant way in which the words of *Ulysses* and its labyrinthine progeny have modified the traditional language of fiction. Related to this innovation of choice is the phenomenon of correction, of retracing narrative paths, which constitutes an encoding of error in the labyrinth of the text. *Ulysses* is seminal here as well; according to Fritz Senn, Joyce's novel may be "the first consistently autocorrective work of literature."[29] All of this labyrinthification of the discourse (if I may invent a term) calls attention to the narrating act, and implicitly defines the reader's project as a labyrinthine quest for meaning.

A second distinguishing characteristic of these recent texts is the extent to which the shape of the discourse reflects that of the stories it narrates. The labyrinths of the novels match the labyrinths in the novels. The same pattern characterizes the physical and mental trajectories of the characters or narrators as well as the design and the texture of the prose in which they exist. Because of this correspondence, the temporal labyrinths that these novels constitute emphasize "how time in the representing is felt to be a necessary analogue of time represented."[30] Furthermore, the matching of the shapes of discourse and story causes the distinction between subject and object to blur. Bachelard's discussion of dream labyrinths, in which he imagines the dreamer not only as experiencing labyrinths but as constituting labyrinthine matter helps to explain the process: "In our dreams, we are sometimes a labyrinthine substance, a substance that lives by stretching itself, by losing itself in its own turnings. . . . The being in the labyrinth is at once subject and object, combined in a lost being" ("l'être dans le labyrinthe est à la fois, sujet et objet conglomérés en être perdu").[31] So it is with a text "in a labyrinth," which not only describes a labyrinthine trajectory but constitutes a labyrinthine discourse, existing as a labyrinthine shape.

In addition to its appearance as a structural design for narrative, the labyrinth also serves frequently as a symbol in modern fiction. The many evocations of labyrinths in the short fictions of Borges are a primary example of this presence. Because of Borges's central place in contemporary fiction, an examination of his work is essential in charting the development of the labyrinth as a dominant figure of thought in the twentieth century and in showing that this development provides insights into the writing and reading of fictions of all kinds. In addition to this exploration of the labyrinth symbol in Borges's writings, I will also analyze a number of modern and contemporary works in which the image of the labyrinth appears in significant ways as symbolic landscape. These appearances of the labyrinth as a symbol generally complement and enrich its embodiment as narrative design as I have discussed it in preceding sections. In conclusion, I will draw on my foregoing analyses in order to discuss theoretical questions raised by the labyrinth's function as a polyvalent sign of the world, the mind, and the text. Many of these are metafictional in nature, others are mimetic.

A discussion of the labyrinth pattern in modern fiction, particularly as it concerns narrative structure, touches on questions regarding the treatment of space and time in fiction. As I have suggested, and as I will demonstrate in my discussions of individual works, especially with regard to Butor, Robbe-Grillet and Borges, part of the labyrinth's attraction as an image results from its potential to oscillate between existence in space and in time. In some sense, it seems to represent the very "shape of time," making explicit the spatial modeling of cultural texts. Similarly, analysis of this mythological pattern illustrates a variety of theoretical attitudes toward the use of mythology in modern literature. In his *Mythic Intentions in Modern Literature,* Eric Gould argues that motifs are less important than the common goal of both myth and literature "as each tries to suppress the void of consciousness, the failure to understand fully."[32] In this context, use of the labyrinth as a symbol and as a structural design for narrative might be seen as an attempt to portray consciousness itself and thus to understand it more fully. In each text it informs, it operates as an overriding design that figures the desire to explore the world, the self, and the processes of writing and reading that embody and transform them.

I have confined my discussion of structural as well as symbolic uses of the labyrinth to works where the term *labyrinth* or a related mythological reference appears in the text, so that the presence of this particular pattern is clearly indicated and thus thematized in varying degrees. Otherwise, given too much latitude, the term *labyrinthine* expands to cover all but the simplest narratives. (This is one reason why I mention Proust, for example, only briefly in my discussion; his novel is generally but not specifically labyrinthine.) Of course, this tendency for the labyrinth to encompass many fictions serves my purposes well; it confirms my argument that it is a potent and ubiquitous sign that stands for modern and contemporary fabulation. But it is simply impossible to demonstrate here the labyrinthine nature of every novel to which the term can be profitably applied. Even so, through and beyond my particular analyses, I will be exploring the many ways in which the labyrinth design has become a strong and often-used metaphor for the theory and practice of fiction and for other kinds of discourse as well. Furthermore, it will be clear by now that I am attempting not only to trace the labyrinth's appearance in modern literary texts and to analyze what the history of the image contributes to them, but also to construct a kind of comprehensive portrait of the sign itself as it constitutes a reflection of our landscapes and our discourses.

The correlation between theme and form or mode, which I invoke in my combination of "symbolic landscape" and "narrative design," occurs throughout literary history, either within one text or within one culture between texts. In bridging the realms of the conceptual and the concrete, or of the mind's inner eye and the eye's written page, such correlations realize the full literary potential of an image or an idea. This doubling of symbol and structure thereby also strengthens the presentation of a concept by causing the reader to perceive it in two different ways, in the case of labyrinths and labyrinthine narrative, both spatially and temporally. Joseph Conrad addresses a similar issue in his well-known preface to *The Nigger of the Narcissus,* when he admonishes the writer to appeal to all the senses as well as to the intelligence. While this kind of correlation between image and structure is a common phenomenon, it is not always a factor; in general, it occurs when thematic material contains structures, spatial or temporal in nature, that can be embodied in formal properties of texts—in analogous linguistic terms, when syntactical features correspond in some significant way to semantic ones. The word *configuration,* understood as a process, expresses well this "incarnation" of a figure of thought. Clear examples of this phenomenon include Dante's use of numerology in *The Divine Comedy,* which embodies the trinity in a tripartite text; Chaucer's tales, told through time, beads on a narrative string that corresponds structurally to the pilgrimage it portrays; the wavelike narrative design and style of Virginia Woolf's novel *The Waves,* which portrays the ebb and flow of the characters' lives. To mediate between thematic content and structural design involves an awareness of both domains, a strong sense of analogy, and a considerable amount of shuttling between those domains to demonstrate that the fabric of the text is indeed woven in their threads.[33] The reason that the labyrinth lends itself to such an analysis is that it is an image with spatial and temporal properties that can be embodied in the structural features of texts.

I have chosen to focus here on major works that stand clearly in the mainstream of the established literary canon in order to illustrate the central place of the labyrinth in the modern western tradition. I might note that I do not have a major North American text to correspond to the European ones I analyze, because I have found the image to be more extensively exploited in European and Latin American than in North American fiction. I imagine that this may be related to the continuing force of the myth of the "virgin land" in North America, and the pervasive, almost sacred, value invested in natural forms, of which the labyrinth as defined here is not one.

In my discussion of both structure and symbol I have followed chronological order. Though it is possible to argue that Borges, whose production spans the years from the 1920s through the 1980s, should be placed between Joyce and the *nouveaux romanciers,* I felt that such a placement would disrupt the discussion of narrative form that proceeds from *Ulysses* through *Passing Time* and *In the Labyrinth,* and also that Borges, in his use of the figure, serves as a meaningful bridge between considerations of narrative design and investigations of symbolic landscape.

2 / Labyrinth of Words:
James Joyce's *Ulysses*

WITH JOYCE'S MASTERFUL DEPLOYMENT OF STREAM-of-conciousness narration in *Ulysses,* the literary myth of the labyrinth moves from the symbolic to the structural domain, realizing the iconic potential of the verbal image. This influential reconstruction of the labyrinth in the twentieth century is brought about principally through the reader's tracing of the labyrinthine structure of the text. Though it operates on a different plane, and is less explicit than the Homeric parallels, this experience also represents a mythic presence in the text. The habitual tension in the labyrinth pattern between explorer and designer is central to *Ulysses;* the confusion of the explorer who wishes to achieve the comprehensive vision of the designer encompasses the characters as they explore their city and the reader as he moves through the text. To the labyrinth as a map of Dublin is added the labyrinthine trace of a voice, thus extending the structure of quest into the realm of language. Though it is ultimately of central importance that story and discourse take the same shape, the labyrinths in the text reinforcing the labyrinths of the text, clarity of discussion requires their temporary separation; thus we will investigate first the thematic and then the linguistic and structural labyrinths in *Ulysses.*[1]

The mythological figures associated with the labyrinth are less present in *Ulysses* than in *A Portrait of the Artist as a Young Man* with its clear and central evocation of Daedalus and Icarus.[2] But besides the fact that the novel constitutes an important recreation of the pattern in the most general terms, there is documentary evidence that Joyce still had the labyrinth in mind as he wrote it. A 1915 letter from Joyce to Emma Cuzzi thanks her for two prints of a bas relief (at the Villa Albani in Rome) that shows Daedalus working on a second wing for Icarus. Joyce says he plans to frame one of them, and adds (strangely, since the Icarian flight was hardly a success), "Who knows if the coming into the house of this man will not bring me good news?"[3] It is thus tempting to conclude that Joyce was identifying the start of his own work on *Ulysses* with Daedalus's other, more successful, project, the labyrinth, already envisioning *Ulysses* as a labyrinthine text.

Stephen's wanderings in the labyrinths of school and city in *Portrait* and his subsequent rebirth as an artist may be associated with the ceremonies of ritual rebirth performed in the ancient Cretan labyrinth and with the general death and rebirth pattern of all initiation ceremonies: "Stephen's ambulatory journey is a quest through the labyrinth of the world to the paradise of the heart."[4] In *Ulysses,* we can distinguish this same trajectory in Bloom's Dublin walks; he too wishes to find relief from the labyrinth of the world in the central enclosure of Molly's heart and her bed. But, as we shall see, *Ulysses* portrays a labyrinthine world seen through labyrinthine prose that denies the possibility of center or escape, and associates that wandering with the creation of art.[5]

On the broadest level of analogy, confused peregrinations of wanderers in the labyrinthine city—"seekers on the great quest"—abound in *Ulysses.*[6] As Bloom in Nighttown says, "I who lost my way" (357), and as is said of him later on, "ever he would wander, self compelled" (598). Similarly, Stephen's "centre of gravity is displaced," and as he walks on the Strand he sees labyrinthine forms before absent-mindedly losing his chosen path. The design appears more compelling than his own preconceived itinerary: "Broken hoops on the shore; at the land a maze of dark cunning nets; . . . He halted. I have passed the way to Aunt Sara's. Am I not going there? Seems not" (34). A few pages later, like all walkers in labyrinths, he reverses direction: "Here, I am not walking out to the

Kish lightship, am I? He stood suddenly, his feet beginning to sink slowly in the quaking soil. Turn back" (37). More generally, Bloom reflects, "Think you're escaping and run into yourself. Longest way round is the shortest way home. And just when he and she. Circus horse walking in a ring." (309). These spatial details call up labyrinthine imagery, demonstrating that here, as elsewhere in literature, urban labyrinths repeatedly figure the individual search, for the self and for others, and that they emphasize that this search involves continual reorientation.

As we have seen in these last two examples, besides this scenario of wandering, of losing one's way, people often retrace their steps or follow circular itineraries, both characteristic of labyrinthine paths. Indeed, the metaphor of labyrinthine wandering is extended by Bloom to figure life itself, and the continuity of the generations. Bloom notes that "trams passed one another, ingoing, outgoing. . . . squads of police marching out, back: trams in, out," and then moves without hesitation to the endless cycle of life and death: "Cityful passing away, another cityful coming, passing away too: miles of pavements" (134–35). Here the comings and goings of births and death are directly associated with the linear pattern of the city. This pattern of births and deaths or the succession of generations can be seen as fundamentally labyrinthine. While it is true that life continues on into the future, so that it can be imagined as a linear temporal progression, it achieves this progress through the circular pattern of repetition, of performing the same events over and over. Every generation or individual is thus in this way (though by no means in all ways) back at the beginning, where the previous one began. Similarly, progress through a labyrinth is progress, but progress that depends on circling back, or repeating the same process, sometimes even the same path. The explorer progresses by regressing, reaches new territory by retraversing the old. That is part of the fascination of the figure — its combination of the linear and the circular. Furthermore, symbolically, penetrating a labyrinthine cave for a ceremony and coming out again was a ritual often performed at the passage from life to death, in an attempt to assure the soul's eventual journey in the other direction. According to C. N. Deedes, for example, "above all, the labyrinth was the centre of activities concerned with those greatest of mysteries, Life and Death. There men tried by every means known to them to overcome death and to renew life."[7] The general significance of this labyrinthine renewal for *Ulysses* is often and easily recognized in the doctrine of metempsychosis, in the juxtaposition of Dignam's funeral and Mrs. Purefoy's giving birth, in Bloom's journey into the cemetery and "back to the world again"; in his irrepressible thoughts during the funeral: "Love among the tombstones. Romeo. Spice of pleasure. In the midst of death we are in life. Both ends meet" (89). On the journey to the cemetery, as if to remind us of the labyrinthine streets that lead there, we hear specifically of each turn the carriage makes.

Joyce also recreates another ancient resonance of the labyrinth pattern in *Ulysses,* this one related to the dichotomy of protection and prison. As W. F. Jackson Knight has pointed out, there has existed a continuing tradition of "Troy towns," of labyrinthine designs that are thought to have served originally as ritual protective walls around a city.[8] Such designs, having evolved from actual walls to decorative patterns, from practical to supernatural utility, were sometimes drawn to protect inhabitants from foreign invaders and at other times were used as blueprints for labyrinthine dances or marches at the occasion of the founding of a city, again to protect the future inhabitants from invasion. In our progress through the labyrinthine text of *Ulysses,* we participate in the ritual labyrinthine circlings that mark the founding of a modern verbal city. With all the specific allusions to pubs and businesses, streets, stores, and people in Dublin, which are virtually inaccessible to noninhabitants, Joyce has in one sense effectively erected a labyrinth that protects his city from foreign intruders—even perhaps from natives of subsequent periods of history.

Several additional details in the text of *Ulysses* reinforce the idea of a labyrinthine trajectory through descriptions of both the city and the life within it. The parallel lines of the trams that go in and out of Dublin resemble the parallel paths of labyrinths. Many walkers, like Mr. Kernan, "make a detour" (197). Near the end of the novel, Stephen and Bloom exit from the convolutions of their catechism in the Ithaca chapter "by a passage from the rere of the house into the penumbra of the garden," to "the heaventree of stars hung with humid nightblue fruit" as medieval wanderers in labyrinths were often imagined to emerge into heaven depicted at their center (573). Finally, after Bloom's wanderings have ended, as he settles down with Molly, the lamp and shade above them, "an inconstant series of concentric circles of varying gradations of light and shadow," reflect the approximate shape of a classical labyrinth, reminiscent of Bloom's circular, often Dantesque journeying (606).[9] And as if to remind us that the pattern of the discourse describing those wanderings also traces a labyrinthine shape, requiring us to undergo an ordeal similar to Bloom's, the question that elicits that response is posed in terms of "listener" and "narrator."

Classical Allusions

In addition to the labyrinthine trajectories in the city, several allusions in *Ulysses* resonate back toward the labyrinth myth, reinforcing the reader's experiential labyrinth of city and language, and implicitly encouraging him to reflect on it *as* a labyrinth. Most obviously, of course, is Dedalus's "absurd name, an ancient Greek" (3), which may prompt him later to "watch . . . the birds for augury" and to say that "last night I flew. Easily flew" (179). Since Stephen is still there to tell the tale, presumably he has assumed the name of the "great artificer" he called on at the end of *Portrait* and a few pages earlier in *Ulysses*, rather than that of his son: "Fabulous artificer, the hawklike man. You flew. Whereto? Newhaven-Dieppe, steerage passenger. Paris and back. Lapwing. Icarus. *Pater, ait.* Seabedabbled, fallen, weltering. Lapwing you are Lapwing be" (173). And again, later on in the Nighttown chapter, he seems to evoke the same scene: "No, I flew. My foes beneath me. And ever shall be. World without end. (He cries.) *Pater!* Free!" Yet this time his earthly father, Simon Dedalus, "somewhat sleepy but ready," a kind of diminished Daedalus, "swoops uncertainly through the air, wheeling, uttering cries of heartening, on strong ponderous buzzard wings" (466). In both cases, however, his calling on the father and the mention of Icarus leave room for a fearful identification with the fallen son as well, suggesting the danger of high-flying artistry. Furthermore, with his several references to the "lapwing," Joyce evokes the nephew of Daedalus who, according to Ovid, was so ingenious an artisan that Daedalus became jealous of him and pushed him off a cliff, at which point Athena favored him by transforming him into a bird. Here is another figure associated with the myth of the labyrinth, who, like Daedalus, is rather too ingenious for his own good, but whose ingenuity is rewarded in the end. Still another reminder of Daedalian building appears in a bawled song: "Behold the mansion reared by dedal Jack" (323); and Stephen and his medical student friends on their way out of the hospital are a "dedale of lusty youth," their spatial arrangement mirroring the shape of their city, the sound of their voices, and the ingenuity of their inventor (345).

Moving away from the central figure of Daedalus, another reference to a classical source of the labyrinth story is "the Minotaur which the genius of the elegant Latin poet has handed down to us in the pages of his Metamorphoses." He appears but once clearly, as an example of "the theory of copulation between women and the males of brutes," advanced in a heated argument among the medical students (336), and already transformed by the literary genius of Ovid. The scene of the minotaur's conception is recalled briefly earlier as well, when "queens with prize bulls" are cited as one example of "incests and bestialities" (170). In both cases, Pasiphae appears to be rather a freak of nature. But if we keep in mind the original myth, we recall that Daedalus constructs the device that allows her to satisfy her desire, and thus participates to some extent in engendering the monster birth. *Ulysses*, as a Daedalian labyrinth, also has something of the monster about it; it is a monstrously complicated house, built with an irreverence for God. (Recall that Pasiphae's coupling with the bull was Neptune's revenge on Minos, who did not sacrifice the bull as he was bidden.) Less directly, one might discern the minotaur's shadow, or that of his father, in other references to bulls in *Ulysses*. Whether one adopts the perspective of Frazer and Cook, who argue in favor of a bull-god associated with the labyrinth, or that of Nilsson, who remains unconvinced that the bulls in Crete and elsewhere served in any other capacity than as objects of sacrifice, rituals involving bulls definitely form part of the classical labyrinthine environment.[10] As Diane Fortuna has pointed out, this whole mythological complex lurks behind the cries of Bous Stephaneforos, which we hear in *Portrait* and again in *Ulysses*.[11] The energy of many of the bulls in *Ulysses* — even when they are gelded, or come from the Pope — is generally disturbing, and thus may point to the desire to enclose them in a labyrinth of words. The heavy punning on the word *bull* starts the process, pointing toward the verbal virtuosity of the text itself and away from the sexual force represented by the animal or the spiritual force represented by the Pope's dicta.

All of these labyrinthine trajectories and allusions reinforce the idea of the reader's labyrinthine progress through the text; the labyrinths in the text alert us to the labyrinth of the text.[12] The reader, as we shall see, "makes his way" through a twisting linguistic itinerary. As Harry Levin suggested many years ago, in Joyce's passage from *Portrait* to *Ulysses* he shifted his ground "from Icarian revolt to Daedalian wordplay."[13] The new and unknown arts, prophesied in the quotation about Daedalus from Ovid at the beginning of *Portrait,* arts that link Stephen Dedalus's artistic vocation to that of his mythical namesake, flower in *Ulysses.*[14] They are the labyrinthine forms of stream-of-consciousness narration and ingenious linguistic experimentation. These new literary arts constituted, of course, a radical departure from traditional fiction with regard to reader participation — and still do. According to Wolfgang Iser, in this departure

> lies the main difference between *Ulysses* and the tradition of the novel. Instead of providing an illusory coherence of the reality it presents, this novel offers only a potential presentation, the working out of which has to be done actively by the reader. He is not led into a ready-made world of meaning, but is made to search for this world. Thus reading itself has an archetypal structure which, just like the archetypes in the text, is unable to lead to any defined goal. It is a quest which brings to the surface the possibility of any number of findings.[15]

I am arguing, of course, that this "archetypal structure" in *Ulysses* is the labyrinth.

The innovation here and in the works by Butor and Robbe-Grillet that succeed *Ulysses* is that the labyrinthine potential of the *langue* is heightened by the syntactical shaping of these particular *paroles.* As Iser suggests, narrative is transformed into a trial for the reader. In this sense the text's *paroles* do not provide an escape from the labyrinth of the *langue,* but rather a deeper entry into and an expansion of its potential convolutions. The reader's experiential labyrinth evokes the form of an ancient initiation rite, in which the initiate learns the cultural patterns that enable him to live in adult society. Here, the reader begins as a Thesean explorer, unsure of the pattern of words in the book, then slowly progresses to become a

Daedalian coartisan as he gains experience in designing his progress—making his way—through the text. Fritz Senn describes this
same combination of Theseus and Daedalus (also locating its origin
in the classical world) in his idea that "the reader's function [in reading *Ulysses*] becomes that of a *demiurgos* (from *demos,* people, and
ergos, workman). . . . Readers are mediators who shape, or forge,
the matter at hand. Moving about and righting entails a lot of in-
ceptive groping, trial and error, possibly false steps. Success is never
guaranteed."[16] These processes are slow and difficult and, as Iser
and Senn suggest, never really complete.[17] Furthermore, forces of
linguistic desire are encoded in this narrative structure of initiation,
and the principle of postponed gratification structures our narrative
journey through *Ulysses* as Bloom's unsatisfied desire for Molly
motivates his wanderings through Dublin. It is especially appropriate, then, that the oblique approach of Bloom and Molly to each
other throughout the day of June 16, 1904, the day that Joyce chose
because it represented the entry into his own labyrinth of love,
should take a labyrinthine shape.

It is important to stress, as Iser does, the relative novelty of
Joyce's narrative style in *Ulysses* with respect to traditional fiction.
In historical terms, then, as well as in the cases of individual readers
from 1922 until now, *Ulysses* serves an initiatory function; it provides a pattern for our coming-of-age as readers of much twentieth-
century narrative. It is a simple point, but true, that in the quantity
of guides—of Ariadne's threads—generated by *Ulysses,* we are reminded once again of its labyrinthine nature. Whether the reader
uses a guide or not, a number of related structures will inevitably
define this itinerary through this labyrinth of language. This consideration of the reader's journey through *Ulysses* involves two related
levels. They correspond to the experience of style and the apprehension of structural design.

The Reader's Journey through the Labyrinth: Style

The reader's experience of style in *Ulysses* traces a labyrinthine
shape in that his progress from word to word is often impeded. Connections between words may be unclear, and before he can proceed,
the reader may need to guess what a phrase refers to; he must decide

which branch of the labyrinth he will follow, and to what end he will direct his course.

Before we investigate the specifically labyrinthine shape of style in this text, an initial clarification will be helpful. It is well recognized that in addition to being methodically disrupted, the syntax changes often and radically in *Ulysses*.[18] The prose alternately flows and jumps, so that the sequence may suggest the spatial analogy of various platforms rather than that of a path. A labyrinthine journey is generally imagined to be continuous—there are no breaks in the road; one does not usually hop over a ditch to change direction. The usual form is sinuous, or perhaps angular, as the various paths intersect; the wanderer's progress is not figured as intermittent, but rather as uninterrupted, even as endlessly impelled. But Stephen and Bloom alternate between flowing sentences and more staccato words or phrases. Bloom's "language of flowers" differs in syntax and therefore in narrative rhythm from his subsequent thoughts. The two modes are separated in the following example by two sentences of commentary:

> Angry tulips with you darling manflower punish your cactus if you don't please poor forgetmenot how I long violets to dear roses when we soon anemone met all naughty nightstalk wife Martha's perfume. Having read it all he took it from the newspaper and put it back in his sidepocket.
>
> Weak joy opened his lips. Changed since the first letter. Wonder did she write it herself. Doing the indignant; a girl of good family like me, respectable character. Could meet one Sunday after the rosary. Thank you: not having any. . . . Naughty boy: punish: afraid of words, of course. Brutal, why not? Try it anyhow. A bit at a time. (64)

Connecting words are generally less frequent in Bloom's and Stephen's than in Molly's monologue—perhaps the most truly "labyrinthine" of all. Run-on syntax heightens the reader's sense that he is following Molly's labyrinthine mental journey; the design of the language itself represents a continuous forked path. When the thoughts appear in fragmented style, on the other hand, the reader seems to be given nodes and to be forced to construct connecting paths between them, to decide how to join two words or phrases, for the discourse often suggests alternative versions of the story. Even so, although these "jumps" may seem formally rather unlabyrinthine, disrupting the reader's progress from one word to the next, they do comprise a verbal labyrinth, since the reader must often backtrack and make interpretive decisions along his way.

The path of this linguistic labyrinth thus traces a multicursal pattern where choices are required because a given word may refer to more than one thing: a good example of a corner in the labyrinth of language that requires a choice of referent appears at the start of the second paragraph of the passage immediately above. As we read the second sentence we may decide—correctly—that it is she (not he) who has changed since the first letter, but we are not sure if we've taken the right linguistic path until the next sentence. (If we had thought it was he who had changed, we would need to backtrack and correct our trajectory.) Often, in fact, pronouns form such nodes or corners.[19] A formalized instance of this pattern is the mutual thoughts of Stephen and Bloom in Ithaca, the "he"'s forming the crossroads in the labyrinth of their language: "He thought that he thought that he was a jew whereas he knew that he knew that he knew that he was not" (558). In Bloom's monologues, we soon learn that an ambiguous "he" will many times refer to Boylan, a "she" to Molly. But not always; a wrong turn is possible, and paths of reference may need to be retraced.

Even more often, the branches in the path come between sentences, requiring a logical connection between them. Here is Bloom in the Ormond bar: "Thou lost one. All songs on that theme. Yet more Bloom stretched his string. Cruel it seems. Let people get fond of each other: lure them on. Then tear asunder. Death. Explos. Knock on the head. Outtohelloutofthat. Human life. Dignam. Ugh, that rat's tail wriggling! Five bob I gave" (228). The reader, following Bloom's thoughts, chooses his path, connecting Bloom's imaginary lute string to his feelings about life's cruelty in allowing people to get fond of each other who then must die. He must even supply the ending of the word "explosion," after connecting it to death and before moving on to accept it all as part of life. That makes Bloom think of Dignam again, the rat he saw at the funeral, his own contribution—and so on. A variation on this labyrinthine narrative process is achieved by a kind of contrapuntal structure in which separate narrative lines are maintained simultaneously. The reader must thread his way between two separate paths at once. Here Bloom thinks of the letter he has just received from Martha and calculates the day's expenditures:

> Accept my poor litt pres enclos. Ask her no answ. Hold on. Five Dig. Two about here. Penny the gulls. Elijah is com. Seven Davy Byrne's. Is eight about. Say half a crown. My poor little pres: p. o. two and six. Write me a long. Do you despise? Jingle, have you the? So excited. Why do you call me naught? You naughty too? (279)

The textual labyrinth of *Ulysses* also contains dead ends; Bloom occasionally reaches such an impasse in the labyrinth of his thoughts, and it often concerns Molly. He has nowhere to turn, because to continue would be too painful. We leave him where he is and exit to a brief narrative interlude. An example of this kind of trajectory occurs when Bloom is recalling a stroll with Molly and her future lover, wondering what secret signs might have been passing between them:

> Wait. The full moon was the night we were Sunday fortnight exactly there is a new moon. Walking down by the Tolka. Not bad for a Fairview moon. She was humming. The young May moon she's beaming, love. He other side of her. Elbow, arm. He. Glowworm's la-amp is gleaming, love. Touch. Fingers. Asking. Answer. Yes.
>
> Stop. Stop. If it was it was. Must.
>
> Mr. Bloom, quickbreathing, slowlier walking passed Adam court. (137)

At such a moment, the prose switches from an internal to an external perspective, from the labyrinth of the mind to the labyrinth of the streets. This kind of shift in levels is obviously a privilege of verbal labyrinths not available to explorers in visual manifestations of the design.

Of course not all of *Ulysses* is comprised of disrupted syntactical structures or interrupted narrative progressions. Frequently, the ease with which we pass from one sentence to another produces the effect of corners turned in a unicursal section of the labyrinth; in this respect, all language can be imagined as a temporal labyrinth, and the design of the prose in *Ulysses*, with its excursive meanders, simply provides the reader with a greater sense of exploration than in most other texts. This is the case at the end of Bloom's thoughts about death, Dignam, rats, and his contribution, and here, where he ponders a bat:

> Birds are like hopping mice. What frightens them, light or noise? Better sit still. All instinct like the bird in drouth got water out of the end of a jar by throwing in pebbles. Like a little man in a cloak he is with tiny hands. Weeny bones. Almost see them shimmering, kind of a bluey white. Colours depend on the light you see. (309)

The associative connections between the end points of one sentence and the beginning of another in this passage suggest another labyrinthine quality of language in *Ulysses:* its autogenerative nature ("tiny hands. Weeny bones" and "bluey white. Colours depend"). One path of thought opens directly onto another, via a particular corner of words; where you've been determines where you can go—your freedom is considerable, but it is circumscribed. The long lists in the Cyclops chapter, where each term in the series exists primarily as a function of the preceding one, are a clear example of this tendency, but it also appears on a smaller scale, as when a woman Stephen sees "trudges, schlepps, trains, drags, trascines her load" (40).

A complementary labyrinthine movement is the detour (really a variation of counterpoint): a thought or phrase begins, is interrupted by another, and then continues. "High wall: beyond *strings twanged.* Night sky moon, violet, colour of Molly's new garters. *Strings.* Listen. *A girl playing one of these instruments* what do you call them: *dulcimers*" (47; my emphasis). Bloom's self-interrogation forms another mini-detour, similar to many. For example: "He had no wed. All trio laughed. No wedding garment" (220). Another: "It is amusing to view the unpar one ar alleled embarra two ars is it? double ess ment of a harrassed pedlar" (100). Bloom's capacity for verbal exploration of small problems, for figuring things out, traces a similarly labyrinthine path of trial and error, of linguistic choice. And here, the small labyrinths of language seem to have centers, which are reached when the problem is solved:

> Glass flashing. That's how that wise man what's his name with the burning glass. Then the heather goes on fire. It can't be tourists' matches.

What? Perhaps the sticks dry rub together in the wind and light. Or broken bottles in the furze act as a burning glass in the sun. Archimedes. I have it! My memory's not so bad. (309)

The existence of such narrative detours is explicitly signaled when Mr. Kernan expresses his intention to "turn down here. Make a detour" in the labyrinth of the city, immediately before the narrative makes a small three-line detour from the primary path of Kernan to describe Dennis Breen (197).

The reader traverses a larger kind of labyrinthine narrative path when he follows the words of a song or another quotation through several pages or paragraphs of text. In this context, the other sentences of surrounding prose temporarily become wrong turns, detours, or dead ends. The method is clearest in the Sirens chapter with Simon Dedalus's song; indeed, the entire chapter is built on this kind of tracing. It begins with "Bronze by gold heard the hoofirons, steely-ringing. / Imperthnthn, thnthnthn" (210); and after a page and half of repeated words and phrases, the design of the sentence becomes clear: "Bronze by gold, Miss Douce's head by Miss Kennedy's head, over the crossblind of the Ormond bar heard the viceregal hoofs go by, ringing steel" (211). Joyce's verbal approximation of musical counterpoint here, because it entails mentally tracking a line of thought, returning from digressions, keeping it in mind along with several others, resembles a labyrinth with its interrupted trajectories. The symmetrical "tap"'s of the blindman's cane represent a similar kind of path. A clear smaller example comes early on in the Nestor chapter. Stephen is in Mr. Deasy's office, juxtaposing the eternal and the present: "As on the first day he bargained with me here. *As it was in the beginning, is now.* On the sideboard the tray of Stuart coins, base treasure of a bog: *and ever shall be.* And snug in their spooncase of purple plush, faded, the twelve apostles having preached to all the gentiles: *world without end*" (24; my emphasis). This linguistic labyrinth, requiring active participation by the reader to articulate a syntactical sequence, intensifies the reading process on a microcosmic level, the text proposing itself as a temporal puzzle in the same way that a maze of city streets does in space. In *Ulysses*, then, as in earlier, more "primitive" labyrinthine initiations, impeded progress paradoxically engenders new knowledge and competence in the reader; the longest way 'round turns out to be the best way to a new home.

The Reader's Journey through the Labyrinth: Structural Design

Repetitions and allusions, which function on an immediate stylistic level to orient the reader within the labyrinth of language, play a similar role on a larger scale in the structure of the novel. The repeated words that the reader can place in an increasingly meaningful context within a sentence, and the syntactical units that he can place in the larger narrative units of paragraphs and sections, as well as the themes or images or allusions that he can relate to each other within the novel as a whole, are like familiar branches of a labyrinth, signposts in the narrative geography.[20] The wanderer recognizes them each time with a sense of *déjà vu* and with the hope that soon he may gain a better sense of how they connect with the rest of the labyrinth. He must construct paths between these thematic and imagistic or allusive stopping points or nodes in the same way he disentangled the pronouns and provided connectives and referents in the smaller units of the linguistic labyrinth.

These suggestions of a design in the labyrinthine fictional universe include large schemes like the Odyssey, grand themes like paternity, love, cycles of death and rebirth, and smaller concerns like food, or even a cake of soap. Continual use of this allusive method as a structural principle creates the reader's insecurity and assures its continuance even as it limits it: he must follow a partially prescribed, yet not an entirely fixed design. Richard Kain traces such a labyrinthine path of flowers in *Ulysses:*

> Virag has anglicized his name to Bloom, and Bloom uses the pseudonym Flower in his clandestine correspondence. Martha Clifford sends him a flower in her letter, and compliments him on his lovely name. As he reclines in the bath, his genitals are described as "a languid floating flower." He consummated his love for Molly amid the rhododendron on the Hill of Howth. Molly, "flower of the mountain," loves flowers. Rose of Castile, The Last Rose of Summer, the gardens at Gibraltar—*Ulysses* is a poem of flowers.[21]

But the words of this poem are not contiguous as they would be in a lyric. The reader must construct the connections between them as Kain has done. The pattern of the reader's journey toward this "poem," which itself has no completely predetermined shape, comprises a similar version on a larger scale of the more syntactically oriented two-page labyrinth that leads to a coherent sentence about the barmaids and the parade. In each case, after the reader has traversed the labyrinthine prose, figuring out his path, he can then perceive a comprehensible pattern.

In following these paths, however, we often have considerable trouble telling a potentially significant detail from an insignificant one when we first encounter them, just as it is impossible to know at first which path will lead onwards and which one will prove to be a dead end in a labyrinth. This uncertainty calls forth the suspicion of a deceptive designer, a Daedalian architect who has deliberately planned textual dead ends (like the potato and the man in the mackintosh) to entrap us. Such a suspicion heightens the tension between Thesean or diachronic reader and Daedalian or synchronic narrator even as it narrows the gap between them; it also increases the dynamic interplay of confusion and coherence that inheres in the temporal progress of all fiction. Furthermore, just as a labyrinth with multiple centers confounds the traditional distinction between correct and incorrect paths, so Joyce's text ultimately questions distinctions between significant and insignificant details.

The Wandering Rocks chapter presents a special case in the consideration of the labyrinthine structure of *Ulysses*, for Joyce, in the schema he provided Stuart Gilbert, called the "technique" of that chapter "labyrinthine." Gilbert does not make too much of this, nor have other commentators—rightly, I think. Presumably Joyce chose that chapter because it encompasses by far the largest number of personal trajectories, which consequently cover a wide geographical area of Dublin, and also because the wanderers encounter many obstacles in their paths.[22] This is the only chapter in *Ulysses* where trajectories are so clearly specified. Thus in his selection of a technique Joyce is stressing the labyrinth of streets rather than the labyrinth of language: he is using the term to refer to the labyrinth of the city rather than to the mental labyrinths that structure the novel. Because the narrative voice orients the reader here, creating for him a comprehensible pattern, a bird's eye view of the action, the narrator and the reader share a Daedalian stance. I would argue that this section is really no more profoundly "labyrinthine" than the others, for why is a labyrinth more of a labyrinth because we look over it as Daedalus, rather than threading it as Theseus? It is simply labyrinthine in a different way. The labyrinth pattern is central to the history of narrative primarily as a symbol for the novel itself and as a blueprint for its discursive shape, rather than as an image of the city.

The reader of *Ulysses* and of other modern novels written in its wake combines the stances of Theseus and Daedalus, progressing from wanderer to designer, as he perceives more and more patterns in the text, though never fully leaving one role for the other. To approximate a labyrinth well, this transition from Theseus to Daedalus must be slow, and is incomplete. The reader in the labyrinth, as Samuel Goldberg says, receives "a pervasive suggestion of an unapprehensible order beyond any actually perceived."[23] Not only does the reader explore the labyrinthine prose slowly, he is forced to enter it slowly at the beginning of the novel; the narrator provides stage directions when we are first introduced to Stephen. Later on, the stream of consciousness prevails.[24] The reader as Theseus must conquer his desire to treat *Ulysses* as a conventional novel, and learn to read it slowly, to appreciate its stylistic convolutions: the only central point he approaches in his voyage through the labyrinthine text exists outside it, in his own understanding and delight. The emphasis here falls on the complications of the journey, not on the arrival at a center—on process, not product.[25] In contrast to the mythical Theseus, the hero who needs to find his way out of the labyrinth of Crete, a successful reader of *Ulysses* will have learned to explore the convolutions in its labyrinth of language, to live within them rather than to escape from them. Part of living within the linguistic labyrinth that is *Ulysses* involves an acceptance of constant revision. Senn recognizes this principle as the "dynamic of corrective unrest," a principle that functions at all levels of story and discourse, and that, like the pattern of the labyrinth, illustrates Joyce's tendency to create "dense verbal equivalents for the mind's groping."[26]

The importance of the labyrinth as a metaphor for fictions like *Ulysses* where the reader takes an active role in structuring his progress through the text is that in its capacity to embody simultaneously the freedom and the compulsion, the undetermined and the determined nature of the process, it pictures the sense in which we readers are free to wander, to structure our own paths, but not in a free field, rather in an always already constructed labyrinth of language and thought. Furthermore, while such fictions increase the quotient of reader participation, making the processes of linguistic and structural discovery more apparent than in more traditionally constructed prose, they also implicitly highlight the labyrinthine nature of all language in which the *paroles* of individual speakers create their own paths within the previously patterned labyrinth of the *langue*.

The Center of the Labyrinth?

The labyrinthine design of *Ulysses* lacks a central enclosure. Instead, it reveals various nuclei — common words and themes to be passed and repassed as the reader traverses the text. The presence of these nuclei may tempt the reader with the traditional hope of reaching the center of the labyrinth, but their number and their inconclusive nature simultaneously deny this expectation. Structurally, the placing and presentation of the Nighttown chapter make it the central part of *Ulysses*, and the reader might feel that he has arrived at the crucial narrative location. We sense a shift in literary space at this point, as the narration opens onto a stage. Bloom's cry of "Rudy!" at the end of the episode is central to the paternity theme, and, indeed, to Bloom's whole existence. However, the center of a labyrinth is traditionally more precise than this, and it is generally differentiated from the labyrinth that contains it. The length of the Nighttown chapter alone disqualifies it. Neither characters nor reader feel that they have arrived anywhere definitive; rather they continue to wander in a region that, despite the distinctions I have noted, resembles the rest of the novel. In a sense, the theatrical presentation does not differ so radically from what precedes it, for much of the stream-of-consciousness narration approaches a dramatic mode. The same themes continue before and after the scene. And recurrent problems — Bloom's relationship to Stephen, or to Molly, for example — are not resolved.

Several other possibilities for a center exist. Stephen and Bloom's meeting over cocoa might be considered to constitute the central point of their two interconnected labyrinthine journeys. But this meeting is anticlimactic, their communion incomplete. The scene does not center the entire novel because it includes Molly only peripherally. Another possible center is the house on Eccles Street. Molly is there, and Bloom's steps and thoughts return there and end there. We say good-bye to Stephen in its kitchen. But again, though Eccles Street may constitute an emotional center, the sense of division within it is also strong. And within the novel, the house functions like many other images, as a familiar landmark rather than as a definitive turning point or a final resting place. Bloom is anchored there, rather than progressing toward it; if it is the center, he has been there before. Molly's final Yes must also be considered as a center for the labyrinth of *Ulysses*, but again, though it is literally more conclusive than Bloom's cry of "Rudy!" or the cup of cocoa, it excludes other concerns.[27] Bernard Benstock has suggested Stephen's and Bloom's cross-trajectories of urination under the light from Molly's window as a possible center for this labyrinth.[28] In its inclusion of all three figures and its sense of a restful pause after the day's wanderings, this intersection is the best central point of any I have considered. And yet it is still inherently inconclusive, given the uncertain nature of the relationships it proposes, so that it remains one of several moments of connection or comprehension. Leo Knuth and George Lord see the Wandering Rocks chapter and within it Bloom's purchase of the novel *The Sweets of Sin* as the center of the text.[29] Among other things, the purchase is a sign of peace, a means by which Bloom renews his relationship with Molly, and his manhood. It is true, as Lord contends, that the center of chapter 10 is very close to the novel's center; and in this interpretation structural and thematic centers coincide. I would still argue, though, that this moment is pivotal rather than central and that if we wish to imagine a center for the novel, we might well imagine it to be somewhere between chapters 9 and 10—displaced, nonexistent within the text itself, exemplifying the inconclusive nature of the experience it portrays. These multiple proposals in themselves—many of them very reasonable—really deny the existence of a single center. As we shall see in the cases of Butor's and Robbe-Grillet's even more specific verbal labyrinths, the distinguishing character of such modern uses of the design is that they are decentered; a center is always proposed, recalled, desired, imagined, but always finally denied.

The Shapes of Ambiguity

As I have suggested, Joyce modifies the traditional object of the labyrinthine journey, the escape, or the finding of a center, by habituating the reader to convolutions, by inducing him to live for a time in a labyrinth of language. In addition to the procedures I have already discussed for exploiting language as a form of exploration, he also achieves this revision of the labyrinthine journey by highlighting language's intriguing ambiguities. Bachelard's contention that the labyrinths of which we dream are endowed with the attributes of both hiding place and prison applies to *Ulysses* as well. The labyrinthine language in *Ulysses* may serve as protection against a hostile world, but it may also entrap the inhabitants. Both Bloom and the reader enjoy the company of attractive mental configurations as they wander through Dublin. Bloom daydreams about his daughter, flowers, or good times with his wife. The reader is often carried along for a while by rhythms and images. But both Bloom and the reader may occasionally feel trapped in the flow. Bloom will inevitably remember that his wife now has a lover; the reader will wish to move outward beyond Bloom's interlocked daydreams. Here Bloom's pleasant thoughts about his daughter turn into painful memories of his dead son:

> Fifteen yesterday. Curious, fifteenth of the month too. Her first birthday away from home. Separation. Remember the summer morning she was born, running to knock up Mrs. Thornton in Densille street. Jolly old woman. Lots of babies she must have helped into the world. She knew from the first poor little Rudy wouldn't live. Well, God is good, sir. She knew at once. He would be eleven now if he had lived. (54)

This sensitivity to the associative powers of language, which structures the labyrinthine progression from one word to the next, offers alternately freedom of expression and enclosure within self-reflexive discourse. In this duality Joyce's interior monologue resembles the Freudian technique of free association to which it is often compared, and in which the individual's freedom to follow any associative path is circumscribed by the pattern of his own personality and experience so that many routes may eventually lead to the same impasse.

Similarly for the reader, alliterative games, processions of images, and plays on words create a sense of delight in language, a delight that inevitably reflects back on the world it portrays and transforms it. For example, he can follow Stephen's rational thoughts as they flow into a poetic "wavespeech":

> I shall wait. No, they will pass on, passing, chafing against the low rocks, swirling, passing. Better get this job over quick. Listen: a four-worded wavespeech: seesoo, hrss, rsseiss, ooos. Vehement breath of waters amid seasnakes, rearing horses, rocks. In cups of rocks it slops: flop, slop, slap: bounded in barrels. And, spent, its speech ceases. It flows purling, widely flowing, floating foampool, flower unfurling.
>   Under the upswelling tide he saw the writhing weeds lift languidly.
> . . . Day by day: night by night: lifted, flooded and let fall. Lord, they are weary. (41)

Note in passing that the impulse to progress to a goal—to the center of the labyrinth of life or of language—that Stephen expresses as "better get this job over quick" is impeded, really redirected into the process inherent in speaking itself in his exploration of the sounds of the wavespeech; this is a small example of Joyce's reorientation of the labyrinthine journey as he causes the reader to live within the labyrinth of language rather than to reach its center or its end. Here again we experience autogenerative language, the sounds of the words generating variations on themselves. But such language, like the sea, ebbs as well as flows; the exuberance fades, the initially active wavespeech ceases, the weeds become weary after days and nights of movement. As we have seen before, the poetry of a wandering mind can lead to unhappy or simply unattractive memories or phrases.

In addition to the ambiguities of protection and prison, delight and despair, two further kinds of ambiguity pervade the text as well: the oscillation between chaos and order and between rhetorical structures that reveal unconscious thoughts and those that reflect conscious artistry. Through the reader's experience of confusion mitigated by incipient and increasingly perceptible patterns, *Ulysses* maintains a balance between the forces of chaos and those of order. The design of the labyrinth constitutes a formalized expression of confusion; it is the sign *par excellence* of one thrust of modern narrative, which seeks to portray the world's chaos in the necessarily ordered world of a text. It thus contributes in its own way to T. S. Eliot's well-known contention that in employing the underlying structure of the *Odyssey*, Joyce was making the chaotic modern world the possible subject of art.

Whether or not Joyce's streams of consciousness penetrate below the conscious layers of the mind, revealing more of the unreachable realms of the psyche than other narrative modes, is impossible to establish. But in comparison to the forms of narration that precede *Ulysses*, the reader senses that he is being permitted to enter a region that lies below the habitual domain of fiction. The linguistic geography in *Ulysses*, which consists of points from which different paths branch off, is analogous to the Freudian idea of nodes, or points of contact between different thoughts. Even more specifically, the linguistic overdetermination in *Ulysses*, where one manifest signifier may refer to a group of latent signifieds, corresponds to Freud's explanation of the "nodal points" in dreams upon which several dream thoughts converge, some of them unconscious.[30] In a sense, then, in entering Joyce's paths of prose, we can imagine ourselves penetrating the unconscious of the novel, where its language is being formed. Like cave labyrinths whose paths symbolically explore the earth's depths, this labyrinthine text reveals a formerly inaccessible literary realm. On the other hand (and here the ambiguity), the fact that there are several streams in *Ulysses*, and that they are highly differentiated, incorporating an unusual number of intertextual allusions and stylistic tours de force, calls attention to the supremely conscious process of verbal construction. Thus, *Ulysses* mediates between the unconscious labyrinths of the psyche and perhaps even of fiction itself, of their barely defined instincts and impulses, and the self-conscious labyrinth of art, with its self-reflexive verbal acrobatics.

This mediation leads us to notice a related dichotomy of method in *Ulysses:* the stream-of-consciousness technique, regardless of what it describes, because it narrates from within an individual's mind, tends to isolate that individual from his fellow citizens, and thus serves as a sign of solitude. However, the intermingling of the streams mitigates this solitude, gathering the separate labyrinths of individual minds into the collective labyrinth of the social world and the literary text.

Joyce's transformation of labyrinthine trial into linguistic adventure depends to a large extent upon the verbal exuberance that surges up even out of dejection. In this respect he constitutes a modern Rabelais as Bakhtin describes him. The ritual traversal of the labyrinth becomes a carnival of words, where the linguistic verve overflows the confines of satirical discourse. At this point we might recall also that certain labyrinthine dances are thought to have been fertility rituals. Here in this modern labyrinth of language, it is primarily the fertility of language that is celebrated — though human fertility is by no means neglected, and in the Oxen of the Sun chapter it provides the pattern for the verbal dance.[31]

Molly's Labyrinth

Bloom's journey, with the reader following him, duplicates in some respects that of the traveler in a distinguished early labyrinthine journey, *The Labyrinth of the World and the Paradise of the Heart*, by the seventeenth-century Czech churchman John Comenius. There, after exploring the labyrinthine city (representing the world) where he discovers a pit of "nothingness" filled with terrifying animals, the traveler falls to the ground in a paroxysm of despair, at which point God's voice counsels him to "return whence thou camest to the house of the heart, and then close the doors behind thee."[32] As we do with Comenius's dreamer, we leave Bloom at the end of the day, in the temple of his heart, so to speak, resigned but not despairing. And we can define that temple as his own heart or as Molly's bedroom. The dreamer in Comenius's text must remove his glasses to see things truly; in the end, he, like Bloom, achieves his vision not by threading but, paradoxically, by shutting out the labyrinth of the world and entering the paradise of the heart, by strengthening the known rather than by exploring new territory. In both cases, however, the labyrinth has served its initiatory function: the knowledge of the world it represents prepares for the final choice of voluntary enclosure. As Bloom thinks about his future course of action, we see that, like Gide's Theseus, his trip through the labyrinth does not change his behavior, but rather affirms his past as a basis for future action.

It is true that we leave Bloom with Molly, in bed. But in another sense, Bloom remains at the gate of a temple he cannot enter, the space of Molly's monologue, a space which is, in turn, also another labyrinth. Molly's monologue at the end of *Ulysses* revives mythological resonances of the labyrinth in a particular way, for the labyrinth is traditionally imagined as a feminine domain, a domain guarded by a woman. As often in *Ulysses*, the experience of the text parallels the experience in the text. Molly's roundness and the centrality of her bed are experienced by Bloom and the reader both. Bloom's physical wandering stops when he reaches Molly and lies down beside her. The reader's journey does not stop, but it does change mode, as he enters yet another labyrinth, an apparently warmer, softer variety than he has encountered before, containing sentences with ample, extended curves and meanders.[33] If an important characteristic of Joyce's labyrinth as it prefigures much modern fiction is a correspondence between story and discourse, this final monologue might be considered to represent this correspondence best, that is, to be the most labyrinthine of all; as Dorrit Cohn has pointed out, Molly's "continuous interior monologue is based on an absolute correspondence between time and text, narrated time and time of narration."[34]

Because of the run-on style in this section, the reader has a sense of following a continuous path, not of jumping from one impression to another. Each "yes" in the last passage represents a turn nearer the center of a labyrinth. The last eleven "yeses" are placed increasingly close to each other, the paths becoming smaller and the branches at each "yes" more frequent as we approach the labyrinth's central "Yes." Its capital "Y" is as important as the period. Both put an end to the series, and the fact that the signpost words are all the same increases the sense of inevitable progression toward a central point—a narrative path through a unicursal labyrinth.[35]

Jung's remarks about the end of the novel, though idiosyncratic, nevertheless provide us with an illuminating perspective on the reader's journey through the labyrinth of the text, connecting it implicitly with ancient myth and ritual:

> Let us assume that the consciousness of *Ulysses* is not a moon, but an "I" which possesses judgment, understanding, and a feeling heart. Then the long way through the eighteen chapters would not only spell discontent but in all truth would be a road to Calvary; and this wanderer, over-

come by so much suffering and folly, would break down at nightfall and
sink despairingly into the arms of the great mother, who signifies the beginning and end of life.[36]

In Jungian terms, the journey through the labyrinth is thought to
represent the journey of the individual soul as it extricates itself
from the labyrinthine entanglement of the overpowering mother
figure. In the passage above, Jung appears to describe the failure of
a reader's soul to differentiate itself from that maternal matrix, the
labyrinth of the text, where it is finally comforted, and yet in some
sense defeated, overwhelmed. This description of the labyrinthine
textual trajectory by this early reader of *Ulysses* emphasizes the
reader's weakening of resolve rather than his acquisition of narrative
competence as he passes through the text, stressing his exhaustion
rather than his development as a decision-making individual. In this
instance the masculine consciousness (significantly he is "not a
moon") experiences the female desire encoded in this labyrinth as
such in terms of enclosure rather than departure, remaining at the
end in a final nocturnal labyrinth.

As Jung suggests, Molly's affirmative ending may provide an
emotional relief for the reader; it also supplies a thematic resolution
of sorts. But this final poetic affirmation is not unqualified, nor is it
logically anticipated by the rest of the novel.[37] The "Yes" may be a
center for *this* labyrinthine mental journey, and even perhaps for
Bloom's, but it is not a universal center, and it is displaced and qualified by the present nonunion of its former participants. Its final
position is essential, but it cannot outweigh the rest of the text or
resolve the problems posed in it. Bloom wanders in the labyrinth of
Dublin in search of Molly as the reader wanders in the labyrinth of
the text in search of meanings; in both cases the respective goals are
partially achieved and partially denied.

Joyce has written of the ending that "the last word (human, all
too human) is left to Penelope. This is the indispensible countersign
to Bloom's passport to eternity. I mean the last episode *Penelope*."[38]
His emphasis is on the episode, not on the figure; the *way* Molly is
portrayed at the end, the language used, is crucial. And she has the
last word, a kind of power over the labyrinth *of* the text, if not control over the present world, the labyrinths *in* the text. Later, Joyce
writes: "I have rejected the usual interpretation of her as a human

apparition—that aspect being better represented by Calypso, Nausikaa, and Circe. . . . In conception and technique I have tried to depict the earth which is pre-human and presumably post-human."[39] In another letter Joyce gives the episode a qualified definitive position in the novel: "*Penelope* is the clou of the book. . . . It begins and ends with the female word *yes*. It turns like the huge earth ball slowly surely and evenly round and round spinning. . . . Though probably more obscene than preceding episodes it seems to me perfectly sane full amoral fertilisable untrustworthy engaging shrewd limited prudent indifferent Weib. Ich bin der [sic] Fleisch der stets bejaht."[40] A *clou* is not a *clef,* however; it fastens but does not necessarily open the text to decipherment, or complete it. Joyce's string of adjectives indicates a deliberate tentativeness.

Part of the magic of the novel's ending is of course that Molly is not idealized.[41] During the course of her monologue, she is vulgar, and often contemplates tricking Bloom, and the end of the book does not depart from that representation by portraying an abstract notion of Molly's love for Bloom. It portrays, in fact, her rush of physical passion for him. In this final flourish Molly carries the reader along so fast that we have no time to judge her; we simply feel her as a forward-moving force. The rush of words convinces us she is spontaneous in her seduction of Bloom, the rhythm and language beautifying part of a life often described earlier as calculating and almost bestial. The affirmative spirit of Molly's emotion, and hence of the final passage, emerges magically yet convincingly, like "flowers all sorts of shapes and smells and colors springing up even out of the ditches" (781–82). The language of the passage contains modern versions of conventional "happy love" symbols: night rendezvous, sunsets, Spanish gardens, a red dress, and flowers. In the context of the monologue, this sweetness does not jar unduly with the earlier irony, or even with Molly's statement that "I thought well as well him as another," although it contrasts with them (643–44). The phrase contributes to the theme of universal, or generalized, rather than individualized love. Even the houses are transformed by love into springlike pastels: ". . . and the glorious sunsets and the figures in the Alameda gardens yes and all the queer little streets and pink and blue and yellow houses and the rosegardens and the jessamine and geraniums and cactuses and . . . " (643). Our final emotional response to Molly depends largely on our immediate involvement with the poetry of this ending. Critical reservations about that positive image of Molly come earlier in the monologue and in reflecting subsequently on it after finishing the book. Goldberg points out, for example, that Molly's acceptance of everything is reduced in pure joy by her accepting it all equally, as well as by her pettiness.[42] Still, the reader's original, immediate sense of affirmation balances the critical afterthoughts. Neither view can cancel its opposite.[43] In fact, the many contradictions in Molly's discourse contribute to its generally labyrinthine nature, to its representations of alternate pathways of thought and expression.[44] The end of Joyce's labyrinth, like its texture throughout, is a fusion of contraries, a play of ambiguities. Epiphanic moments of vision take place within the complex structures of explorative thought that surround them, creating a narrative design of intertwined labyrinths and proliferating temples, labyrinths of the world and paradises of the heart.

3 / The Labyrinth of Time and Memory in the City: Michel Butor's *Passing Time*

Building on Joyce's innovations, Michel Butor develops specifically the labyrinthine structure of the literary work of art as it exists in urban time and space. In focusing intensively on the artist in the labyrinthine city, he reactivates the ever-present ambiguities of protection and prison, of freedom and entrapment that we encountered in *Ulysses*.

Butor's essay, "Short Cruise Preceding an Exploration of the Joycean Archipelago," while it is largely an introductory piece, connects *Passing Time* to *Ulysses* in significant ways. Clearly familiar with Joyce, Butor uses the metaphors of exploration that are central to Joyce's labyrinthine discourse in his own explication of Joyce's texts. He maintains that Stephen and Bloom, like Revel (the narrator of *Passing Time*), have lost the support of certitude or transcendence, and are "haunted by the debris of old systems," often in the form of classical myths.[1] Butor, not surprisingly, explains the *Odyssey* as a pre-existent grid on which Joyce structures *Ulysses*, and then builds his own novel on classical and biblical narratives. More generally, both *Ulysses* and *Passing Time* are intensively focused on the topography of a city.[2] And both texts reveal a particular consciousness of time in the narrating act. We see this in

Ulysses because the time of its discourse follows quite closely the time of its story; while this is not strictly true in *Passing Time*, the concern is there, for the structure of that novel plays explicitly on the impossibility of achieving such a temporal fit. Finally, Butor believes that the central focus of *Ulysses* is language.

An extension of this last idea is the most significant point of contact between Joyce and Butor for my purposes here, because it signals the progressive thickening of the line of narrative discourse into a labyrinth. Butor's description of *Finnegans Wake* as a branching narrative—a multicursal labyrinth of language—prefigures the generative mechanisms in both his own and Robbe-Grillet's texts. According to Butor, the way Joyce combines words from two different fables in that book means that "each of these words can become like a railway switch, and we will go from one to the other via a multitude of routes. Whence comes the idea of a book which doesn't just tell one story but a sea [or a labyrinth] of stories."[3] This Joycean network of verbal railway switches, of alternate narrative paths, is just what we encounter in various ways in *Passing Time* and *In the Labyrinth*.

Butor has said that a novelist is someone "who perceives that a structure is in the process of sketching itself in its surroundings, and who pursues this structure, makes it grow, perfects it, studies it, until the moment when it will be readable for everyone."[4] The environmental structure that emerges from *Passing Time* in this way is the labyrinth. It provides a visual image for a city and an experiential equivalent for the perception and the recording of time that passes there. Jacques Revel, the French narrator of *Passing Time*, keeps a diary of his sojourn in the town of Bleston, England. He does this in order to stay sane in what he perceives as an unusually alienating city. But he starts the diary late, after several months have passed, and so, like Tristram Shandy before him, he discovers that his efforts to record time past are doomed to fall ever farther behind, and to become increasingly complicated. Thus the narrator's keeping of his diary and the reader's tracing of the narrator's path as he reads the diary both resemble a journey through a labyrinth—in Revel's words, "the labyrinth of my days in Bleston."[5] And in addition, the town of Bleston itself reveals the same labyrinthine shape as these temporal journeys. In Revel's diary, then, the space of the city and the time of writing and reading are compressed into one symbol, and the experience of entrapment is intensified by that condensation.

Butor's topographical impulse, his awareness of the metaphorical interplay between space and time, has led him to speak of books in spatial terms: "In fact I walk around in a book as I would walk around in a house. Some have grand entryways, some have series of well lit parts, dark parts, narrow corridors that I have to traverse in order to come out suddenly into a large space." He maintains that to study time in its continuity one must apply it to a space, consider it as a trajectory.[6] The structure of the labyrinth enables Butor to achieve this portrait of time as space in *Passing Time*, for Revel's diary, written and read in time, is analogous to a labyrinth perceived in space, though, finally, of course, the reading process recasts the pattern in time. In an interview Butor discusses this aspect of *Passing Time* and explains his use of the labyrinth as a desire to portray the monotonous atmosphere of a town without sunlight. He notes that where no shadows exist, one cannot mark passing time. If shadows—on a sundial, or elsewhere—are the most basic way of telling time, then a city without sun is a city without time:

> One is in a kind of wandering state just as much as regards time as regards space.
>
> Moreover, that is why the theme of the labyrinth is so important in this book, not only a labyrinth in space (the classical labyrinth, the Cretan labyrinth constructed by Daedalus to house the Minotaur and which Theseus succeeds in figuring out thanks to the thread that Ariadne has given him), but a labyrinth in time; the whole book is a labyrinth inside time, the thread of sentences playing the role of Ariadne's thread.[7]

City and Diary

The city of Bleston constitutes the primary spatial labyrinth in *Passing Time*, a labyrinth in which we see Revel wander right from the start, speaking continuously of being lost, of making wrong turns, of taking wrong buses, which return him to his point of departure, whence he sets out again. The very fact that Butor has included a map of the town as a frontispiece to the book questions Revel's ability to describe it clearly, highlighting the tension between diachronic explorers and synchronic perceivers or designers in the labyrinths of city and text that follow. Revel clearly needs guides to orient himself in the labyrinthine city of Bleston—a map, or his friends Horace Buck, James Jenkins, and the Bailey girls. But even with their aid, he still fears entrapment in the "pitiless" metropolis.

It is easy to see that Revel's actions are those of a bewildered wanderer in a labyrinth; his descriptions of the city itself reinforce its labyrinthine qualities. It is a city "which is still unfamiliar, which conceals other folds, which shuns scrutiny as though the light scorched it, like a woman"—a recognizably labyrinthine realm, and one which even has a park with a small maze (103, 47). This urban labyrinth is one that Butor imagines as ubiquitous, for in a mechanistic version of the labyrinth pattern, Revel pictures Bleston as the center of a wheel that shares spokes with other wheels, and when he can find no real countryside on his walks, he imagines that that set of interlocking wheels extends across the entire earth.

More specifically, Revel compares Bleston with Crete and its labyrinth both explicitly and implicitly. He says at one point that he is Theseus and that Ann Bailey is Ariadne; it is she who sells him the map that helps him through the streets. The Bleston cinema runs a travelogue about Crete; Revel compares and contrasts it with Bleston. Just before he describes the Cretan labyrinth in the tapestries in the museum at Bleston, he mentions the streets, houses, and railroad tracks of Bleston on the other side of the museum wall. We shall see later why the identification of the two towns is necessarily incomplete, but the tentative equation, which underscores the controlling metaphor of the labyrinth, is established.

On close investigation, the interplay between the novel's labyrinthine structure and the city's labyrinthine plan becomes increasingly complicated. The book describes the city-labyrinth and hence in some sense serves as a possible blueprint for Revel's survival in it and an ally in his final escape from it. The process is at once concrete and metaphorical: the greyness and fogginess of Bleston, and its grid of similar streets, are real dangers at the same time they are manifestations of Revel's inner disorientation, exterior and interior landscapes modeling each other:

> The rope of words that uncoils down through the sheaf of papers and connects me directly with that moment on the first of May when I began to plait it, that rope of words is like Ariadne's thread, because I am in a labyrinth, because I am writing in order to find my way about in it, all these lines being the marks with which I blaze the trail: the labyrinth of my days in Bleston, incomparably more bewildering than that of the Cretan palace, since it grows and alters even while I explore it. (183)

This passage presents the idea of the novel as a labyrinth. But it also demonstrates the way in which the two labyrinths, of the city and the book written in the city, tend to merge, emphasizing their interdependence, for Revel often describes his walking around the city and his writing of the book in similar terms, such as "track," "trajectories," "lines," "exploration," and so forth. He has already said that Ann Bailey is Ariadne, but now he claims that his "rope of words is like Ariadne's thread." Furthermore, even if on a second reading it becomes clear that Revel is talking of his diary tracing the labyrinth of the *days* in Bleston rather than of Bleston itself, the first impression we have is of *spatial* progression: "I am in a labyrinth," "I am writing in order to find my way about in it," "I blaze the trail." As he suggests in his essays, Butor is clearly applying time to a spatial trajectory, and inducing us to identify the town with the diary written there by having Revel refer to them with all-purpose spatio-temporal terms. Here, for example, he is speaking about the New Cathedral, which he was unable to appreciate initially, not realizing that "it offered another clue in that puzzling, evasive trail which I had been following for some time and the end of which I have not yet discovered, for it has vanished into the winter's fogs" (111). Butor conflates town and text in this way because to be an efficacious investigation of the labyrinth of Bleston, a true understanding of it, and hence a protection against its insidious power, the book must resemble it. Furthermore, to be a true mirror-investigation, the writing must achieve a temporal fit as well, and thus can only be done in Bleston; it starts as the train pulls in and ends as Revel leaves. Constructed in this way, the novel constitutes the string that has traveled Revel's mental and physical itineraries, a string that will retain their pattern and subsequently guide the reader in his wake.

Our awareness of the novel's specifically labyrinthine structure develops in two ways, one symbolic, the other experiential. Direct statements like the preceding ones by Revel concerning his writing emphasize the confusion he feels and suggest symbolic resonances for his activity. This confusion reinforces the reader's own experience as he progresses diachronically from word to word. Revel's structuring of the diary-novel, on the other hand, constitutes a more orderly form of dated memory and the reader's synchronic perception of that structure provides an experience that mitigates his confusion, so that the comprehensive effect resembles a journey through a labyrinth pattern whose structure is confusing for the duration of the journey but finally perceptible at its end.[8]

Narrative Structure: Design and Confusion

An investigation of the structural organization of *Passing Time* reveals what Butor means by a structure becoming "readable." Georges Raillard notes a tendency toward regular arithmetic progressions of increasing complexity in the narrative structure of Butor's novel; this progression means that Revel's bewilderment, "implied by the content of the text on each page, is nevertheless not rendered by the disorder of the narration."[9] The increasing temporal complications of the general plan express the growing complexity of Revel's situation:

I	II	III	IV	V
May	June	July	August	September
October	June	May	June	August
	November	July	April	July
		December	August	March
			January	September
				February

In May Revel writes about October, in June about November, but also about June, since that is when he is writing. Revel writes in consecutive order during the top underlined month about the bottom underlined month: in May about October, in June about November, and so on until he is writing about February when he leaves Bleston in September. But as he progresses, he finds it increasingly difficult to limit himself to this scheme, and so after the first month he starts writing about the month he is writing in (the month second from last in the diagram) as well as the months with which he may see connections while he is writing. Since the diary is written about October through January during May through September, we miss February through April. We also miss numerous days within the months of narration. The various time sequences do not flow together.[10] As in a labyrinth, some paths remain unexplored forever. Revel's confusion does grow in the pattern of arithmetic progression, but it is still confusion. Similarly, even though the reader may perceive the order of the dates, he wanders in a confusing written labyrinth, following some of the same paths over and over, never completely certain of how they connect with each other. Here again, the labyrinth's confusing paths within an overall pattern embody the tense balance between confusion and order in a life.

Further particularizing our description of the novel's design, we might imagine that in reading the novel the reader explores a labyrinth that is for the most part unicursal in its overall design, because his choices have been limited by Revel's decisions. There is an important exception to this, though, for the reader encounters one major set of forking paths in the plot, the various details surrounding the mysterious car accident of George Burton, which are never resolved into a single explanation. Revel, on the other hand, in leaving the trace of Ariadne's string that constitutes the diary, himself has had to chart a multicursal path of trial and error through the city streets, through the time he spent in Bleston, and through his thoughts as he writes of his activities. For the reader following him, then, the concept rather than the experience of multiple paths obtains in this labyrinth, so that with regard to events in the novel, he shares the narrator's bewilderment ritually. In this respect Butor's text recalls the unicursal mosaic labyrinths on church floors (certainly familiar to Butor, with his knowledge of architecture), which are thought to have been used in penetential processions: while the turnings of the penitents symbolized their confusion and their need of God's guidance, the formalized and unicursal design of the labyrinth assured them of his existence.[11]

Not only these trajectories but also Revel's manner of narration resembles the experience of a labyrinth, and in this case the pattern approximates a multicursal path. The outstanding features in this respect are deviations that are so long that we are afraid of losing the narrative thread. The examples are numerous, formalized, and of varied length; and large digressions may contain further digressions within themselves. Take this passage, for instance:

> With what relief, on the morning of Sunday, November 18th, did I thrust into my one and only *suitcase the few articles* I had taken out of it, *the few articles* I had bought in Bleston, *the map* of Bleston identical with *the one* now lying folded on the left-hand corner of my table, *that map* which I had bought from Ann Bailey, the plan of bus routes of which I had not needed to buy a second copy, and *that novel* by J. C. Hamilton (whose real name I had not yet discovered), *The Bleston Murder,* which was still in my possession that day (for I only lent it to James, I remember quite clearly, the day after our first visit together to Pleasance Gardens), *that copy* of *The Bleston Murder* which must now still be at the Baileys' house, which their cousin had returned to them (it was Ann who let him take it, . . .) — *that copy* which I had thought lost, identical in text with *that I possess at present* and only, at that time, a trifle cleaner-looking.
>
> With what relief did I shut my heavy *suitcase,* my one and only suitcase, which now lies empty. (109; my emphasis)

The reader has almost forgotten the journey and the valise during the long enumeration of the latter's contents. Within this detour, there are three shorter ones starting from and returning to the novel: "that novel by J. C. Hamilton . . . that copy of *The Bleston Murder* . . . that copy . . . that I possess at present." Even within the first few lines here, the text retraces its steps to produce labyrinthine convolutions: both objects and map appear once, are followed by a few narrative steps, and then re-encountered, before the sentence moves on.

At other times, a detour never returns to its starting point, indicating that we have left that narrative path behind. When Revel is eating with his French friend Lucien, for example, his thoughts about the waiter prompt him to describe a past dinner with James Jenkins in the same restaurant. The Jenkins time sequence then continues without further mention of the dinner with Lucien. These two sorts of deviations, the circular and the continuing, create a temporal labyrinth, and their repetition traces the kind of increasingly familiar yet not completely predictable pattern that is characteristic of labyrinthine itineraries.

Butor's essays are helpful again here, for in them he explains how for him an attempt at complete narration inevitably tends to become a labyrinthine pattern with parallel paths, backtracking, new starts, crossroads:

> Let's imagine that the narrator keeps not only a double but a quadruple diary. . . . Parallelisms, reversals, repetitions . . . each event seems as if it could be the starting and merging point of several narrative sequences, like a central point whose importance is increased or diminished according to what surrounds it. Narration is no longer a line, but a surface in which we isolate a certain number of lines, points, or noteworthy groupings.[12]

As we have seen, time sequences in *Passing Time* do become increasingly complicated, because not only has Revel to describe his past actions and feelings, but also, when he comes to describing the days when he wrote his diary, he must recount the effect that this process had on the events in his life that he has just set out to describe. In terms of the governing metaphor, this means that having arrived at a temporal node, he has difficulty deciding whether to proceed forward in narrative time or to retrace his steps—in Genette's terms, whether to try for a narrative prolepsis or an analepsis. Given this impasse, the tension builds, and Revel suffers from a feeling of enclosure, "[because of this text that I pursue, this search that exhausts me, in which I enclose myself, and which] has taken up all my evenings ever since the beginning of May" (194).[13]

For Revel, then, choice does not necessarily constitute freedom. Furthermore, in his literary labyrinth, even if he does choose which path to take, that choice may lead him through familiar terrain; in labyrinthine terms, he has wandered into a passage which he has already encountered—discouraging if his object is to progress, or to escape. When he mentions the map, for instance, he usually repeats the same information about Ann selling it to him, Jenkins taking him to her store, and often his own burning of it. Similarly, the Chinese restaurant or the cathedrals have their own associative sequences. It is as if Revel has constantly to retrace his steps before coming out of a given path into new territory. The technique formalizes the associative thinking that characterized the labyrinthine thought patterns of Stephen and Bloom in *Ulysses*.

Characters and Centers in the "Labyrinth of Time and Memory"

Butor has followed the classical myth of the labyrinth in *Passing Time*, and hence we can easily find analogues for the mythological figures in the novel. Revel's youth conforms to the initiatory resonances of the labyrinth pattern, which explains in part why he identifies himself explicitly with Theseus rather than with Daedalus, even though he resembles the latter in his methodical construction of a book-labyrinth: "I myself [was] Theseus" (169). The figure of Ariadne reveals a similar duality. Ann Bailey is a would-be Ariadne; losing her may have forced Revel to adopt another guide—this time a narrative thread without a woman at the end. "Ariadne represented Ann Bailey" (169); but, as we have seen, "this rope of words is like Ariadne's thread." Horace Buck serves as yet another Ariadne figure, for he makes Bleston more accessible and hence conquerable for Revel by finding him a decent room, though he contrasts with Ann because he enables Revel to concentrate on the city and its problems (by writing about it) rather than to escape from its coils. If he had attached himself to the other Ariadne's thread—to Ann Bailey—Revel might not have undertaken the task of writing, might have left the labyrinthine city without attempting to understand and to transform it. Indeed, he claims that if Horace hadn't directed him to his current abode, he would not be writing now, nor would he have been able to appreciate the New Cathedral, or to realize that it might serve as a source of understanding in his exploration of the city.

Moving on to another mythological figure, the minotaur, we note that here, as in Joyce and Robbe-Grillet, he is less important than the labyrinth itself. If we were to name him as the main danger within Revel's labyrinth of city streets and narrative paths, he would be an internal monster called lassitude, and would imply a loss of selfhood. Near the beginning of the novel, Revel dreads a "darkening of consciousness," and is "overwhelmed by an absurd wish to draw back, to give it all up, to escape"—to escape not by conquering but by retreating (8). Later on, he speaks to Bleston, asking the town, "Do you imagine, puny alchemist, that you can so quickly, so easily free yourself, free me from my vast powers of darkness, from that monstrous lethargy which corrodes your resolution and which, if you ignore it, will ruin you the more completely?" (262). The monster seems to be inspired by a Baudelairian ennui, which threatens the artist's will to transform the city. The heroism needed to conquer this monster is persistence rather than force, or even genius — the kind of painstaking artistry Baudelaire required of himself. Butor has said in an interview that *Passing Time* was for him "an exercise of continuity and above all of slowness," not airy flight above the labyrinth but earthly toil within it.[14]

Like the design of *Ulysses,* the painstakingly formed narrative structure of *Passing Time* lacks an analogue for the central enclosure that characterizes many visual labyrinths. Though the novel is divided into five parts, the central chapter has only an arbitrary claim to structural significance. And Revel's point of exit is similarly arbitrary and inconclusive. Revel's decision to begin writing might constitute a more likely "center," a point from which he begins his journey out of the labyrinth of Bleston in which he has become increasingly entrapped. But that decision, though central, occupies two narrative points — when he announces it in the text, and later, when he recounts its previous occurrence in his mind.

The symbolic structure of the novel reveals a similar lack of central focus. Both the detective novel by George Burton and the New Cathedral designed by Mrs. Jenkins's father might constitute end points for Revel's exploration of the town. But Revel's encounters with them lead on, or back in, to further exploration. Burton's detective novel *The Bleston Murder* (the novel within the novel) at first appears to contain vital directives, but in following them, Revel becomes more and more confused. Revel slowly realizes the danger of *The Bleston Murder* as a wrong path, yet he and the reader following him persist in pursuing it.[15] We half expect an answer to the mystery of the Burton car "accident," and to have it connect with the detective story, for the chapter on the accident is located, deceptively, at the center of the novel. We therefore experience the danger of being in a dead end by expecting a dénouement from the detective story because Revel refers to it continually. But it is the story we are reading that may be a key to Bleston and what goes on there.

Original effort—Revel's own writing, or our own reading—develops understanding; no one can traverse the labyrinth for you or give you a plan to follow, for a successful initiation is an individual event.[16]

Revel illustrates this value of figuring things out for oneself when he speaks of the tapestries in the Bleston museum that portray the stories of Theseus and Cain and Abel. He understood them after a "zigzagging search"—another small labyrinthine quest.[17] He says that "if I had had at my disposal a catalogue . . . the tapestries would not have played so important a role in my life" (152). The labyrinth of inquiry is necessary, and there is no shortcut through it. The same is true with regard to Burton's book, though it does give him some important points of orientation. He explains how he had discovered *The Bleston Murder* through a poster, and how it had led him first to the Murderer's window in the Old Cathedral, which had in turn led him to the New. He thinks it was "as though a trail had been laid for me, at each stage of which I was allowed to see the end of the next stage, a trail which was to lead me hopelessly astray" (79–80).

In the description of Revel's paths between these symbolic nuclei we recognize a labyrinthine journey, a design where the explorer perceives only partial paths. Though the New Cathedral is a powerful symbol and a promising ingredient in understanding the town, Revel must continue to traverse the labyrinth of his own intellectual quest. The church is not its center; it is "a crippled work of art, but a profoundly imaginative one, . . . poignantly striving towards freer and happier creation" (118). It, like Burton's novel, is a model to be surpassed, a stage on the artist's journey, not a central resting place; and it is protected, as were ancient temples, by labyrinthine convolutions of streets in the town and of time in the mind.[18] Revel's attempts to center his search for meaning in Bleston around images he thinks may explain the city to him—*The Bleston Murder,* the map, the guide book, the windows, the tapestries, and finally and more successfully the New Cathedral—are thus destined to fail; none of them is sufficient because he must create his own meaning. The same is true for his related project, to account for the time he has spent in Bleston; the account will reflect the design of the time as he has passed it.[19] Paradoxically, this man, like Gide's Theseus, must lose himself in his own labyrinth if he is to emerge from it at all. This aspect of Revel's experience, in conjunction with his loneliness, like Bloom's, underlines the fact that the labyrinthine adventure is essentially a solitary one.

The Presence of Myth

Resonances of ancient myths in *Passing Time* function like other symbolic works of art such as detective novel, cathedrals, or maps. And the hermeneutic status of those very resonances conforms to the governing metaphor of the labyrinth. Interpreted too literally, given too much importance, they could be dead ends in the labyrinth of Revel's thoughts as he explores the city and accounts for his time there, or impasses in the reader's labyrinth of interpretation. But as they are understood to represent only partial truths, or incipient models, they can serve as passages leading part way out. Revel's self-doubt does not disappear when he identifies himself with Theseus, though the identification helps him describe his discomfort and thereby lessens it somewhat. (It also mitigates his loneliness.) Revel's labyrinth is different from Theseus's, and requires a different thread for him to escape.

The constant comparison of the blue skies of Crete with the grey skies of Bleston, as we have said, establishes the identification of the two cities but prevents it from being complete. The cinema where Revel goes to escape temporarily from Bleston has a documentary color film about Crete. Even the color contrasts with grey Bleston, as do Revel's reveries about Greece, where he imagines that "day must be bright . . . glittering on the translucent waters at their feet, bathing the whole of that steep, jagged coastline . . . which we followed . . . staring through the dense, smoky, sooty air" of Bleston (99). Butor achieves these comparisons with gentle modulations from one region to another, the reader sharing Revel's mood through the concentrated, poignant, yearning lyricism of the passages. At one point, Revel remembers

> the princesses who to the Greeks became Ariadne and Phaedra . . . just as the palace itself became the Labyrinth: princesses . . . with breasts exposed in low-cut, close-fitting bodices, breasts like sensitive peaches, such as I imagine Rose's to be . . . under her high-necked sweater. (101)

The ending betrays Revel's disappointment and yearning. The last six words brutally close the rippling sentence as Rose's high-necked sweater covers her breasts and cuts short Revel's drifting reverie about them. That Revel recognizes the "mythic" dimensions of his situation and yet is still troubled suggests that the recognition does not solve his problems. The well-defined contours of the myth, like the center of a labyrinth, while comforting to contemplate are not available to Revel as he represents a modern Everyman. Revel's word-play with Ann's name, associating it with Ariadne, almost suggests an attempt to give the comparison substance, to make his anguish disappear, in a sense, under the myth: "If you will become my Ariadne once more—faraway Ann, Ann whom I can scarcely make out" ("si vous redevenez mon Ariane, Ann lointaine, Ann que je distingue à peine"; 234, 354). Her real identity is "Ariann"—related to, yet not defined by, the myth. The myth is seen through filigree, not as a solution to Revel's anguish, but as a component of his growing comprehension of his situation.[20]

Transformation and Initiation

The structural design of Passing Time resembles a labyrinth that varies in complication but conceals no definite center. Some passages inevitably lead to others already explored; others do not. The reader's labyrinthine journey through the text constitutes a more highly structured path than Revel's earlier wanderings in the labyrinthine city, or in the "labyrinthine ways of [his] own mind" as he writes his diary, for we follow the thread he has laid down. But the complex and ordered structure of the story has been achieved just for the story, and just barely. Revel's reiteration of his own confusion is crucial to the concept of creation—a difficult and dangerous transformation of chaos into order. To express the difficulty involved, bits of chaos must remain to endanger the order. The time sequences, for example, seem confused at close range though they constitute a pattern. And the narrative thread nearly disappears in lengthy deviations. Both of these characteristics are embodied in the form of the labyrinth.

After having traced the design of Revel's verbal labyrinth, we need to assess the consequences of this narrative journey. Those consequences are partially obscured by the journey's apparently circular design, for Revel ends, as he begins, in a train compartment. But this time he is leaving Bleston, not re-entering it; and while it is true that not much has happened since his arrival, Revel, and with him the reader, have confronted the difficulties involved in measuring and recording the passage of time—no small feat.

In exploring these temporal problems and others that he encounters in Bleston, Revel changes the shape of the labyrinth of urban experience by accounting for it. Knowledge of confusion is differentiated from the original confusion by the five-part ordering of time in the novel, whose complexity, as we have seen, progresses arithmetically and thereby describes graphically the difficulty of Revel's task, so that in one sense the narrator's words transform the language of the city. The text congratulates this conscious, ordering mind, and yet in the end it also questions its value. Is Revel saved by his diary or by his predetermined departure? Nevertheless, his account of life in Bleston encompasses and surpasses several others. Alternative attempts to understand the town—the map, the guide book, and the detective story—are always on the corner of Revel's writing table, other Ariadne's threads, already formulated solutions to the problem of confronting the Blestonian labyrinth by retracing it.

That Revel resists burning his pages in anger represents both a triumph of meticulous—Daedalian—art and a denunciation of it, an ambiguity we met first in Ovid's description of the labyrinth as a structure too clever for its builder. The pages have saved Revel from drowning in the fogs of Bleston, but they have also caused him to suffer. He claims that it is mainly their number, that is, the time and effort invested in them, rather than their quality, which saved them, but later he is grateful to have kept them, since burning them would have meant succumbing to Blestonian despair.[21]

In addition to the personal implications of Revel's journey, *Passing Time* suggests a more social result—perhaps a future ideal. In his essays Butor maintains that literature has a social function "as a methodical experience."[22] Revel refers several times to his "dark pact" with Bleston. The relationship is difficult to follow, for it goes through many reversals; Revel claims that Bleston tries to kill him or his will, but that it also shows a secret desire to see him survive the death it has planned for him, its sarcasms "strangely turned into entreaties" (254). Baudelaire and the artistic transformation of a city come to mind again in this context when Revel imagines that Bleston says to him, "When shall we see our velvet spread out, our metals gleaming? When shall we be cleansed, and you too, Jacques Revel?" (256). Revel continues talking to the city and says that his work—"my exploratory description, the basis for a future [deciphering]"—needs other such efforts to make the town comprehensible, and hence livable (256). The goal is for Bleston to become conscious: "Through the eyes of these two sisters, you yourself Bleston may begin to [decipher this deciphering] of yourself which I have begun" (259). This repeated deciphering—the uncovering of hidden social identity through a literary text—corresponds to Butor's sense that "literature envisions the creation of a collective consciousness" and that this collective consciousness will be self-reflexive.[23]

Just as Revel has in a sense died—to a "normal" life, including love—while he is in Bleston, in order to achieve through his writing a more complete comprehension of the city and the life there, so Bleston manifests a "desire for death and for deliverance, for light and for fire" (259). Passage through a labyrinth often symbolizes this kind of transformation, the passage through death to another life. As Eliade has said, it is an arduous road, "a rite of passage from the profane to the sacred, from the ephemeral and the illusory to reality, and to eternity, from death to life, from man to the divinity." In this secular text, we do not reach that last step, but even though Revel may have survived by *not* burning his diary literally, his written critique serves symbolically as a kind of purgation by fire for the town, refining its essence, so to speak, even pushing it toward the status of an eternal city as it exists in print. At one point, for example, as he thinks of his text, the writing and the town seem to combine, and to undergo a sort of transformation into a flame: "Bleston, [whose carapace I erode by this writing, by this] slow relentless flame issuing from your own innards" (285). In this way, Revel's journey is a collective as well as an individual trial, his hatred for Bleston and his literary destruction of the town constituting social analysis as well as individual vengeance.[24] At the very least, Revel has made what was at first for him an impersonal city into a personality with whom he is intimately hostile. From this perspective, then, *Passing Time* represents a communal labyrinth of initiation.

In personal terms, as he himself has suggested, Revel's diary is the

rope of words that leads him out of the urban labyrinth in Bleston.
It is, and yet it isn't. Revel does preserve his sanity in the grey labyrinth by writing, by creating his book-labyrinth, which mirrors the
city-labyrinth, and this precarious sense of control over his labyrinthine environment is his primary form of escape from it (in the sense
that it enables him to live within it). However, even though he finally
escapes from the labyrinth, his physical form of escape—departure
by train at the end of his contract—was prearranged, and hence
tends to undermine the effect of his effort at psychological escape.
Confirming this idea, Revel's tone at the end of the novel suggests
relief rather than triumph.

An even more important issue is the clearly negative conse-
quence of Revel's journey; his verbal achievement seems to stifle his
emotional fulfillment during the period of time it encompasses,
literary activity becoming a substitute for love.[25] Talking of Bleston,
Revel claims that "I shall still be prince over you since, by acknowl-
edging my defeat, I have managed to survive (as you secretly wished
me to) the fate you had in store for me, I have not been engulfed"
(253). This is his rational side working, and it does triumph, but
perhaps it would have been better to loosen his hold on his literary
Ariadne's thread and concentrate more on an emotional thread held
by Ann or Rose. Like Oliveira in Cortázar's *Hopscotch,* Revel has
caged himself in his labyrinth of words, with the Bailey girls on the
outside.

Butor suggests this situation in passages where Revel's loss of love
is associated with his loss of will; in many cases, slight variations
modifying a repetitive rhythm create a lyric sadness. Here Revel is
meditating on his situation:

> But my voice fades away, stifled by the storm, Oh Ann. . . .
>   I sat for a long time without writing, with my eyes closed, and if I still
> linger here, at this table, before this sheet of paper, beside this window
> to which the melting snow and the January fogs once clung, it is because
> I am reluctant to admit that any attempt to pursue this exploration is
> vain tonight, and that I must drag my pen from the page over which it
> is crawling, must rise and undress, put out my light and sleep. (217)

The last phrase flows to a final and smooth close, revealing Revel's
pensive and delicate misery. This lyrical style appears most often in

descriptions of the Bailey sisters, or as above, in descriptions of Revel's situation just after he thinks about having lost them. Such a lyrical vein contrasts with Bleston's bleak streets, and with Revel's rational desire to recapture every moment systematically in his diary, with his writing as a sort of protection, a "rampart of written lines" he erects around himself (195). The lyrical style thus sets a tone that implicitly evaluates Revel's experience as the builder of a labyrinth, a labyrinth of words.

Butor has stated that he deliberately sets lyric power to work for him in his novels, that

> by using structures which are sufficiently strong, like those of poetry, like geometrical or musical structures, and systematically causing the elements to play in relation to each other until they achieve that revelation which the poet expects of his prosody, one can incorporate the powers of poetry into a description taking off from the merest banality.[26]

In Revel's case, the lyrical repeatedly grows out of the banal; poetic reveries about Ann or Rose rise from the banality of Bleston's streets. Similarly, Butor masterfully plays two rhythms against each other in this text: the consecutive arithmetic rhythm of daily memory and the tempo of lyrical, nostalgic love—two modes of viewing the past, one organizing it, the other crying over it.

These two aspects of Revel's experience, the rational effort and the yearning for love, are often modulated in one passage; he passes almost imperceptibly from one to the other. Usually the progression is from the writing to the love and suggests that subconscious emotional longing has asserted itself despite Revel's concentration on his diary. For example, from the passage already cited about his "exploratory description, the basis for a future deciphering," Revel continues one sentence during seven paragraphs, all of which begin with "cette Ann" ("that Ann"). The piece becomes a kind of love plaint, ending with "[that] Anne whose grey eyes which looked so kindly at me last winter now haunt me, now are closed to me, those eyes to which, despite all our estrangement, something bitter like the mist of those days still binds me indissolubly" (257). Similarly, earlier in the novel, Revel slips from writing rationally of his work to poeticizing about Rose: "What is the good of pursuing this futile, dangerous work of exploration and analysis, of trying to mend the broken thread? What is the good of reviving my pain by thinking of that evening when I went out with Rose—my Rose who should have been my Rose" (185). And again, later on, Revel moves from his journal to a reverie about Ann: "On my table I can only make out the pages as paler rectangles and the written lines as faint streaks at which I must peer closely to read them; I can't go on without my lamp. O my Ann, the Ann I knew in January, Ann who was so close to me then" (216).

Writing does become an Ariadne's thread for Revel, as Jean Roudaut suggests, but it is not an entirely satisfactory one for two main reasons.[27] First, the string takes on qualities of the labyrinth it attempts to conquer; Revel is lost within a labyrinth of words as he writes his diary as well as in the city where he wanders from place to place,[28] so that instead of providing an exit from the labyrinthine city with its foreign cultural codes, Revel's words really achieve a further labyrinthification of their language. His labyrinthine rampart has turned out to be both protection and prison. Second, there is no woman at the end of his string, and literature is unable to replace her. Again like Cortázar's Oliveira, who wishes La Maga could lead him out of his labyrinth, Revel regrets his inability to use the thread offered him by "Ariann" Bailey, in imitation of his legendary prototype, when he journeyed to another city. Instead, he feels compelled to create his own guide in the form of a written record. This labyrinthine initiation, then, is not a sexual one, as the original myth might suggest. The possibility of sexual fulfillment arises, but the initiation here is into art. Whether or not Revel freely chooses this artisitc initiation in preference to a sexual one is unclear. He blames the town of Bleston for his separation from Ann, but admits also that he did not know how to love her; the failing may lie within himself, in his tendency to construct himself a protective labyrinth of words. No need of a minotaur in such a labyrinth.

In his excellent article on Butor's techniques, Leo Spitzer also examines the ambiguous nature of Revel's labyrinthine activity. He emphasizes Revel's inability to capture time rather than his loss of love: "The Proustian solution, the past becoming book and art is no longer valid for Butor, who records the hopelessness of ever recovering the past." Still, even though Revel's long meandering sentences drown details in a "sea of atemporality," he saves himself from despair through the processes of thought and writing. According to

Spitzer, "French Cartesianism still remains intact, at least in the rational attitude of the writer, who still knows how to dominate the chaos of the modern world by his description."[29] While Revel may have failed in his effort to account fully for his time or to love a woman, his rational, painstaking mind survives a year in debilitating Bleston, and structures the diary-novel according to the convolutions of its thought. The resulting labyrinth thus represents Revel's initiatory journey into the complex realm of writing and in including the sexual resonances of the labyrinth as it does, it highlights what Revel misses in this particular kind of initiation. We readers follow closely behind Revel, of course, and throughout the novel striking images from the scene of writing focus our attention on the narrative process.[30] Here, for example, Revel describes (in a particularly brilliant metaphor) the writer's inevitable self-portraiture:

> As for the blank sheet of paper on which I am writing, it too is a thick mask of paint . . . but a mirror lies beneath the thick layer of paint that I am scratching with my pen as though with a knife . . . and gradually, through the cracks that my words make, my own face is revealed . . . and yours behind it, Bleston. (267)

Butor has said that he wishes to work at the point of language articulation. He is troubled that interior monologue does not always deal with the ways language and thought are formed, and that it therefore frequently remains similar to third-person narration: "It is this dynamic relationship between consciousness and the awareness of consciousness in its acquisition of language, for which it is impossible to account."[31] The labyrinthine form of *Passing Time* and the images it contains represent the effort to overcome this impossibility, to expand Joyce's labyrinth of language, so to speak, by increasing its metafictional dimensions; both structurally and symbolically, Butor's forms and images describe the problematic acquisition of a narrative language, an arduous initiation into the realm of the storyteller, into the world of his words.

Postscript: Ariadne's Disappearance, or
Labyrinths Are Not for Lovers

Like Revel, Ambrose M— in John Barth's story "Lost in the Fun-house" experiences an artistic rather than a sexual initiation in his journey through a labyrinth.[32] The reader senses Ambrose's dissatisfaction with this result through a stylistic pattern of alternation between concern with women and concern with literary problems comparable to the one which characterizes *Passing Time*. In this way and others, Barth, like Butor, exploits the metafictional dimensions of the labyrinth. "Lost in the Funhouse" recounts the adventures of thirteen-year-old Ambrose during a day with his family at Ocean City. The theme of youthful initiation is even clearer here than in *Passing Time*, for "Ambrose was 'at that awkward age'" and is much concerned with his growing sexuality (69). His feelings of inadequacy and desire are heightened by the presence of his older brother Peter, and Peter's girlfriend Magda, with whom Ambrose had some kind of sexual encounter when both were younger. After various adventures in Ocean City (like Crete, near the sea), the story ends with a trip by the three young people through a funhouse. The funhouse consists primarily of a maze, containing "labyrinthine corridors" (92). It is an ironic modern version of Renaissance garden mazes—also labyrinths of love, though more gracefully designed and more elegantly explored.

The first sentences of "Lost in the Funhouse" separate Ambrose from the lovers who enjoy the funhouse: "For whom is the funhouse fun? Perhaps for lovers. For Ambrose it is a place of fear and confusion" (69). The last sentences of the story echo the first and explain Ambrose's position; they classify him as a labyrinth maker, that is, an artist—a person who observes life rather than participating in it. And at that point, even more than Revel in *Passing Time*, Ambrose thinks his position is second best: "He wishes he had never entered the funhouse. But he has. Then he wishes he were dead. But he's not. Therefore he will construct funhouses for others and be their secret operator—though he would rather be among the lovers for whom funhouses are designed" (94). Even here, Ambrose thinks in a labyrinth-like mode. He locates himself at bifurcations in life's paths, imagining the roads not taken, and confirming the ones he is following.

In order to observe the technique of alternation between amorous and literary concerns in Barth's story, and then to compare that dialectic with Butor's, we need to examine briefly the relationship between Ambrose and the narrator in "Lost in the Funhouse." During the course of the story, we increasingly identify Ambrose's experiences in the funhouse with the narrator's experiences in the "house of fiction." Both figures are overly self-conscious; neither can act because of wondering how to act; neither can live in the present dimension of action — real or fictional — because the past or future intrudes; and neither can prevent clichés from periodically taking over his experience. Just as Ambrose cannot get on with his life, the narrator cannot get on with the story. Near the end of the text, two sentences that separate the narrator's reflections about writing and Ambrose's fantasies about death in the funhouse could refer to either activity. The narrator has just been describing the plot line of "conventional dramatic narrative," which a writer ought not to abandon unless he is willing to forsake the effects of drama, "or has clear cause to feel that deliberate violation of the 'normal' pattern can better can better effect that effect. This can't go on much longer; it can go on forever. He died telling stories to himself in the dark; years later" (91). Note again the suggestions of labyrinthine bifurcations in life's narrative path (the situation can't go on or it can; Ambrose dies or lives until "years later"). Immediately following this juxtaposition of fiction and funhouse, the funhouse is described as "labyrinthine," a term that characterizes the activities of both the narrator and Ambrose. This labyrinth, the funhouse of the title, represents the complications of this story, and by extension, of fiction in general, as well as the pattern of Ambrose's adventures. This identification is implicit near the beginning of the story when the narrator worries that "we haven't even reached Ocean City yet: we will never get out of the funhouse" (74). The "funhouse" here is obviously the funhouse of fiction, for we haven't sighted the "real" one in Ocean City yet. When at the end of the story Ambrose says that he'll content himself with constructing "funhouses for others . . . though he would rather be among the lovers for whom funhouses are designed," the statement comes from the narrator as well and is symbolic of the writer's stance. And conversely, we associate Ambrose's lack of success in the lovers' funhouse with the narrator. Literary art and sexual satisfaction seem to be incompatible.

If the labyrinth is traditionally a structure of initiation, successful passage through it often indicating readiness to enter a new phase of life, the journey to the center of the self that Eliade envisions as coinciding with passage to sacred and eternal life is interrupted here. Instead of going through the funhouse and coming out on the other side, Ambrose ends up still inside it, or behind its decor, lost in his reveries about his own adventures in and out of the funhouse or about the clever funhouses he will construct for others:

> He wonders: will he become a regular person? Something has gone wrong; his vaccination didn't take; at the Boy Scout initiation campfire he only pretended to be deeply moved, as he pretends to this hour that it is not so bad after all in the funhouse, and that he has a little limp. How long will it last? He envisions a truly astonishing funhouse, incredibly complex yet utterly controlled from a great central switchboard like the console of a pipe organ. Nobody had enough imagination. He could design such a place himself, wiring and all, and he's only thirteen years old. (93)

Another narrative forking path—it's an impossible task/he can do it—and a vision of Daedalus as an electronics whiz kid. Ambrose will not become a "regular person." He will not be helped through the labyrinthine funhouse by a woman, into a full sexual existence, toward union with her and a normal middle-class or even a heroic life. Even as he asks the question, "How long will it last?" he is transformed, reluctantly, into a Daedalus rather than a Theseus figure. His question is not answered; instead the focus shifts, and his creative imagination takes over, but it turns Ambrose temporarily into a misfit. He fails to participate in any initiation beyond his Boy Scout one, and that was a fake. He does not enter the adult sexual world yet. But, like Revel, he accomplishes a different rite of passage, into the realm of art; and again like Revel, he isn't sure he likes the transformation. Worse than being lost in the labyrinth of love is to remain outside of it.

Underlying the thematic oppositions in Barth's story between writers and lovers, or literature and sexuality, is a less evident pattern—a stylistic technique of alternations between the two. These shifts usually take the form of abrupt juxtapositions: self-conscious discussion of a literary device precedes or follows mention of a specific woman (most often Magda or Ambrose's mother) or of women in general, or sexual activity. These modulations achieve two complementary effects: on the one hand, they link writing and sexuality because of their proximity in the text; on the other hand, they suggest a contrast betwen the two activities because of the disjunctive nature of the transitions between them, implying a shift in the speaker's focus.

Examples of this technique abound. On the first page of the story, just after the narrator has described "Magda G——," the next sentence begins, "Initials, blanks, or both were often substituted for proper names in nineteenth-century fiction to enhance the illusion of reality" (69). Twice shortly following this, physical descriptions of the boys' mother follow observations on the literary techniques being used. Here is the first:

> when a detail from one of the five senses, say visual, is crossed with a detail from another, say auditory, the reader's imagination is oriented to the scene, perhaps unconsciously. This procedure may be compared to . . . a process known as triangulation. The brown hair on Ambrose's mother's forearms gleamed in the sunlight. (70)

The much remembered scene in the toolshed between Magda and Ambrose is also preceded immediately by a metafictional comment about using "the first person narrative viewpoint" (74). Similarly, just after Ambrose has commented on the use of "serious wordplay" in fiction, his flashlight picks out two lovers under the boardwalk. And so on.

Like Revel's shifts from writing about his diary to writing about one of the Bailey sisters, this pattern in Barth's text suggests an unconscious conflict, or the suppression of a desire, in the narrator's mind. In both works, the Ariadne's string of the narrator's words does not lead back to a woman. "Escape" from these labyrinths of language and the labyrinthine worlds they describe consists, rather, in mentally recreating them. Another man gets the girl, so to speak, while the narrator's head is turned toward his story. The implication seems to be that one either threads the labyrinth of life with a woman, or shifts to another labyrinth—the labyrinth of art—and stays out of the labyrinth of love, often reluctantly. Just as it is thought that the Cretans sacrificed bulls or even human captives at the heart of the labyrinth to propitiate the forces of the earth embodied in its tunnels, so here Revel and Ambrose, albeit perhaps unwillingly or unwittingly, have sacrificed their more animalistic instincts to achieve precarious mastery over their respective labyrinths. The artist, the builder of the labyrinth, is contrasted with the explorer, the lover. The first is above, alone, smarter and sadder; the second finds a wife as his reward and participates happily if unreflectively in life. Perhaps because of his sensitivity and visionary powers, this artist can see, and may wish to play, the alternate role, preferring the more "normal" initiation rite to his esoteric variety.

In juxtaposing these two rites of passage, Butor and Barth illustrate what appears to be a recent tendency to associate the labyrinth with overly conscious, even sterile artistic elaboration, rather than with unconscious desires or amorous initiation. Three points of comparison between the two works emerge in this context: the narrator's solitude, including the possibility of solipsism; a pattern of linguistic confusion between art and life; and the elusive nature of the women figures.

Both narrators suggest the isolating qualities in the modern labyrinth of art. Revel encloses himself in a labyrinthine wall of words that is a blueprint of his mental journeys; Ambrose will create funhouses for *others* to play in, while he remains behind their walls to operate them. In neither case can a lover approach; both figures are condemned to solitude, to amusing themselves with their own labyrinth making — superior, maybe, and very clever, but disappointed.

At several points in both texts the reader is confused about whether a word or a phrase refers to a physical action or to the writing process itself. Just as we ask ourselves from time to time whether Revel's "track" is a literal path (in the city) or a mental one (in the diary), so in "Lost in the Funhouse" we may wonder if a word belongs to Ambrose's thoughts about his situation or the narrator's description of his method. We have seen this with the sentence "This can't go on much longer; it can go on forever," which refers both to Ambrose's fantasies inside the funhouse and to the narrator's discussion of plot lines; it is also true of the title of the story itself. Most important, this linguistic confusion conflates the narrator's labyrinthine story and the labyrinthine life it reflects, underlining the interdependence of the word and the world, and in doing this it also highlights his isolation.

Both stories include women who drift in and out of the characters' fields of vision and who represent a tempting yet unattainable alternative to their intellectual literary activity. They recall the sexual initiation the labyrinth often designates, but only to signal the lack of such sexual fulfillment for these heroes. In each case, the man loses the desired woman, though she wanders strangely near him, a kind of Ariadne manquée. In *Passing Time*, the Bailey sisters become engaged to other men while Revel painstakingly records the events; in "Lost in the Funhouse," Magda remains Peter's girlfriend, though Ambrose secretly feels he should have her.

In these fictions the labyrinth suggests intellectual activity, which, while valued as such, may have overextended itself; the pattern produced is too formal, even threatening, and defines its creator as a dissatisfied outsider, though perhaps endearing to the reader. The funhouse Ambrose imagines he could construct is "incredibly complex yet utterly controlled from a great central switchboard" (93). Similarly, though Revel may be confused, he records this confusion in a patterned structure. In both cases the resulting labyrinth is complex and confusing but controlled, and embodies, as labyrinths often do, an intriguing amalgam of freedom and compulsion. It suggests each narrator's fear of overintellectualization; he has planned too elaborate a labyrinth, which separates him from other people. Because these labyrinths also mirror their surroundings, they reflect a post-Romantic fear of a world that is too complicated, even too orderly, too constraining. A writer's mind traps him in its labyrinth by reflecting the mechanical environment and the mind's patterns of thought, rather than leading him toward the lover he desires.

4 / The Minimal Labyrinth:
Alain Robbe-Grillet's *In the Labyrinth*

IF WE CONTINUE BUTOR'S ANALOGY OF EXPLORING novels as he does houses, we might imagine that *Ulysses,* remarkable for its inclusiveness, represents a labyrinthine dwelling filled with people and furniture, and that *In the Labyrinth,* stripped down to reveal the labyrinthine processes of narrative itself, resembles a similarly designed but spare and empty house. In his articulation of narrative space, Robbe-Grillet brings the labyrinth farther along the road from literary symbol to structural design, from image to icon, than either Joyce or Butor, who include a higher concentration of symbolic resonances and intertextual allusions in their novels.[1] Here, only two oblique references to the classical myth appear ("labyrinthe" in the title and "dédale" in the text), so that the labyrinth becomes significant in *In the Labyrinth* primarily through its presence as a structural principle. *In the Labyrinth* thus fulfills the potential for a labyrinthine text in a more singleminded way than does *Ulysses* or *Passing Time,* proposing the labyrinth even more explicitly as a model for modern narrative than they do. Furthermore, Robbe-Grillet's novel is more rigorously autogenerative than the other two, a labyrinth that weaves itself from itself. As we read *In the Labyrinth,* we follow a soldier wandering lost in a strange city, apparently attempting to deliver the possessions of a dead comrade, finally being shot and dying himself. At the same time, we witness what appears to be a narrator's construction of scenes and narrative sequences out of an engraving in his room.

Thus the title *In the Labyrinth* defines the soldier's exploration of the city, the narrator's construction of the story, and the reader's passage through the text.[2] In this way, Robbe-Grillet's sense of narration as quest, his idea that "the writer, by definition, doesn't know where he's going, and he writes to try to understand why he writes" is formalized and experienced directly by the reader as he traverses the novel's labyrinthine structure.[3] In discussing this process, I will look first at the text as it, like *Ulysses* and *Passing Time*, imitates in its temporal structure the spatial experience of a labyrinth, and then examine how it describes labyrinthine forms and movements in a city.[4] Finally, I will extend this analysis briefly toward the relevant mythical and symbolic resonances the text evokes.

First, a word about the narrator. The reader habitually perceives the narrator's trials and errors in the way he recounts the wanderings of the soldier. He knows only what the narrator is experimenting with at any given moment. As he progresses, he learns pieces of what seems to be a story about a soldier searching for an address in a strange town, as well as information about the present situation of this narrator. But as we shall see, the narrator's immediate surroundings and the events he describes become entangled.

Several questions regarding the narrator's identity and activity trouble the surface of the text.[5] He may be imagined as a writer who attempts to construct a story using only the elements that surround him — an engraving, a box, and certain other decorative motifs in his room. Perhaps this writer sees a soldier in the street and integrates him into the story, or invents a "doctor" whom he invests with his own voice for a time. This narrator may "be" a doctor who was once called to attend a soldier or was interrupted during his writing to attend a soldier. Robbe-Grillet himself has suggested that there are several narrators, the first a writer, the second a soldier, the third a doctor who re-enters the room by the movement of the soldier's writing.[6] Repetition near the end of the novel of sequences that appeared near the beginning suggests the existence of a single narrative voice, or at least one that reappears.[7] Lucien Dällenbach maintains that the Robbe-Grilletian narrative in *In the Labyrinth*, unlike other *récits* that may be assigned fictive fathers, denies this possibility and proclaims itself a-causal, a bastard, a parricide, because of its *équivocité*. For Dällenbach, the "I" of *In the Labyrinth* remains unanchored:

> When is he writing? When is he imagining? Which is the text that we are reading? Who is "behind" him? Questions without answers, because we are at a complete loss. As soon as it is proposed, the equation author-narrator is revised. The narrative alternates between allegory of literary creation and writing in process. And it is the indetermination — which is to say the "labyrinth" — which presides here at that doubling.[8]

Whether one naturalizes the text by positing a single narrator, or (as I would prefer) deconstructs the narrative voice by accepting the notion of an autogenerative text whose narrators displace each other, the labyrinth remains the structure (in Todorov's words) of "the quest of narrative," the voyage toward a text. In this labyrinth of language, then, the reader participates in the quest of a voice in search of itself, a self forever postponed, forever denied. The revolutionary nature of Robbe-Grillet's project, this willful erasure of narrative origins, disrupts the critical idiom as well, calling into question our habitual analytic assumptions and terms. Even so, since the actions of the figures exist within the novel, whatever their ontological status, in discussing those actions we need to lend the agents a consistency denied them in the novel itself.

Labyrinthine Discourse

The labyrinthine nature of Robbe-Grillet's text is established early on by both the design of the discourse and the shapes of the referents. To begin with the first of these, in *In the Labyrinth,* as in *Ulysses* and *Passing Time,* passage from word to word as well as perception of larger structural units resembles a journey in a labyrinth. The procedure of backtracking to particular words or phrases appears in the first paragraph and continues rigorously throughout the novel. Here is the beginning of the text:

> I am alone here now, under cover. *Outside it is raining, outside you walk* through the rain with your head down, *shielding your eyes with one*

hand while you stare ahead nevertheless, *a few yards ahead,* at *a few yards* of wet asphalt; *outside* it is cold, the wind blows through the leaves, rocking whole boughs, rocking them, rocking, their shadows swaying across the white roughcast walls. *Outside* the sun is shining, there is no tree, no bush to cast a shadow, and *you walk* under the sun *shielding your eyes with one hand while you stare ahead,* only *a few yards* in front of you, at *a few yards* of dusty asphalt where the wind makes patterns of parallel lines, forks, and spirals. [my emphasis][9]

As in the passage we looked at from *Passing Time,* the underlined words are the familiar corners or passageways, which we encounter more than once and from which alternate routes branch out. The "Outside" at the start of each sentence, combined with the clause after the semicolon beginning with the same adverb, announcing first rain, then cold, and then sunshine, are analogous to three alternate routes branching off from the same node of "Outside," but leading eventually back to the same path of "shielding your eyes with one hand." The same principle applies to the phrase "a few yards," which constitutes another crossroads or corridor from which the alternate passageways of "ahead" or "wet" or "dusty" asphalt lead on. In this pattern, even though the resulting texts are so vastly different, we can see that Robbe-Grillet and Butor close the gap between story and discourse as Joyce does, by focusing on the generative qualities of verbal signs, and forming their syntactical arrangement into a labyrinth of language.

As we shall see, the same pattern writ large structures the entire novel: familiar figures and phrases are passed again and again before new narrative paths branch off, many of them to merge later on. For example, after retracing separately the narrative paths describing the dusty room to which we return many times, and the entryway of the building where it is located, we emerge into a passage of prose that connects them: "At the top is the closed room where the gray film of dust gradually settles" (95). At this point, the description of the room trails off, after a few of its contents have been mentioned, as if to acknowledge that the reader now knows this corridor of the labyrinth well enough to dispense with the rest. Similarly, a room where the soldier attempts to make his way through a gesticulating crowd appears three times before it is joined definitively to the café. But in neither case do these passageways constitute more than partial paths in the more extensive labyrinth of the text. As if to specify this procedure, we hear of the latter scene, "But this scene leads to nothing"—a dead end in the labyrinthine prose (134). Near the end of the novel, a number of résumés join formerly separate narrative paths; the plan of the labyrinth is becoming more familiar.

Although the labyrinth that results from these narrative journeys represents confusion, it reveals the structural formality characteristic of labyrinths. Repeated returns to recognizable points via definite paths imply entrapment within a pattern. An order may exist, even though the explorer cannot perceive it. This pattern repeats scenes, and particular objects often induce modulations from one scene to another. And as it did in *Passing Time,* this process further distinguishes the labyrinth from a more random sort of confusion. As in Butor's text, scenes include invariable sequences; when a certain object in one scene is mentioned, the others follow in a progression, as if when one turned into that tunnel of the labyrinth, it were necessary to go past all its contents before emerging into new territory. Again, this procedure further formalizes the mode of associative thinking that we observed in *Ulysses.* When the room is mentioned, for example, the paths in the dust, the bureau, the fireplace, the lamp, and the rest of the furniture follow. The same thing happens in the café, with its inevitable red-checked tablecloth, winestains, its glasses, its soldiers drinking. The narrative is hedged, confined; its progression is channeled, not free, its labyrinthine trajectory in this respect resembling our experience of language itself.

The objects that form points of modulation between scenes resemble forks in a labyrinthine path in the same way that repeated words in the first paragraph did. This technique is most evident at the beginning of the novel in transitions between the narrator's room and the outdoors. Descriptions of shiny tracks on the floor repeatedly precede descriptions of tracks outside in the snow: "On the marble top of the chest, on the day bed, on the waxed floor where the felt slippers . . . / The tracks continue, regular and straight, across the fresh snow" (95). The red curtains also provoke transitions to the outdoor scene: "and for the greater part of its width by thick red curtains made of a heavy velvety material. / Outside it is snowing" (30).[10]

In addition to the repetition of scenes with slight variation, a complementary scriptural procedure achieves a conceptual merging, a narrowing of possibilities. The author's room merges with that of the young woman, which in turn joins the café and the hospital, later confused with each other. The young woman in the room blends with the waitress in the café, and the soldier with the young woman's husband. The streets themselves also give the impression of coalescing, when we are shown "another row of identical windows and doors which look like the reflection of the first, as if a mirror had been set there" (36). Multiplied scenes and superimposed places are both analogous to familiar crossroads or paths in the textual labyrinth; combined, they create the sense of a large yet contingent universe. We may ask ourselves whether there is "really" one woman—or table, or corridor, or street—which expands into several, or several which are conflated into one, but the question is irresolvable in a self-generative fiction in the same way that an explorer in a labyrinth cannot tell whether a particular passage or crossroads is the same one or another. Robbe-Grillet's narrative labyrinth thus distinguishes itself by playing relentlessly on the mutual contamination of "iterative" and "repeating" narrative (something which happened several times but which is recounted only once versus something which happened once but which is recounted several times).[11] Robbe-Grillet disrupts the convention of writing that comes into play when we say that this scene happened many times and imply that ones like it repeatedly took place. As in a labyrinth, where many corridors look the same, even though they may not be the same (though they may be), here we are presented with the question of whether the scene is repeated in the story or only in the discourse. Indeed, this labyrinthine text questions the possibility of distinguishing between them. Here Proust precedes but does not go so far as Robbe-Grillet. As Gérard Genette argues, Proustian narration frequently eludes the clear joining up of temporal sequences. Still, in Proust, "the characteristic and very marked tendency toward inflating the iterative is intended to be taken in its impossible literalness" (i.e., this same scene "really" did happen many times even though the wealth of its detail suggests the contrary),[12] so that we can still distinguish this iterative from the repeating narrative. In Robbe-Grillet's text, however, the labyrinthine principle of referential choice, again more radically deployed than in Joyce or Butor, prevents such a distinction.

Since a characteristic of labyrinthine journeys is the action of re-tracing a path or reencountering a corner, the functions of choice and of repetition are closely linked in these labyrinthine texts. As we have been seeing here, a corner of a labyrinth may look the same as another, and yet be different; or it may look different—because the explorer approaches it from a different direction or in a different light—and yet be the same turning he has encountered before. Thus the labyrinth confounds the distinction between sameness and difference. As Genette recognizes, Robbe-Grillet's labyrinths exploit this aspect of the design with particular insistence: "The labyrinth, privileged space of Robbe-Grillet's universe, is this region that already fascinated the baroque poets, a disorienting region of being where the reversible signs of difference and sameness meet in a kind of rigorous confusion."[13] In passing, I note Genette's confirmation of the labyrinth as an emblem of the paradoxical rigor and confusion that characterize the process of literary discourse as it articulates a text. As we shall see, the reversibility of sameness and difference in Robbe-Grillet's novel extends to the specifically human frame of reference, resulting in an interchange of self and other.

Decor and Movement

Appropriately, the first paragraph of *In the Labyrinth* (quoted above) ends by evoking the component parts of visual labyrinths, parallel lines, forks, and spirals, all of which reappear on the third page along with a truncated circle—another element of a classical labyrinth shape. After that come more labyrinthine forms, "uncertain, overlapping shapes" (31). Similarly, the repeated conjunction of circles and squares in the third and fourth paragraphs also recalls the curved paths and squared corners of many labyrinth designs, as does the configuration of the lamp base—a circle on a square.

Such visual reminders of labyrinths continue throughout the novel: concentric rings and intertwined ivy encircle the lamppost; "a crisscrossing of meaningless lines" characterizes the intersection of two streets in the town; wine glasses leave numbers of incomplete circular traces on the tablecloth at the café; crisscrossing paths in the snow traverse the sidewalks (32). The entryway of a building consists of one long corridor giving onto another darker one. The wrinkles on the soldier's hand, accented by traces of something black, comprise a generally labyrinthine design: "The forefinger is crisscrossed with short black lines, mostly parallel or only slightly divergent, the others variously oriented, surrounding the first lines or cutting across them" (63). The soldier worries about the young woman in "the long series of hallways, narrow staircases, and more hallways turning off at right angles, where she may easily get lost before reaching the street" (145). The careful scrutiny of footprints in snow, with attention to how long they remain recalls the laying down of Ariadne's thread, and suggests the desire for a guide in the labyrinth. Yet in this case guide and guided change places: at one point the soldier follows the boy's footsteps, at another their positions are reversed.

In similar fashion, figures following prescribed circuits (as they would in a labyrinth) or the evidence of such trajectories appear frequently; inside, the fly on the lampshade "reappears and continues its circuit," and "on the waxed floor, the felt slippers have made gleaming paths" (30, 32). Outside, "a yellowish-gray straight path also indicates the snow-covered sidewalk. Produced by the footsteps of people now gone, the path passes" (34). Most obviously, the emphasis on walking, and on finding the right path, the measuring of steps, plus the soldier's evident disorientation, and his efforts to distinguish one place from another, establish a labyrinthine environment. "Having arrived at a crossroads," for example, "the soldier hesitates," unable to locate the street signs at a corner (42). In any case, they would not help him much, we are told, since he doesn't know the town. Completely lost, the soldier goes "in circles through the maze of identical streets" ("le quadrillage des rues identiques"; 46).[14] As he walks with the boy, "the crossroads and sudden changes in direction increase in number" (138). When the soldier first tries the wrong door to get a drink in the barracks, he must retrace his steps; he also mistakes another bed for his own. He finally gives up, not having the strength "to make another attempt to walk through the labyrinth of unlighted hallways ["le dédale des couloirs"] until he reaches this infinitely distant and problematical water" (97, 121).

Not only trajectories on foot but verbal trajectories within the story are also reported in terms that suggest labyrinthine paths, though less frequently. When he meets a man in the street, the soldier's speech is characterized as having a labyrinthine form, a linguistic equivalent of his uncertain spatial itinerary: "And he continues talking, losing himself in a plethora of increasingly confusing specifications, suddenly conscious of this, stopping at almost each step in order to start again in a different direction" (116). This conversation continues in the same vein, presenting a labyrinth in which the soldier founders, attempting to follow two branches simultaneously: "The soldier had to choose between two solutions: to speak more openly or else to beat an immediate retreat. But he had not had time to choose one course or the other, and he had persisted in both directions at once," and so finally he stops talking, defeated by the labyrinth of his own speech as he is by the streets in the town (117). At one point, the boy's speech also follows alternative routes; when the soldier asks him if he will reach the same boulevard whichever way he goes, the boy first says yes and then no.

Finally, fissures in the urban decor further particularize its labyrinthine qualities. The repeatedly described crack in the wall of the narrator's room and the various barely open doors suggest the desire of the wanderer to find a way out of these familiar corridors of city and prose, or perhaps even the desire to escape inevitable entrapment via a flaw in their structure rather than by deciphering them. But no; even the crack turns out to be another labyrinth, to produce a labyrinthine glance: "It would be necessary to follow [the crack] with application from one turn to the next, with its curves, vacillations, uncertainties, sudden changes of directions, inflections, continuations, slight regressions" (154). In this next example, doors are described tentatively, and the smallness of the opening is emphasized; the doors leave "perhaps an inch or two of space between them, a vertical stripe of darkness" (36). Such a description visualizes the hope for escape, as does the narrator's imagining an exit to the café; there his desire is so strong that he begins the description as if the door actually existed: "The main entrance, with white enamel letters spelling out the word 'café' . . . can be nowhere else but in the wall not shown in the print" (52–53). Just following the description of the crack between the doors, looking in the opposite direction — as if the explorer had turned around in his search for an escape — there is another door, whose opening seems to elicit the wanderer's hope again: "a dark interval wide enough for a man, or at least a child, to slip through" (36). The emptiness of the town reveals a similar anxiety, this time the wish to discern a guiding figure in the labyrinthine streets: "And the entire scene remains empty: without a man, a woman, or even a child" (37). The decor, like the structure of the labyrinth of city or text, provides actual or imagined possibilities for escape but no definitive exit. It is the scenery of trial and error, of frustrated desire.

Explorers and Centers

In the Labyrinth opens with the narrator alone in a room. He surveys part of the labyrinthine city, and creates a labyrinthine text out of what he sees: in the room, the wallpaper, the table, the box, the rifle, the bed, the fireplace, the bureau, the light, the engraving of the café scene, the curtains, and so forth; outside it, the street lined with buildings, the snow, the intersection with a lamppost under which a soldier may be standing. These are the components of the soldier's labyrinth, created for him to wander in. But, as I have suggested, the narrator's process of writing resembles *his* being lost in a labyrinth, the labyrinth of his literary imagination—a "labyrinth of his own devising," as Gide will tell us in *Theseus*. In devising his labyrinthine text, that narrator reveals a certain method, but also a certain madness.

The urban labyrinth *in* the story, which the soldier explores, is more relentlessly monotonous than the textual labyrinth *of* the story, which the narrator creates and the reader follows in his wake, but not much more. The principal difference between him and them is of course that whereas he dies in the labyrinthine city, we can close the labyrinth of the book and the narrator can lift his pen from the labyrinth of the page; in the speed of his exit at the very end of the novel, we can even imagine that narrator, like the original Daedalus, flying out of the labyrinths of city and text, leaving the blurred image of "the inordinately delicate pattern of the wallpaper and the indeterminate edges of the gleaming paths made in the dust by the felt slippers, and, beyond the door, the dark vestibule where the umbrella is leaning against the coat rack, then, once past the entrance door, the series of long hallways, the spiral staircase, the door to the building with its stone stoop, and the whole city behind me" (160).

The labyrinth of streets that the soldier explores exists within the labyrinth of the prose, which, because it is patterned on imaginative journeys, provides a bit more variety for its explorers. Nevertheless, since the components of the text are rigorously limited, our experience in it duplicates the claustrophobia of the soldier in the town. Thus the distinction between the soldier as Theseus and the narrator as Daedalus, which we are tempted to posit, is suggested only to be denied. As he composes his text, the narrator approaches the danger against which we will hear Gide's Daedalus warn Theseus, the danger of self-enclosure in the labyrinth of art. As Jean-Pierre Vidal recognizes, this danger stems from allowing himself the freedom to experiment, from voluntarily relinquishing complete control.[15] As we have seen before, the liberty to wander includes the possibility of becoming lost. And in the same way that the distinction between sameness and difference is eroded, the categories of Theseus and Daedalus are blurred, the difference between the subject and the object of the discourse questioned.

Throughout Robbe-Grillet's novel, the reader is reminded that he follows the narrator "in the labyrinth" of the scene of writing. Certain passages in the prose refer to the structure of the story as if it were already composed, or had some form toward which it should move. For instance, we hear that the soldier "must be dead for the others to leave him like this. Yet the next scene shows him in the bed" (148). Or an abrupt "no" stops at a dead end and necessitates a retracing of steps, a re-creation of the scene. (In this second case it is not possible to tell whether the uncertainty belongs to the soldier, who has forgotten just where he is, or the narrator, who has had a lapse of memory.): "Instead he will wait until the attendant in the canvas duffle-coat and the hunter's boots comes back. No, that's not it: here, it is the woman with the low voice who is taking care of him. It is only at this moment that he is surprised to be back in this room whose setting belongs to a much earlier scene" (143). Several pages later, the phrase "but in the drawing there are so many other garments hanging on top of each other" recalls the engraving that serves as one of the points of departure for the story; it, too, refocuses the text on the narrative process (159). In threading his way through this narrative labyrinth, in contemplating questions like Was there an address for the soldier to find? Are the narrator and the doctor the same person? Is there one woman or several? the reader must choose which alternative path of interpretation to take, or choose not to choose and allow the possibilities to exist simultaneously, recreating the labyrinth of the text in his mind.

In the Labyrinth, like *Passing Time,* contains neither a structural nor a symbolic center. At the end of the book, as we have seen, the narrator takes flight in a kind of zoom-lens motion, leaving his narrative trace and "the whole city behind" him. The point of exit is clearly random and arbitrary, not a well-defined or a significant center of the narrative labyrinth it terminates. In contrast to this final flight, the Daedalian task of inscribing and decoding that the text embodies has been of a slow and painstaking nature — in Revel's words, "a dangerous work of exploration and analysis." As in Joyce and Butor's texts, we have been led to consider possible centers for the narrative sequences that comprise the novel's labyrinthine design — in this case the engraving, the box, the decor of the room, the café, the narrator's mind, the death of the soldier, the exit of the narrator; but here, as in those other instances, they resemble forks within the labyrinth, rather than a central enclosure, forks that the narrator, with the reader following him, passes repeatedly. Again, as in *Ulysses* and *Passing Time,* these "centers" are nostalgic spaces, reminiscent of a vanished order, proposed only to be denied; the novel's best spatial analogue is a labyrinth with multiple nuclei but no single center. As the labyrinthine text represents the articulation of discourse itself, the erasure of a single narrative voice — another kind of centering device — and the denial of a traditional origin for this fiction confirm the profoundly decentered nature of the postmodern imagination.

Initiation

The question of what constitutes the center of the labyrinth, the object of the narrative quest, leads to the related question of what is accomplished by this journey. The book ends with the soldier dead and the narrator intact. Literature prevails, one might say. But what was at stake in the first place for the narrator? Unlike the soldier, his life seems not to have been in danger; he has remained comfortably in his room, writing. The circular design of the text, beginning with "I" and ending with "me," highlights Robbe-Grillet's contention that at the end of the novel nothing is solved—only unimportant details are revealed.[16] The ending of the story is anticlimatic, not triumphant.[17] We can object here that during his narration the narrator has been trapped dangerously in his own labyrinth of fabulation, for it is true that a certain anxiety and feverish activity pervade the text. And we can imagine that he is concerned somehow with the soldier's fate and therefore compelled to reconstruct his story. But, as in *Le Voyeur,* where we also follow relentless experimentation with narrative segments, this kind of identification is disrupted and we hesitate between alternate evaluations of the narrator's activity: meticulous, even disinterested, or compulsive. In either case, though, that narrator remains in control of his situation—albeit in dubious control—rather than at risk, and he ends up where he began.

The novel's decor of similar forms and neutral colors underlines the lack of change in this environment, and heightens the strange tension between stagnation and compulsion transmitted by the text. The soldier's face is "grayish," "the eyelids are gray, like the rest of the face," his coat is of no distinguishable color, and the book begins on "a dull day which makes everything colorless and flat," a day on which "the falling snow depriv[es] the scene of all relief" (33, 32). Similarity extends not only to color, but also to perspective. The confusion of objects, their merging, begins as a result of the gray uniformity near the beginning of the novel. The shape of the small dagger covered with gray dust on the table is repeated on the wallpaper, also gray: "A similar design also embellishes the wallpaper. The wallpaper is pale gray with slightly darker vertical stripes; between the dark stripes, in the middle of each lighter stripe, runs a line of small dark-gray identical designs" (35). Even within this gray wallpaper, the differences between the stripes are hardly visible—more uniformity. The sentence continues, and re-emphasizes the identity of the wallpaper design with the dagger, as it did at the beginning with the words "similar" and "also." The monotony extends to motion with the fly, whose "speed is always the same: slow and steady" (33). The snowflakes also "descend gently in a steady, uninterrupted, vertical fall" (32). This decor harmonizes with the soldier's point of view: "'Anyway,' the soldier says, 'it all comes down to the same thing now. Sooner or later they'll get us'" (133). Moreover, this sense of personal failure is increased by the background of national defeat.

This decor of inertia reinforces the anticlimactic side of the soldier's and the narrator's experience within the story, but the labyrinthine narrative structure itself, a trajectory of trials and errors,
counters that inertia with its characteristic suggestion of progress,
often progress toward a new state of being or awareness. Although
they do traverse their own labyrinths—of city and text—neither the
soldier nor the narrator really completes such a rite of passage.
Indeed, the lack of progress, the absence of initiatory experience for
the soldier and the narrator, focuses our attention more closely on
our progress as readers, for this is the primary initiation that takes
place within this labyrinth of language.[18] An initiation teaches the
initiate the patterns he will need to know in the realm to which it
gives access. In Robbe-Grillet's textual labyrinth we learn about the
process of writing, the construction of discourse, having witnessed
the normally hidden bifurcations of a narrator's thought.[19] This, of
course, is a reading that in its constructive design resembles a writing, making In the Labyrinth, in Barthes's terms a writerly more
than a readerly text, one that requires active participation by the
reader. The reader's labyrinthine rite of passage, like Revel's, leads
not into individual or sexual maturity but rather into the realm of
writing, into the privileged space of narrating, into the domain of
the signifying process. This space is a rigorously labyrinthine space,
filled with convolutions and complications, not the restful temple of
the *mot juste,* but the disconcerting marketplace of the everchanging, self-transforming, and multivalent verbal sign. Like Gide,
Durrell, and Nin, who use the mystery of the journey in the labyrinth and the battle with the minotaur to symbolize inner exploration and confrontation with unconscious forces, enlarging interior
landscapes with telluric dimensions, here Robbe-Grillet focuses that
journey and that battle on the process of reading, transforming the
reader into the hero of those adventures. The labyrinth he must
thread is the syntax of the narration and if there is a monster he
must slay it is the labyrinth's resistence to yield a meaning to his
mind. Clearly, such a writerly text proposes the interdependence of
narrators and listeners. In this case, initiation into the writer's labyrinth of the signifying process coincides with emergence into the
reader's labyrinth of interpretation.

Before moving on to more general concerns of symbolic resonances in Robbe-Grillet's text, let us examine the reader's labyrinth

of interpretation for a moment. As we have seen, since we experience the labyrinthine wanderings of the soldier in the town through the narrator's labyrinthine attempts to record them, we are often unsure whether the repeated trajectories mirror the narrator's writing or the soldier's walking. Does the soldier "actually" return various times to the lamppost, for example, or does the narrator try repeatedly to perfect his description? Does the soldier meet the boy several times or only once? Sometimes it seems clear that the repetitions belong to the narrator because the words, the narrator's medium, are the same, and only the order changes, but sometimes not.[20] Most readers will realize sooner or later that there is no such thing as "actually" or "really" in such a text, but the realization does not erase the cognitive efforts to start solving these referential tangles.

Besides blurring the distinction between iterative and repeating narrative, the confusion of the writer's and the soldier's activities amounts in a general way to a confusion of time and space.[21] The writer's labyrinth of his text is temporal, the soldier's labyrinth of the town is spatial. But we cannot always tell them apart. Even so, Robbe-Grillet keeps us trying, inviting our efforts to decipher the soldier's story, presenting new elements for the narrator to arrange. That we can never fully recreate a coherent story keeps our attention focused on the labyrinthine process of composition, on the journey *toward* a story. Thus we see that, as suggested earlier, Robbe-Grillet escalates the merging of story and discourse that we have noted in Joyce and Butor. By repeating the same actions, sometimes even in the same words, he conflates "the world in which one tells" and "the world of which one tells," confounding once again our habitual distinctions between different fictional spaces, between subjects and objects of narrative, ultimately between selves and others.[22]

The Symbolic Landscape

In his early essay on "Nature, Humanism, Tragedy," Robbe-Grillet proposes to renounce the depth of meaning often lent objects or even life itself in favor of surfaces presented in a nontragic spirit. Tragedy for him is an effort to recoup the distance between man and things. Instead of this project, he wishes "to propose objects as purely exterior and as composed of surfaces," and argues that this "is not—as people have said—to deny man; but it is to resist the pananthropic idea contained in traditional humanism. . . . It is only in the end to develop the logical consequences of the affirmation of my freedom."[23] Robbe-Grillet reveals the post-Existentialist nature of his thought by basing his theory on his freedom. He differs from earlier Existentialist thinkers, of course, in that he experiences no anguish in this freedom, in objects that present him with surface texture rather than hidden significance.

The allegorical title of *In the Labyrinth,* layered with a depth of cultural resonances, in conjunction with the spare labyrinth of the text, empty of specific allusions, situates the novel at the heart of a central question regarding Robbe-Grillet's works—whether or not to ascribe symbolic meaning to his minutely described structures. The preface to the novel also reveals a purposeful ambiguity; it informs us that the text presents "a strictly material [reality]; that is, it is subject to no allegorical interpretations." But the strong allegorical resonances of the word *labyrinth* are bound to surface nonetheless.[24] The preface warns the reader not to give the novel "either more or less meaning than in his own life or his own death." Again, a contradiction, a fork in the labyrinth of interpretation that precedes our entry into the formal labyrinth of the prose. In effect, this admonition serves as an invitation to attribute any and all meanings we perceive, for what could be more significant than one's own life and death? In the book's unanchored symbolic title, then, Robbe-Grillet encourages diverse symbolic explorations. The title of *In the Labyrinth* thus presents a culturally bound image; the "objective" description within the novel pursues a phenomenological exploration of that image. And so the book invests a symbolic configuration with its experiential manifestation as text.[25] Conversely, the resonances in the title reverse the erasure of symbolic traces in the text; through it, the reader begins to reinvest the minimal textual labyrinth with allegorical meaning. Like the carefully constructed wings of Daedalus, or the carefully designed labyrinth that contained a monster, the intricate meanders of Robbe-Grillet's text support multiple flights of the allegorical imagination, not the least of which is the necessity to invent them, which is to say to confront their presence as absence.

Here, as in *Passing Time*—and in continental mosaic labyrinths on church pavements—the minotaur seems to have disappeared. As Cortázar's Theseus says in *The Kings,* even if he kills the minotaur, "the problem remains; his death makes [Theseus] the lord of a prison," and he must still find his way out.[26] The explorer must trace a pattern rather than conquer a monster; for this he needs tenacity and intelligence rather than physical strength. Furthermore, as Borges implies in his poem "Labyrinth" (where he warns the inhabitant not to expect a bull) and his city in "The Immortal" (which is empty and chaotic), the labyrinth without a minotaur may be more frightening than one built around a beast, the void of meaning more disquieting than its excess. This idea, which applies to Robbe-Grillet's text, also appears in a poem by Philip Booth entitled "Cold Water Flat," where it serves as a sign of contemporary alienation:

> Come to conquer
> this living labyrinth of rock,
>   young Theseus of Dubuque
> finds he is mazed without a minotaur,
> without his Ariadne in the dark.
> . . . .
>   How now, Theseus? How send
>   word home you are confined
> with neither wings nor lover's thread
> in the city that a murderer designed?[27]

For the reader of the poems by Borges and Booth, though, the mythological figures do appear in the texts, even though they are denied there, and to some extent by their very presence they subvert the demythologizing projects of the poems. In this context, *In the Labyrinth* more fully empties the labyrinth of minotaurs and Ariadnes, though not, in the end, of existential significance. In the absence of specific mythological figures, which in some strange way justify its existence, humanize it, the verbal labyrinth encloses us all the more tightly, constituting as it does so a powerful symbol of urban disorientation and textual experimentation.

Postscript: Comparisons

In the Labyrinth and *Passing Time* are strikingly similar in their use of the labyrinth pattern. In focusing our attention on the process of composition, these two texts tend to foreground the narrating instance, specifically denying what Genette claims is "one of the fictions of literary narrating," which is that it comprises "instantaneous action, without a temporal dimension."[28] Thus they explicitly illustrate our sense that in much modern fiction the line of narrative discourse has thickened into a labyrinth. Both narrators finally escape from their labyrinthine cities and texts, though during the process of composition they take on the Thesean qualities of explorers, blurring, as we have seen, though not abolishing, the distinction between Daedalus and Theseus, designer and wanderer, synchronic vision and diachronic exploration, writers and readers of texts.[29] In both cases, modern urban life-as-a-labyrinth is gray with uniformity, and the power of these foggy or snowy labyrinths suggests the partial eclipse of the masculine solar hero and the cultural values he represents. As in *Ulysses,* figures of women hover tantalizingly near the wanderers. But these texts are even farther from love's labyrinth than Joyce's; the Cartesian imperative to constitute the self through thought stifles voluntary entry into the labyrinth of love, and we follow the hard roads of reason rather than the soft paths of the heart.

The most significant parallel between *In the Labyrinth* and *Passing Time* is that both novels follow the same "garden of forking paths," the same labyrinthine narrative design; the initiation pattern structures the processes of writing and reading. Thus, like Renaissance garden mazes, which exploited the labyrinth's potential for intricate patterns, Butor and Robbe-Grillet focus on meanders rather than monsters, and like those secular mazes, their textual labyrinths move the design out of the cathedral onto the streets. Yet the playful quotient of the earlier gardens is lessened in these urban texts. We sense the legacy of Kafka's fearful labyrinths and of French Existentialism. Anxiety escalates within the convolutions rather than dissipating at a central resting place.

Two final similarities concern ancient resonances of the labyrinth. First, the narrators of these texts have replayed the ancient game of

Troia, where men traced ritual labyrinthine designs on the ground during the founding of the city to protect it from supernatural enemies or during wartime to insure it against the entry of enemy soldiers. As founders of these textual cities, having performed these functions, they now take their leave. The second resonance is that in associating the design with the acts of writing and reading, Butor and Robbe-Grillet renew one of the ancient aesthetic roles of the labyrinth, which, because of its importance as a ritual space, according to C. N. Deedes, "fostered the development of all art and literature."[30]

These two narrative labyrinths are not identical, however. For one thing, *In the Labyrinth* viewed in its spatial capacity as a verbal icon suggests greater angularity and coldness than *Passing Time.* First of all, in the referential domain, the grid of streets in the town is rigid, the pattern is square, hard-edged, the corners turn right angles. In addition, the mind of the narrator and the city he describes are more closely identified with each other than in Revel's case. Both mind and town contain the same furniture of corners, lamps, and fissures; the physical scene and the emotional tone are similarly bleak.[31] The narrative is empty of overt affective elements, which soften the contours of material reality. The reality of *Passing Time* is less "strictly material"; it functions in a more conventionally humanistic manner, revealing an emotional depth within its labyrinthine prose and thus presenting softer, more welcoming, albeit also more melancholy, corridors of lyric warmth to the reader. According to Bachelard, both of these labyrinths have their dangers: A "hard labyrinth is a labyrinth which hurts: it differs from the soft labyrinth where one suffocates."[32] He contrasts the "crystalline chemistry" and empty corridors of the first variety with the "flowing chemistry" and full passageways of the second.[33] In contrast to the labyrinthine monologue of Molly Bloom that ends *Ulysses,* and which, as Jung suggests, may tend to suffocate the reader who explores it, and to Butor's narrative and symbolic labyrinths in *Passing Time,* Robbe-Grillet's labyrinths of city and text are of the first, the hard variety, minimal labyrinths, relentlessly minimal labyrinths, spare, hard, empty, labyrinths of alienation rather than labyrinths of nondifferentiation.

In comparing the labyrinths of Butor and Robbe-Grillet, we can also discern a difference in the textual patterns they form. Because of the greater disparity between city and mind, between story and discourse, Butor's structure is less confusing; the reader is normally able to separate events from accounts—in Genette's terms, he can distinguish between iterative and repeating narrative—generally understanding what happens before what and to whom. The pattern of this labyrinth thus comprises a tortuous path with few choices. Robbe-Grillet's narrator, on the other hand, confounds iterative and repeating narrative, and leaves open questions of time and identity. The reader is never sure what happened to whom or when. The narrative labyrinth here contains many forks from which diverging paths of interpretation branch out. The reader's progress through these labyrinths of language thus forms a multicursal pattern for *In the Labyrinth*, a unicursal path for *Passing Time*. Even so, we have seen that the labyrinthine style of *Passing Time*, where Revel starts from one point and digresses, to return or not, and even more significantly, the existence of unresolved details (concerning Burton's car accident, for example), suggest the existence of alternate narrative paths, even though they are not exploited formally to the extent that they are in *In the Labyrinth*.

We should note here that this kind of narrative structure, the branching, expanding, parenthetical style, the self-reflexive design of the prose in these novels, their extensive use of narrative detours, their reactivation of the structures of initiation in the realm of literary discourse, owe a great deal to Proust's example. The most strikingly labyrinthine characteristic of Proust's prose that Butor and Robbe-Grillet develop is its incessant narrative detours, which, like the passage about Revel's suitcase and the beginning of *In the Labyrinth*, take off from one element, explore a path, and then return to the original element. More generally, Butor and Robbe-Grillet also continue Proust's interest in heightening the tension, present in all fiction of course, between the diachronically wandering character and reader in their respective labyrinths of life and text as contrasted to the synchronically designing writer hovering over them, a tension that they highlight, as Proust does, paradoxically, by simultaneously questioning it through the mediation of a narrator who participates in both perspectives, and that, like the form of the labyrinth itself, is ultimately an elaborate game of time and space.

Finally, the presence of the labyrinth as a symbolic structure in *Passing Time* and *In the Labyrinth* raises two significant theoretical issues; they concern the tracing of mythological patterns in literature and the idea of the mise-en-abyme (a miniature model of a text contained within that text). The use of myth in these two novels resembles much critical discussion of the mythical structures that underlie literary texts. Butor and Robbe-Grillet do not retell a classical story, but rather they allow particular elements of a myth to appear beneath an ostensibly independent one. The project corresponds in the narrative domain to Roland Barthes's contemporaneous *Mythologies,* which exposes social myths underlying ostensibly neutral commercial texts. Butor and Robbe-Grillet create artificially this same situation in their novels. The critical reader looks within the story to discern an underlying mythical pattern. These novels thus resemble the "unconscious survivals" of mythological patterns that Harry Levin claims are more powerful than "conscious revivals" of ancient texts.[34] In achieving this effect willfully they simultaneously deny the unperceived presence of mythical structures in contemporary society and affirm their continuing force as descriptive metaphors and even regulators of experience.

The labyrinths in *Passing Time* and *In the Labyrinth* illustrate the notion of the mise-en-abyme in several related ways. First, as we have seen, specific references to the labyrinth myth suggest an analogue for the reader's progress through the text that contains them.[35] Second, the labyrinthine narrative structures of the novels mirror, in addition to exterior landscapes, the processes of their own compositions.[36] Finally, this very self-reflexive design of the texts represents a labyrinthine doubling back, a series of convolutions, a hollow center, so that these narrative labyrinths suggest a metamorphosis of fictional subject matter into fictional process. Lucien Dällenbach maintains that readers generally use the mise-en-abyme as something like a model for an all-encompassing moment of understanding, as a "criterion for selecting and structuring" as they read.[37] The mise-en-abyme of the labyrinth in these novels functions in this way, because by allowing us to picture the design of the text as a garden of forking narrative paths, it provides a recognizable model that enables us to understand our confusing verbal trajectories as a quest for narrative itself. Particularly in the case of *In the Labyrinth,* however, rather than selecting among alternatives, the reader holds the possibilities presented to him suspended, recognizing that the alternatives themselves constitute the labyrinth he explores, a labyrinth whose multicursal nature is thus rigorously affirmed.

5 / Too Many Labyrinths:
Jorge Luis Borges

BECAUSE THE LABYRINTH APPEARS WITH UNUSUAL frequency in his work, Borges adds to the labyrinth as we have known it a dimension of obsession.[1] Unlike some obsessions, however, the distinguishing characteristic of this one is the variety of the forms it takes, for Borges often thinks in terms of labyrinths, but not always the same kinds of labyrinths. Thus Borges exploits with special intensity the ambiguities that make the labyrinth a powerful and versatile sign. Furthermore, the writings of Borges, who knows intimately the topographies of both ancient cities and his own, constitute an outstanding contemporary example of the labyrinth as a sign of the interdependence of cities, texts, and thoughts. Borges persistently uses the labyrinth to suggest how the shapes of thought and their printout in writing both inform and reflect the shapes of their worlds. Over and over again in his fiction, labyrinths of words or thoughts coexist with labyrinthine itineraries, each variety implicating the other.

The variety of expression that characterizes Borges's use of the labyrinth is well illustrated by two facing poems in his *New Personal Anthology*.[2] They will provide an introduction to the variety of labyrinths Borges creates, and particularly to the dialogue with itself that the image maintains throughout his texts:

The Labyrinth

Zeus, Zeus himself could not undo these nets
Of stone encircling me. My mind forgets
The persons I have been along the way,
The hated way of monotonous walls,
Which is my fate. The galleries seem straight
But curve furtively, forming secret circles
At the terminus of years; and the parapets
Have been worn smooth by the passage of days.
Here, in the tepid alabaster dust,
Are tracks that frighten me. The hollow air
Of evening sometimes brings a bellowing,
Or the echo, desolate, of bellowing.
I know that hidden in the shadows there
Lurks another, whose task is to exhaust
The loneliness that braids and weaves this hell,
To crave my blood, and to fatten on my death.
We seek each other. Oh, if only this
Were the last day of our antithesis!

Labyrinth

There'll never be a door. You're inside
and the keep encompasses the world
and has neither obverse nor reverse
nor circling wall nor secret center.
Hope not that the straightness of your path
that stubbornly branches off in two,
and stubbornly branches off in two,
will have an end. Your fate is ironbound,
as is your judge. Forget the onslaught
of the bull that is a man and whose
strange and plural form haunts the tangle
of unending interwoven stone.
He does not exist. In the black dust
hope not even for the savage beast.

In the first poem, the presumably ancient narrator recalls Borges's own Asterion (whom we will see in a moment), waiting to be delivered from a hateful labyrinth. The tone is a poignant combination of weary resignation and mildly romantic nostalgia. The galleries curve in "secret circles"; the captive has forgotten his former identities but still remembers that he possessed them. The evocative words—"galleries," "parapets," "pale dust," "desolate bellow," "vast solitudes"—contribute to the feeling of nostalgia, to a sense that the world retains echoes (albeit faint ones) of a more meaningful past. The mythological allusions to Zeus and the minotaur enhance this effect.

The second poem, "Labyrinth," provides a counter image. This narrator seems to answer, or rather to attack, to deromanticize—to deconstruct—the vision of the labyrinth presented in the first poem. He denies the mythological references, the secret, the center. In doing this, in implying that we do not need the minotaur to feel the horror of a labyrinth, or that to mythologize our anguish is comfortingly deceptive, Borges also questions the ways we invest our world with meaning. The tone of the second poem is harsh rather than poignant; short, direct words transmit a matter-of-fact voice. No poetic euphemisms romanticize the minotaur; he is denied under the simple name of "bull." The sentences start abruptly and they are definitive. Compare the sharp future, "There'll never be" of the second poem with the softer, more nostalgic conditional, "Zeus, Zeus himself could not" of the first. These two symbolic labyrinths carry on their dialectic, and call into question any definitive interpretation of the labyrinth in Borges's work, while at the same time signaling its importance there.[3]

We can see already in these two poems that Borges's use of the labyrinth reflects his uneasy fascination with it; at the same time he uses the labyrinth as a commanding image for the world, the mind, and art, he also questions what the image represents, and eventually even his own association with it. I will begin my discussion of Borges's fiction by considering where the labyrinth appears there, and then move on to discuss the symbolic meanings with which he invests it. Finally, I will investigate what I see as significant "anti-labyrinth" tendencies in his texts.

A number of Borges's stories focus directly on labyrinths. In these cases, a structure is either called a labyrinth and is described as such ("Ibn Hakkan al-Bokhari, Dead in his Labyrinth," "The Two Kings and Their Two Labyrinths," "The Garden of Forking Paths," "The House of Asterion"), or a structure is described and compared to a labyrinth, though not explicitly identified as one ("Tlön, Uqbar,

Orbis Tertius," "The Library of Babel"). In numerous other texts, the word *labyrinth* is used metaphorically (the labyrinth of a horse's steps in "The Life of Tadeo Isidoro Cruz (1829–1874)," Scharlach's feeling that the world is a labyrinth in "Death and the Compass," the labyrinthine rules of a card game in "The Trick," the labyrinth of the jaguar's spots in "The God's Script"). Because in his work the labyrinth most commonly symbolizes the world, Borges's frequent use of the adjective and the metaphor causes an imaginative expansion; the labyrinthine object or event tends to pervade the literary landscape, to radiate outward into the world-as-labyrinth, merging the one with the many.

In addition to specific uses of the word *labyrinth* to describe particular structures, many recurrent situations in Borges's work recall labyrinths. To the situations mentioned by Emir Rodríguez Monegal—works of art contained in others, the contamination of reality by dream, voyages in time, and doubling—we may add complicated dwelling places (houses or cities), surprise endings to intricately complex stories, and bifurcations in time and space.[4] Furthermore, words such as *contrive* and *weave* are so often used by Borges to describe the creation of labyrinths that whenever we encounter them in another context, we tend to imagine the labyrinth pattern.

While they frequently symbolize the world at large, the actual labyrinths Borges describes occasionally recall primitive stone structures located in remote places, suggesting the sites of abandoned cities, and thus they plumb the archeological depths of the image. Asterion clearly lives in Crete, of course, the two kings with their two labyrinths in Babylon and Arabia; the Immortal comes upon the labyrinth he explores in the middle of the African desert. Though Borges does not mention it specifically, these labyrinths in deserts recall the most ancient known labyrinth, an enormous square building at Fayum in Egypt, which we know through the description of Herodotus.[5] The labyrinth in "The Immortal" most fully develops this connection, for it too represents an antique structure depicted by a classical traveler. As it was often imagined to do in Troy or other ancient towns, the labyrinth in Borges's story forms part of the city's defensive walls designed to perplex intruders. Characteristically, Borges covertly suggests the similarity of this labyrinth to the world around us; the narrator writes that as he explored it he "found it incredible that there could be anything

[else]" and that he confused this atrocious place with his native city.[6]

In "Ibn Hakkan al-Bokhari," Borges sounds ancient resonances of architectural labyrinths in several ways. In this story we hear from an Englishman, Dunraven, the story of Ibn Hakkan al-Bokhari, who built a huge labyrinth in order to hide from his vizir Zaid, because Zaid wished to kill him and steal his treasure. After they have explored the labyrinth where both Arabs have died, Dunraven's companion, Unwin, claims to have figured out that the situation is actually the reverse; the vizir, posing as Ibn Hakkan, has constructed the labyrinth in order to attract the latter and usurp his name and treasure. Most obviously, Unwin refers specifically to the Cretan labyrinth as the dwelling of the minotaur. The labyrinth that the Bokhari—or his vizir—builds is a stone wall enclosing "a single room and . . . miles and miles of corridors, of which the English townspeople remark that Moors use such houses, not Christians.[7] These phenomena, in conjunction with the Bokhari's connections to Africa and the East, again evoke the labyrinth's origins in ancient city defenses, many with presumed magical powers, and carry its use as an exclusionary tactic into our own times. In these reconstructions of ancient settings, as in the refashioning of old tales, Borges asserts our early awareness of the labyrinthine nature of our existence, and our perpetual need to decipher the world's labyrinthine forms. Furthermore, in portraying the three dead bodies in Ibn Hakkan's labyrinth as faceless, their identities obliterated (because their faces have been crushed by a stone), Borges suggests that the world's labyrinth can equalize men and beasts.

Uses of the Labyrinth

Since it is a structure of initiation, of the acquisition of new knowledge, it is particularly appropriate that Borges uses the labyrinth to examine or to redefine traditional concepts of space, time, literature, man's life and death. The idea that a straight line may be more subtly bewildering than a more intricate pattern appears at the end of "Death and the Compass" when Scharlach promises Lönnrot that next time he will approach his execution along a labyrinth consisting of "a single line which is invisible and unceasing." In "The Two

Kings and Their Two Labyrinths," a king humiliates a rival monarch by enclosing him in a labyrinth he has built; subsequently the humiliated king abandons his tormentor in the desert—God's antilabyrinth. In a reversal of the usual, the second king's desert becomes a more effective prison than the elaborately constructed labyrinth of the first king, the efficacy of a labyrinth existing without its characteristic form. As we shall see in more detail in a moment, another reversal of traditional concepts occurs in "The Garden of Forking Paths," in which the temporal bifurcations of a book-labyrinth question the finality of human acts in the present, as well as their portrayal in single time narration that decides between alternate outcomes of given events. Similarly, Asterion, at the center of his labyrinthine house—"it is the world"—is reported to have scarcely defended himself from his killer; this labyrinth, like many in ancient myth and ritual, seems to be a kind of intermediate ground between life and death. Its eerie atmosphere has affected Asterion, taking his will to live away. Borges implies that, in another reversal of commonly accepted ideas, Asterion has welcomed Theseus as his long-awaited redeemer, seemingly preferring death to continued life in the labyrinth. Furthermore, "The Two Kings and Their Two Labyrinths" and "Death and the Compass" are intriguing examples of Borges's use of the labyrinth to question tradition for another reason: in them the labyrinth itself is divested of its traditional form. It is changed; in a sense, Borges triumphs over *it*, by transforming it into a simple structure. In a similar vein, the poet in "Parable of the Palace" abolishes the palace-labyrinth with a simple one-word poem. It is fitting that these conceptual reversals occur in conjunction with labyrinths, since they are metaphysical analogues for the reversals of direction that characterize labyrinthine itineraries.

Although a labyrinth structure figures centrally in only a few of Borges's stories, in others he often alludes to the pattern just before a significant event or dénouement, reactivating its ancient initiatory function in temporal fashion. (As Knight points out, Vergil achieves the same effect in placing a labyrinth on the doors of the temple at Cumae before Aeneas penetrates to the underworld.[8]) In "The Life of Tadeo Isidoro Cruz (1829–1874)," Cruz has been fighting with government soldiers against the Argentinian outlaw gaucho Martín Fierro, but in the end joins Fierro. Just before Cruz recognizes his destiny as Martín Fierro's partner, Fierro "shuttling back and forth on horseback . . . had woven a long maze," followed by Cruz and the other soldiers (*Aleph*, 84). This miniature labyrinthine journey symbolizes a kind of rite of passage toward Cruz's final identity. It also suggests Martín Fierro's attempt to protect himself from his pursuers by constructing a magical protective labyrinth around himself in the manner of ancient city dwellers performing defense rites around their cities. He duplicates with striking similarity one outgrowth of the protective labyrinth associated with the city of Troy, the game called Troia, which, as shown on Greek vases, consisted of horsemen following labyrinthine patterns. (Recall that this game, similar to the dancing of labyrinthine dances, may have been played during the construction of cities to exclude evil spirits and enemies or at funerals to protect the dead from the same forces, because the tracing of the labyrinthine design symbolized guarded access to a strategic realm;[9] Vergil describes such a labyrinthine game at the funeral of Anchises.) Thus the labyrinth Cruz traces on horseback links him with warriors of the classical world, allowing Borges (characteristically) to situate the peculiarly Argentine within a universal context. When Cruz joins Martín Fierro he has found his way through a labyrinth to the immortal realm of heroes and also to his own personal identity.

The labyrinth serves a similar initiatory function in two more stories as well. In "The Immortal," where we hear of a man's wanderings through several ages and identities, the narrator goes through two labyrinths just before he reaches the terrifying city of the immortals. One appears in a dream he has: "an exiguous and nitid labyrinth," which contains an unattainable jar of water at its center (*Labyrinths*, 107). The other provides the protective passageways around the city itself. This labyrinth, in turn, is made of multiple labyrinths, which are, the narrator laments, multiplied the more by his anxiety and his fortune, and is, furthermore, merely the prelude to the overwhelming city of the immortals. In "The End," guitar music, "a kind of meager labyrinth infinitely winding and unwinding," suggests cosmic confusion before a significant event, in this case the imagined death of Martín Fierro.[10] More specifically, in "Conjectural Poem," Francisco Laprida meditates that "the manifold labyrinth of my steps / . . . has brought me to this ruinous afternoon" (*A Personal Anthology*, 193.)[11] At each of these points, the labyrinth highlights a character's feelings of hope and fear as he undergoes an initiation into a new state, increasing the emotional tension preceeding a momentous experience.

With the exceptions I have mentioned, such as "Ibn Hakkan al-Bokhari," and "The Immortal," the reader of Borges's stories rarely accompanies a character on a long trip through a labyrinth. The character may instead live in one like Asterion, wander in one for a brief time like the first king in "The Two Kings and Their Two Labyrinths," see one or hear of one like Stephen Albert in "The Garden of Forking Paths," or experience a combination of these situations like Albert's visitor Yu Tsun in that same story. The lack of long itineraries, the preference for momentary perceptions of labyrinths, results in part from Borges's fondness for the short story; and the labyrinth serves him well in that genre, as a shorthand to signal the passage of time. This same kind of shorthand, where the image of a labyrinth perceived in an instant serves to suggest a hypothetical labyrinthine journey, forms part of the early history of the visual sign. Knight maintains that the meander, or Greek key pattern, on the walls of the palace at Knossos is a vestigial remnant of labyrinthine defenses. The Minoans, he surmises, may have considered a meander appropriate for house decoration because they imagined the convolutions to represent labyrinthine protective walls, a charm to ward off intruders.[12] In the case of Borges, most of his stories are short, though they often contain references to an entire life; Borges's use of the labyrinth in them allows him to avoid detailing a character's progression in time, and still permits him to evoke the power of destiny as it operates through a lifetime or through universal history.[13] As inscriptions of meanders on ancient city walls did, the symbol serves here to figure extended temporal and spatial progression in compressed form. The same is true of what has become a particularly well-known use of the symbol by Borges, the epilogue to *The Maker* (*El hacedor*). There Borges pictures the sum of an artist's creations, either verbal or visual, as a labyrinth comprising the lines of his own face:

A man sets himself the task of portraying the world. Through the years he peoples a space with images of provinces, kingdoms, mountains, bays, ships, islands, fishes, rooms, instruments, stars, horses and people. Shortly before his death, he discovers that that patient labyrinth of lines traces the image of his face.

In addition to the temporal compression the image achieves here, it also serves Borges to take away some of Daedalus's autonomy, to show us, in characteristically poignant fashion, the designer designed, the artist as artifact.

Symbolic Labyrinths: World, Time, Art

Because the labyrinth figures so centrally in Borges's imagination, it symbolizes a number of interrelated phenomena, as is obvious from the stories that I have mentioned already. Stated very succinctly, Borges's labyrinths represent the world, the passage of time, and the artificial systems that man creates in his attempt to understand the world—his works of art.[14] And because Borges often considers the world as a book, as well as because art mirrors the world, the labyrinth of the world and the labyrinth of art merge. A question arises in the case of the world as labyrinth as to whether Borges uses the labyrinth to represent chaos. Critical commentaries have often maintained that he does, and he does; but even more significantly, his labyrinths of the world balance suggestions of chaos and order in the cosmos.[15] Though Borges's incessant playing with systems—religion, philosophy, even time—suggests that they are all fallible, in many of his stories he implies that there may be a system of which we are part yet of which we know nothing. For Borges, this alternative, with its aura of compulsion, may be just as disturbing as the anxieties attendant on the comparative freedom of chaos and choice, but it may also, in characteristically paradoxical fashion, be comforting, because to know that a system exists is reassuring.

"Tlön, Uqbar, Orbis Tertius," in which Borges and his friend Bioy Casares discover a whole imaginary universe in an unknown set of encylopedias, suggests that man constructs labyrinths to explain his universe. But the narrator implies that what is true of Tlön (one of those labyrinths) may be true of our world, for while at first Tlön was believed to be chaotic, it is now known to be governed by laws at least provisionally formulated. At the end of the story, the tone of ironical distance allows us to entertain opposing ideas; no assurance is possible: "It is useless to answer that reality is also disorderly. Perhaps it is, but in accordance with divine laws—I translate: Inhuman laws—which we never quite grasp. Tlön is surely a labyrinth, but it is a labyrinth devised by men, a labyrinth destined to be deciphered by men" (*Labyrinths,* 17). The world-as-labyrinth seems ungraspable, whereas the manmade variety is not; art is more comprehensible than reality, but Borges refuses to separate them clearly. Just as reality is only perhaps disorderly, its laws perhaps existent if undiscernible by us, art is not always fully comprehensible, for it too is a labyrinth. This is also true of the chance, or art, that rules every aspect of the Babylonians' lives in "The Lottery in Babylon," where the labyrinth serves to elicit the central question about whether some kind of order obtains or whether chaos reigns in the universe—in other terms, whether the world's labyrinths are legible or not. Just as the disorientation, the haphazard trials and errors that are designed into a labyrinth's plan differ from completely uncharted trials and errors, so the chance in "The Lottery in Babylon" changes in nature because it is the result of a strategy. All of this underlies Borges's observation that the Babylonians are not very speculative, and that "it does not occur to them to investigate fate's labyrinthine laws" (*Labyrinths,* 33). Here Borges again holds out the hope, even more than in Tlön, that the world may be understood; if the Babylonians would investigate the laws, perhaps they'd understand them. Or perhaps not.

Borges parodies systems like the lottery in Babylon, showing them to be arbitrary, even fraudulent, but the way in which he presents them suggests the troubling possibility that we may live in just such a fraud, on a larger scale. The labyrinth is essential to this project, because it pictures this very dilemma: a traveler cannot see a pattern, but he suspects that one exists. Borges demonstrates this idea again in "The Immortal," when he makes an important distinction between a labyrinth and complete chaos: "I had crossed a labyrinth, but the nitid City of the Immortals filled me with fright and repugnance. A labyrinth is a structure compounded to confuse men; its architecture, rich in symmetries, is subordinated to that end. In the palace I imperfectly explored, the architecture lacked any such finality" (*Labyrinths,* 110). In characterizing the architecture as lacking any purpose, Borges in one sense disqualifies it as a labyrinth, for in no other instance does he eliminate altogether the possibility of a plan in his labyrinthine symbols for our world.

Borges has commented on the labyrinth as posing the question of order or chaos in the world, seeming to tease himself and us by changing back and forth between the alternatives, following his own forking paths of speculation:

> I think that in the idea of the labyrinth there is an idea of hope also, because if we knew that this world is a labyrinth then we would feel secure, but possibly it's not a labyrinth, that is to say, in the labyrinth there is a center, even though that terrible center is the minotaur; on the other hand we don't know if the world has a center; possibly it's not a labyrinth, but simply a chaos and then yes we are lost. But if there is a secret center of the world, this center can be divine, it can be demoniacal, then we are saved, then there is an architecture.[16]

If we could decide definitively either way, we could rest more easily, but Borges refuses both himself and his readers such a rest. The labyrinth of the world will not be justified or explained in the equilibrium of classical forms but only explored in all its baroque complexity, for as Dunraven says in "Ibn Hakkan al-Bokhari," mysteries are divine, their solutions merely pedestrian. Firmly rooted intellectually in ancient sacred traditions of all kinds, Borges is unwilling to abandon the idea of a universal order, though he is also unwilling to uphold it with complete conviction either. He humorously characterizes his ambiguous relation to religion in this way: "Catholics (read Argentine Catholics) believe in a world beyond this one, but I've noticed that they aren't interested in it. With me it's the opposite: I'm interested in it but I don't believe."[17]

"The Garden of Forking Paths" is one of Borges's most labyrinth-filled stories, and as such merits our attention for a moment here. Borges himself thinks that his initial impulse for writing the story came from "the idea of the labyrinth which has always obsessed me, and of the world as a labyrinth," combined with the idea of a man who kills a stranger to call attention to himself, a notion that comes from detective fiction. For Borges, more important than the detective story is "the presence of the labyrinth, and then the idea of a lost labyrinth. I had fun with the idea not [only] of losing oneself in a labyrinth, but in a labyrinth which loses itself as well."[18] Here again Borges uses the labyrinth to question though not to destroy a tradition. He himself has said that he is fond of the detective story because it is the most end-oriented of all fiction, and yet in this neatly solved mystery story he proposes a book/labyrinth that denies that fictional orientation.[19]

In "The Garden of Forking Paths," we witness the journey of Yu Tsun, a German spy of Chinese descent, as he locates and finally kills the English scholar Stephen Albert, in order to indicate that the Germans should bomb an arsenal in the town of Albert in France. As he speaks with Albert, Yu Tsun learns that Albert has deciphered an enigmatic—a labyrinthine—text left by Yu Tsun's ancestor Ts'ui Pên. Here again, we might note, as Borges has, that he turns the labyrinth on itself, so to speak, and triumphs over it; instead of losing someone in a labyrinth, the labyrinth is lost—and found by a rather Borgesian recluse. The most suggestive "presence of the labyrinth" in the story is of course the labyrinthine novel of Ts'ui Pên. But besides this principal concern, Yu Tsun is surrounded by echoes of labyrinths as he travels toward his ancestor's "garden of forking paths." He remembers he grew up in "a symmetrical garden," and as he starts out for Albert's house, he enters "a solitary road" (*Labyrinths*, 20, 22). Soon he is told by some children that in order to reach the house he should turn always to the left, a piece of advice which reminds him that "such was the common procedure for discovering the central point of certain labyrinths" (*Labyrinths*, 22). As he nears Albert's house, "the road descended and forked among the now confused meadows," and "the damp path zigzagged like those of my childhood" (*Labyrinths*, 23, 24). The world-as-labyrinth surrounds the book-as-labyrinth; the gardens of forking paths multiply, their potency always increasing.

The presence of Ts'ui Pên's labyrinthine novel as it stands behind the events of the story heightens the tension we feel throughout "The Garden of Forking Paths" between Yu Tsun's adherence to a path of destiny and his freedom to act as he chooses; Yu Tsun himself notes this dichotomy between the limited self and infinite possibility, between chosen and potential paths of action: "Countless men in the air, on the face of the earth and the sea, and all that really is happening is happening to me" (*Labyrinths*, 20).[20] In some sense Ts'ui Pên's temporal labyrinth serves a protective function with respect to his descendent. Before he knows just what kind of a labyrinth his ancestor has constructed, Yu Tsun implicitly intuits the temporal labyrinth Albert finally describes to him: "I thought of a labyrinth of labyrinths, of one sinuous spreading labyrinth that would encompass the past and the future and in some way involve the stars" (*Labyrinths*, 23). A labyrinth of time itself. And thinking about this labyrinth, or, as he says, about those illusory images, affords him temporary insulation from his anxieties of the moment; he forgets his limited victim's path, imagining other alternative forks in his life's labyrinth, becoming momentarily an abstract perceiver of the world. But in the end, such insulation fails him; as Borges has said of the story, "the reality of war wins. It's sad, but it has to be that way."[21]

With Ts'ui Pên's labyrinthine novel Borges suggests a reinterpretation of linear time in fiction. The clue that helps Stephen Albert discover that the novel is "an enormous riddle, or parable, whose theme is time" is the letter Ts'ui Pên left with it which said "I leave to the various futures (not to all) my garden of forking paths" (*Labyrinths*, 137, 126). He cannot leave them to all futures because all futures do not materialize; they exist only potentially in the events that precede them. The "forking paths" in Ts'ui Pên's novel are events that normally would be portrayed as mutually exclusive because a character's opting for one action would cancel his other possible actions. But "in the work of Ts'ui Pên, all possible outcomes occur; each one is the point of departure for other forkings. Sometimes, the paths of this labyrinth converge: for example, you arrive at this house, but in one of the possible pasts you are my enemy, in another, my friend" (*Labyrinths*, 26). The labyrinth of Ts'ui Pên and the itinerary of his descendant Yu Tsun begin to converge as Albert draws the labyrinth out of the realm of art and applies its laws to his and Yu Tsun's life not once but twice. Here he is again:

> [Ts'ui Pên] believed in an infinite series of times, in a growing, dizzying net of divergent, convergent and parallel times. This network of times which approached one another, forked, broke off, or were unaware of one another for centuries, embraces *all* possibilities of time. We do not exist in the majority of these times; in some you exist, and not I; in others I, and not you; in others, both of us. In the present one, which a favorable fate has granted me, you have arrived at my house; in another, while crossing the garden, you found me dead; in still another, I utter these same words, but I am a mistake, a ghost. " (*Labyrinths*, 28)

Borges prefigures Ts'ui Pên's labyrinthine view of time in his "Examination of the Works of Herbert Quain," whose books contain chapters where alternate events stem from one event. Quain's detective novel *The God of the Labyrinth* apparently resembles Ts'ui Pên's novel, for it culminates in one major bifurcation. The reader realizes at the end that he has not reached the correct solution to the crime and then must reread the text to discover it. In Quain's regressive and forking novel *April March,* three mutually exclusive stories branch off from one initial conversation, and from those three, three more. In somewhat the same spirit in which we see Asterion's labyrinthine house appear to extend poignantly over the world, we learn Quain's prediction that demiurges and gods chose infinite bifurcations: "infinite stories, infinitely branching" (*Ficciones,* 85). Even though the Spanish word *historias* would generally be translated as *stories* in this context, the word does also mean *histories,* and so we are left wondering about the labyrinthine nature of both fiction and history, of books and the world. And appropriately enough, this story ends with a reference to Borges's own volume, *The Garden of Forking Paths*—yet another fork in the neverending path it portrays.[22] Because of their multicursal bifurcations, their disruption of unicursal, or linear, temporal progress, all of these labyrinths, actual and imaginary, contribute to Borges's exhaustive reassessment of chronology, his continually renewed refutations of time.

The many correlations between different kinds of labyrinths in this story—between concrete and imagined, spatial and temporal structures, for example—suggest the labyrinth's pervasive presence in the world of objects and the world of thoughts, as an organizing principle of both events and discourses, and consequently also a sign of their interdependence.[23] The labyrinth attracts Borges, as it does Butor and Robbe-Grillet, because it permits contradictory suggestions of order and confusion, or compulsion and freedom in the world.[24] It signals these questions at crucial points in the stories. And Borges, again like Butor, Robbe-Grillet, and Joyce, heightens the anguish the labyrinth evokes by multiplying the labyrinthine structures in his texts. Thus we see that, like many of his contemporaries, Borges exploits the dualities in the sign of the labyrinth; they are eminently suited to his philosophical speculations because they allow him to inhabit the space between contradictory views, to explore the gap between visions of universal chaos and worldly order, between a diachronic wanderer's and a synchronic designer's perception of the world and the word.

In "The House of Asterion" and "Ibn Hakkan al-Bokhari" Borges focuses on the minotaur as the inhabitant of the world/labyrinth. Although, as we shall see, Borges's narrators often identify with Daedalus, it is a particularly Borgesian innovation to present the point of view of the minotaur sympathetically, an innovation that implies a dislike of labyrinths as well as a fascination with them, a tendency to identify with the victims as well as the perpetrators of artifice. Like the figure of Borges in the epilogue to *The Maker,* who looks out through the labyrinth of lines composing his own face, Asterion surveys the world across his labyrinthine house. In this story, Borges—like his successor Cortázar in *The Kings,* a work written shortly after "Asterion"—adopts the minotaur's perspective, a stance not attempted by authors in the ancient world. The classical myths view the journey in the labyrinth as an exceptional event. The minotaur was a monster indigenous to his island, a unique freak. Borges, on the other hand, like many modern rewriters of this myth, reflects our sense that we are enclosed in a labyrinth, not just on a temporary visit, that in this respect we are all minotaurs in one way or another. Hence the empathy with the minotaur that Jaime Alazraki considers a new dimension in Borges's works.[25] We might apply to Asterion what we hear in "Ibn Hakkan al-Bokhari," that "what matters is that both the dwelling and the dweller be monstrous. The Minotaur amply justifies its maze" (*Aleph,* 123). In "Ibn Hakkan al-Bokhari," Zaid is presumably the monster, for Unwin decides that he is the coward who stole the treasure of his king and then plotted the king's murder. In him, then, Borges achieves a new and strange mixture of the minotaur and Daedalus—a monstrous artisan. Again, like the storyteller at the end of *The Maker,* whose fictional labyrinth traces the lines of his own face, this man has constructed a dwelling that conforms to his own psyche. In part, then, Borges's interest in the minotaur may be seen as stemming from his perception of the monstrous and entrapping nature of artistic life. On the other hand, his portrait of Asterion (typically) punctures that theory. Unlike the figures of Borges and Zaid, Asterion does not appear to be responsible for designing his own prison. In fact, in contrast to many of Borges's builders or explorers of labyrinths, he has no affinities to Daedalus, and he is an avowedly nonliterary creature. He thinks that nothing is communicable by writing, claims not to know one letter from another, and asserts that impatience prevented him from learning to read. In such a figure we see that for Borges, as for Revel in *Passing Time,* the best solution to living in the labyrinth of the world — imperfect as that solution may be — is to create a mirroring labyrinth of words, as many of us cannot; Asterion is poignantly hemmed in by the labyrinthine world, unable to fulfill whatever potential he might have had — a potential he might have developed had he had the patience to learn to read.

It is evident from these stories, and from others as well, that Borges uses the labyrinth to picture the complex confrontation between works of art and the world. The labyrinths described in "Tlön, Uqbar, Orbis Tertius," "The Garden of Forking Paths," "The Library of Babel," and "The Two Kings and Their Two Labyrinths," for example, are artificial creations, and yet they are confusing in the same way the world is, their narrators often implying that they have been created as the world was.[26] The "elegant hope" (which gladdens the narrator's solitude at the end of "The Library of Babel") in considering the world a labyrinth is that someday someone may understand its design instead of being obliged to impose various imagined patterns — or labyrinths of art — on the world. As I have been suggesting, it is precisely its ability to hover between these opposing suggestions of chaos and order in the world and thus to imply the kind of endless question Borges cherishes, which explains the labyrinth's dominance of his interior and exterior landscapes.

In his suggestive article on Borges's labyrinthine fiction, Nicolás Rosa studies the labyrinth of art in Borges's texts, focusing most intensely on the labyrinth's self-referential function. For Rosa, in Borges's texts, the labyrinth "is simply the space where literature can reveal itself and develop its own contradictions. . . . Literature as a *labyrinth* . . . begins and ends in itself."[27] Rosa contrasts this phenomenon of rigorous self-signification with medieval and Renaissance conceptions of the world and the scriptures as symbolic texts validated by a higher reality. The labyrinth, like literature in general, now symbolizes itself rather than hiding another higher meaning or a sacred reality. The argument is convincing because the labyrinths in Borges's texts are consistently self-referential, and yet Rosa's interpretation narrows the referential function of Borges's labyrinths more than I would wish to, impoverishing them by dismissing their mimetic qualities and thus disconnecting them from their early precursors — always important presences for Borges.[28]

Borges's labyrinths oscillate continually among the referents of the text, the world, and the self, though as we have seen, the primary symbolic resonances change from story to story.[29]

We have already examined an outstanding imaginative representation of Borges's conception of labyrinthine art in "The Garden of Forking Paths." Ts'ui Pên's novel really constitutes a conceptual model for the labyrinthine narrative structure in the novels of Joyce, Butor, Robbe-Grillet, and others like them where the reader is given the choice of following alternative paths through the text. "The Garden of Forking Paths" is not alone in this respect, for Borges indirectly proposes the model of labyrinthine narrative discourse elsewhere in his fiction as well, confirming our sense that the labyrinth is indeed a pervasive sign of writing and reading in our time, and that Borges has enriched it significantly. A few examples will confirm this idea. A book in the library of Babel is described as "a mere labyrinth of letters," and fictions in Tlön reportedly "contain a single plot, with all its imaginable permutations" (*Labyrinths*, 53, 13). Moreover, the Borges narrator of "Tlön" says that he owes his discovery of the imaginary labyrinthine fiction that is Tlön to the conjunction of a mirror and an encyclopedia, the mirror, we are told, troubling the end of a corridor, causing the passage to replicate in same labyrinthine fashion as the passages in the books of Tlön. Thus the labyrinthine configuration of Tlön can be seen as a self-reflective structure of invention and exploration, generated by Borges and Bioy Casares (habitual collaborators) out of materials at hand. Just after we hear about the mirror, the encyclopedia, and the corridor, we learn that they had imagined a fictional labyrinth, "a novel in the first person, whose narrator would omit or disfigure the facts and indulge in various contradictions" (*Labyrinths*, 3). And the historian of Uqbar, Borges informs us in a note, has also published a general history of labyrinths, an appropriate apprenticeship for his role as historian of Tlön. Similar echoes of textual labyrinths resonate through "Ibn Hakkan al-Bokhari": Dunraven narrates the story of Ibn Hakkan as he and Unwin traverse a labyrinth, so that in a topographical sense his words can be imagined to trace a labyrinthine design through space as the men walk along the corridors of the labyrinth. In addition, Unwin thinks that they will have to sleep "in the labyrinth, in the 'central chamber' of the story, but that in time this uncomfortable experience could be looked back on as an adventure" (*Aleph*, 121). The "'central chamber' of the story" of course refers primarily to the central chamber of the labyrinth as described in the story of Ibn Hakkan, but the ambiguity of Unwin's phrase, which could refer to the central chamber of the story itself, as well as to the labyrinth in it, remains. The self-reflexiveness of Unwin's reference is particularly appropriate here, for Unwin is already fictionalizing his own experience, imagining how it will seem when it has achieved the status of a memory. Here again, as he does following Yu Tsun down his labyrinthine paths, the reader moves in and out of the labyrinths of verbal art and worldy action, following a line of discourse that thereby perplexes the distinction between the scriptural and the geographical, between the text and the world.

The End of the Journey

In stories where the labyrinth figures centrally, a character's voyage through it usually ends in death; this is the case in "The Garden of Forking Paths," "The House of Asterion," "Death and the Compass," "Ibn Hakkan al-Bokhari," and "The Two Kings and Their Two Labyrinths." But death does not always await Borges's wanderers; the immortal, the explorer of the library of Babel, and the second king in "The Two Kings and Their Two Labyrinths" remain alive. Logically, the deaths that occur are not so strange, because if life is a labyrinth, its end point will be death.[30] And Borges refers several times to the labyrinth of steps composing a life's trajectory. The deaths that take place at the hearts or the exits of Borges's labyrinths, like the voyages preceding them, often reveal valued hopes and truths. Recall in this context Borges's comment that though the labyrinth is frightening because we realize we are lost in it, it can also provide "a hope because there is a center, because there is a plan, because there is an architecture."[31] Before dying, an explorer of a labyrinth may have a significnt vision, or a revelation about himself that causes him to die happy. The classical labyrinth, as we have noted before, often represented a rite of passage in which the dead entered a new life or in which an initiate risked death in order to reach a new stage of life; in his use of the labyrinth to explore the nature of death, Borges again exploits the classical resonances of the image. For the reader of Borges's stories, as for the inhabitants of the ancient civilizations Deedes describes, the labyrinth is the symbolic space where man confronts the great mysteries of life and death, attempting to renew the first and overcome the second.[32]

The death of the captive Aztec priest Tzinacán in "The God's Script" is one of the more hopeful deaths in Borges's stories, and of great interest as the culmination of a symbolic labyrinthine journey. Tzinacán, captured by the Spaniards, awaits his death in a cell beside a jaguar's cage; at the end of the story, he deciphers on the skin of the jaguar his god's message, which would presumably enable him to escape. But the perception of the message so overwhelms him with the sense of his own insignificance and the grandeur of the universe that he does not pronounce the word that would free him. While Tzinacán's prison is not shaped precisely like a labyrinth, its floor is similar in pattern to labyrinths composed of interrupted circles, "somewhat less than a great circle, a fact which in some ways aggravates the feelings of oppression and vastness"; its patterned enclosure thus produces the paradoxical combination of confinement and extension that we associate with labyrinths (*Labyrinths*, 169). But as often before, this is not the only labyrinth in the story; the labyrinth of the world-as-prison is duplicated in the text on the tigers and in the dream in the mind of Tzinacán. After Tzinacán deciphers the mystery written on tigers—"that teeming labyrinth of tigers"—with the aid of his "labyrinth of dreams," he appears to lose all sense of individual self in favor of communion with the universe, until at the end of the tale his vision seems to have deprived death of its sting.[33] Of course the undercutting irony remains; is this merely Tzinacán's way of justifying to himself his inaction in an impossible situation, rather than a divine vision? Or does Borges suggest that death is the best thing that could happen to an Aztec priest who has been captured and conquered by Spaniards? In any case, Tzinacán's relinquishing of his individual identity continues the ancient tradition of some kind of sacrifice (of an animal, of Athenian youths) to sacred forces at the heart of a labyrinth.

Here again, Borges's treatment of the labyrinth also recalls part of the early Christian history of the design, where most frequently man does not conquer a particular monster—a deed that would tend to glorify individual strength—but rather strives for unification with divine power. In Christian symbolism the labyrinth commonly represents the world, and the center, heaven. The pattern assumes a successful initiatory journey, though it also serves as a warning of possible dangers in the world. The unicursal nature of most church labyrinths minimizes individual will: a man reaches the center only after he has followed a prescribed path, a discipline that implies some abnegation of the individual self. Similarly, Tzinacán *reads* rather than *invents* the message on the jaguar's skin. But even that distinction is questioned in this story, for the labyrinth of dreams within Tzinacán and the labyrinth of the sacred text embodying the world's divine mystery outside him on the jaguar are both paths to the self, since in the end his ego dissolves in a universal vision. In the moment of comprehension, then, Borges achieves for Tzinacán a masterful blending of self and other—of Tzinacán's understanding of his own destiny and his reception of the god's message. The moment is, of course, a kind of epiphany, a divine revelation at the heart of his life's labyrinth—an unusual event in modern labyrinths.

Other Borgesian characters are also granted understanding at death via labyrinthine journeys of various kinds. Tadeo Isidoro Cruz imagines a more highly individual identity than Tzinacán's, which is nevertheless achieved, like Tzinacán's, in an instant at the heart of a labyrinth. After he and Martín Fierro trace their labyrinths on horseback, Cruz, in what seems like a joyous burst of enthusiasm, fights to the death beside Fierro because he suddenly knows that is where he belongs. Again, during this "moment in which a man finds out, once and for all, who he is," Borges's character seems to have ascended to a plane where death is secondary to identity (*Aleph,* 83). Though we may ask ourselves whether these men may simply be justifying inescapable fates, whether their self-revelations might be no more than ironic self-deceptions, the labyrinth nonetheless persistently represents a path to the self. The case of Asterion is less dramatic, but his death does approach deliverance, and Yu Tsun and Albert are offered some hope by Ts'ui Pên's labyrinthine novel: in another possible past (or future?) they are friends. In "The Two Kings and Their Two Labyrinths," though the first king's journey through the desert-labyrinth will eventually cause his death, the process will achieve a poetic, if terrible, justice. And finally, the traveler through the labyrinthine library of Babel ends with the "elegant hope" that one day someone may understand it.

As we have seen, the frightening discovery of self at the heart of a labyrinth is often a denial of the unique individual, and in this way it recalls the medieval tradition of labyrinthine pavements that picture heaven—symbolizing union with God—at their center. In Borges's fiction, the labyrinth figures a journey to a sacred space beyond the privileged position of the modern Western individual, and thus achieves a circular return to ancient or non-Western beliefs, and also, as we shall see, a prefiguration of postmodern critical theories of literature. Borges has said many times that man is everyone and no one—"my Shakespeare . . . like myself [you] are many and no one" (*Labyrinths*, 249). He splits his own personality in "Borges and I" and the personalities of others in "The Immortals" and "The Theologians" into two or more identities. But behind this expansion or negation of the individual personality lurks the fear that we are more limited than we would like to think after all, that the individual self cannot be denied: "The world, unfortunately, is real; I, unfortunately, am Borges" (*Labyrinths*, 234). Thus in several stories, a character does not achieve a merging of self and universe at the center of the labyrinth; that rite of passage remains incomplete and the individual dies an individual death. The immortal and Ibn Hakkan—and Borges himself, perhaps, in the epilogue to *The Maker*—experience the labyrinth's claustrophobia without its redeeming epiphany.

As I have implied in this discussion, in contrast to the narrative labyrinth proposed in "The Garden of Forking Paths," Borges's symbolic labyrinths frequently contain centers. Though the action varies from story to story, in most cases a decisive event, a revelation, occurs there. (This very configuration is what Borges's own poem "Labyrinth" cries out against, in warning and despair: "nor circling wall nor secret center" [*In Praise of Darkness*, 39].) Nevertheless, Borges, like Gide, often veils exactly what happens at the center of a labyrinth, or why it happens, guarding with narrative secrecy the sacred nature of that ancient space. We hear just the report of Theseus's battle with Asterion; the first king's death in the desert is only projected; the precise circumstances of the final killings in Ibn Hakkan's labyrinth are not completely explained; the labyrinth surrounding the city of the immortals may be centered, but it is centered on incomprehensible chaos. Once again, Borges prefers the "divine" mystery inaccessible to man's imagination to the "pedestrian" solution he may figure out, and he uses the labyrinth to preserve that mystery.

Narrative Design

Borges's constant use of the labyrinth as a symbol has led critics to propose that he also uses the pattern to structure many of his stories. Borges encourages this view, for he refers to other authors or books as "labyrinthine."[34] L. A. Murillo, among others, terms Borges's frequent use of stories within stories or dreams within dreams the "labyrinthine situation."[35] Frank Dauster sees all the stories in *The Aleph* in terms of a character's twisting through a labyrinthine existence to find his destiny at its center.[36] And Jaime Alazraki maintains that the structure of many of Borges's stories is labyrinthine in a general way: "The structure of the narration is labyrinthine (stories within stories or stories which are part of other stories); in some of them the order and the rhythm of a description suggest the idea of a labyrinth. The labyrinth thus draws itself without being named, the subject matter organizes itself in labyrinthine constructions."[37] While these interpretations are correct in linking the structure of Borges's stories to the design of the labyrinth in a general way, I think it is possible that that link may have been forged largely by the ubiquity of the symbol in Borges's work rather than by their structural design; in the absence of the symbol, the structural analogy might not have suggested itself so strongly. Furthermore, the repeated association of stories within stories with the structure of the labyrinth in Borges's stories seems erroneous to me; I would say that Chinese boxes are Chinese boxes (or simply embedded narrative structures), and not labyrinths.

Borges does describe many labyrinths, but his language for the most part is quite limpid, not, in comparison with Joyce's for example, specifically labyrinthine in proposing syntactical choices to the reader. Similarly, again in comparison to Joyce, Butor, and Robbe-Grillet, Borges's stories are not striking examples of labyrinthine narrative structure either. While his fictions portray complex convolutions of thought and thus roughly resemble the intricacy of labyrinths, Borges does not usually activate in his own texts the idea of alternate futures, of bifurcating narrative paths that he proposes in "The Garden of Forking Paths" and which in either their linguistic or structural form constitute the most distinctive technique in recent labyrinthine fictions. Borges's stories thus belong largely to the symbolic rather than the iconic verbal exploitations of the figure.

John Barth testifies to this nonlabyrinthine quality of Borges's stories in his article on "The Literature of Exhaustion." He suggests that Borges signals rather than succumbs to the labyrinthine self reflexivity of much contemporary fiction. Barth's article forges yet another link between the makers of labyrinthine fictions in the twentieth century, and gives further proof that the labyrinth is a current sign of multiple narrative possibilities. In it Barth pays Borges the compliment of comparing him to the heroic prince Theseus rather than the artistic commoner Daedalus. He maintains that Borges is not "lost in the funhouse" (not caged within his own endless labyrinth of narrative possibilites), whereas more ordinary creators (like Ambrose and Revel and Barth) are trapped there. For Barth,

> a labyrinth, after all, is a place in which, ideally, all the possibilities of choice (of direction in this case) are embodied, and — barring special dispensation like Theseus'— must be exhausted before one reaches the heart. . . . it's the chosen remnant, the virtuoso, the Thesean *hero*, who, confronted with Baroque reality, Baroque history, the Baroque state of his art, need *not* rehearse its possibilities to exhaustion, any more than Borges needs actually to *write* the Encylopedia of Tlön.[38]

As Ronald Christ has suggested, the closest Borges comes to the labyrinthine structural model is to leave us uncertain about the fate or identity of a character at the end of a story or to provide alternate interpretations of given facts: Did Pedro Damián die a hero or a coward in "The Other Death"? Who was the narrator in "The Immortal"? Was Unwin right in declaring that the man who presented himself as Ibn Hakkan was really his enemy the vizir? Is the nameless storyteller in "The Shape of the Sword" really John Vincent Moon?[39] Similarly, in both "The Lottery in Babylon" and "The Immortal," the avowals by the narrators that they have falsified their documents create the labyrinthine situation of narrative alternatives, and "The Lottery in Babylon" ends with a number of speculations about the lottery company's status. On a more micro-cosmic level, the Borgesian tic of stating something one way and then adding "or rather" and an amplification that may contrast with the original formulation creates a labyrinthine bifurcation in the prose.[40] But there is not much more than that in the way of labyrinthine narration.

Although most of Borges's stories do not trace specifically labyrinthine paths, many of them do progress through descriptions of complicated situations or itineraries, places or plans, either actual or imagined, to a simple yet powerful dénouement — in a metaphorical sense, from labyrinth to temple. These endings may surprise the reader by shifting from the intricate theories presented in the story to the contrasting dimension of unresolved emotion. It is this emotion that strengthens the best stories but has received relatively little critical attention.[41] This unresolved emotion implicitly extends the text beyond itself into the lives of its readers in much the same way that the book-labyrinth of Ts'ui Pên extends conceptually beyond its pages to embrace the lives of his descendent and interpreter. Thus Borges continues to ring changes on finitude and infinity in the world and the book, on the endless possibilities of the imagination, and its potential to continue on forever coexisting and contrasting with the finite number of pages in a story. Since for Borges, as for Dunraven in "Ibn Hakkan," a mystery is divine while its solution is merely mechanical, the impulses will remain contradictory, even though infinity, mystery, and resistence to closure predominate. The final movement in the stories away from rational speculation toward emotion results in many cases from the expansion of the reader's perspective to include the narrator. The technique shifts us away from the intellectually engaging complexities in the narrator's tale to focus on the narrator himself; in other words, we move away from the object of the discourse to its scene. The suddenness of this refocusing often unsettles us, for the narrator tends simply to register a surge of emotion, but not to develop it in the context of his preceding story. The text thus administers a powerful affective charge by abandoning the narrator with his unresolved emotion and the reader with his nascent pity.

The ending of "The Aleph," for example, which consists of an unexpected focus on the narrator's sense that "I myself am distorting and losing, under the wearing away of the years, the face of

Beatriz" (*Aleph,* 30), might lead us to consider the tale a love story rather than the philosophical meditation on the nature of infinity and eternity we had thought we were reading. Such an ending readjusts the reader's thoughts about the psychological motivation for the narrator's vision of the Aleph: an effort to revive Beatriz? to compensate for her deficiencies, or for his loss of her? to revenge himself on her? During the vision we become fascinated by the idea of the Aleph, and the possibility of seeing all time and all space in a single moment and a single point; at the end of the story we are brought face to face with an individual emotion.

The same process occurs in "The Garden of Forking Paths." During the story we concentrate on the idea of the mysterious labyrinthine novel of Ts'ui Pên, its relationship to Yu Tsun and Stephen Albert, and finally, on the clever wartime mystery story. But again, what strikes us at the end of the story is a sudden shift to the poignant emotion of Yu Tsun: "He does not know (no one can know) my innumerable contrition and weariness" (*Labyrinths,* 29). Yu Tsun speaks dramatically here; until now he has adopted a more matter-of-fact tone. At the end, after we have enjoyed the ingenious device of a shot "heard" across the channel, Borges points to the narrator, as if to say that what is important is that this human being is miserable, is finished—a perspective that contrasts with the preceding ingenuity. Furthermore, according to Borges, "it's more pathetic that Yu Tsun kills a man who has known how to understand the enigma of his own ancestor, a man who thereby becomes almost a relative."[42] With these shifts in perspective, Borges questions the attitudes of readers, or writers, who are content with intellectual puzzles.

As we are seeing, this shift from cerebral problems to personal emotions characterizes many of Borges's stories. Much of the force in the masterful and very short story "The Two Kings and Their Two Labyrinths" comes at the end when the desert king, restrained up to this point, vents his rage at his rival by leaving him to die in the desert. "The Library of Babel" ends with the narrator's moving admission that "my solitude is gladdened by this elegant hope" (*Labyrinths,* 58). And "Tlön, Uqbar, Orbis Tertius" trails off with the narrator "revising, in the still days at the Adrogué hotel, an uncertain translation (which I do not intend to publish) of Browne's Urn Burial" (*Labyrinths,* 18). The shift from intellect to emotion I have been documenting is perhaps most obvious in "A New Refutation of Time." After fifteen pages of theoretical considerations, in the famous last paragraph the narrator destroys all by turning on himself: "*And yet, and yet* . . . Denying temporal succession, denying the self, denying the astronomical universe, are apparent desperations and secret consolations . . . the world, unfortunately, is real; I, unfortunately, am Borges" (*Labyrinths,* 234). The languorous—or else frantic—mood of the "and yet, and yet . . . ," with the trailing ellipsis, signals a shift in focus, a break with the earlier rational argument. The tone becomes more traditionally poetic. Strangely, the assertion of the reality of the world and of Borges is not in itself particularly emotional. But repetition of the long word "unfortunately" commands the reader's attention and forces him to sympathize with the narrator, to share in his disappointment, a disappointment that depends for its emotional force on the preceding fifteen pages of arguments to the contrary. This narrator, by his apparently impersonal statement about obvious deceptions and secret consolations, solicits the reader's pity indirectly and poignantly.

At the ends of these stories, on emerging from their conceptually labyrinthine convolutions, we readers may experience horror, fear, pleasure, or pity—an emotional reaction rather than the resolution of an intellectual problem. The relation of this point of exit to the preceding story recounting labyrinthine actions, events, or thoughts is delicate. On the one hand, the emotional explosion contrasts with those labyrinths and repudiates them. On the other hand, as I have suggested, the emotion relies for its surprising and apparently "simple" force on the preceding intellectual complications, as the labyrinth of the world precedes the temple of the heart.[43] Once again, the labyrinth performs an initiatory function, this time in the realm of literary discourse itself, orchestrating the rhythm of the reader's response, preparing him to receive the desired effect at the end.

Borges's Dissatisfaction with Labyrinths

As we have seen, the significant experiences in Borges's stories or poems are often short or can be taken in at a glance, but are infinitely ponderable (the Aleph, a consummate moment in a life, the end of a story when perspectives suddenly shift), or the stories may end with the sudden forceful evocation of a personality ("Story of the Warrior and the Captive," "The Maker," "The Dead Man"). The labyrinth, on the other hand, represents a long journey, or in the realm of art, the slow process of elaboration. It contrasts with the epiphanic moment of recognition or the sudden onset of emotion that appears at the endings of many of Borges's stories. These considerations lead us toward Borges's ambivalence about labyrinths and his apparent discomfort with the large number of them in his own work, to what I have called his "anti-labyrinth" tendencies. In an interview Borges says that "I've grown weary of labyrinths and of mirrors and of tigers and of all that sort of thing. Especially when others are using them."[44] There is of course a possibility of irony here, but Borges does add that he wishes to write realistic stories, and in the introduction to Dr. Brodie's Report he says that he seeks to move people, not to create fables, a search that causes him to rewrite some of Kipling's early stories while shunning later more complicated ones.[45]

These statements suggest a contrast with Borges's praise of labyrinthine plots in his prologue to The Invention of Morel by Bioy Casares. The labyrinth in the work of Borges and other modern authors, as we have seen, is often associated with ingenious artifices, and with the cerebral aspects of writing; Daedalus—and Joyce in his wake—were meticulous artisans. In distancing himself from the design, Borges may be expressing his reluctance to join the ranks of labyrinth makers, his dislike of this literary identity. Before examining more closely how Borges uses the labyrinth to suggest these reservations, it is useful to note the chronology of the image's appearance in his work.

The symbol of the labyrinth comes into Borges's writing in the 1940s. It does not appear in his early collections of poems about Buenos Aires—Fervor of Buenos Aires (1923), Moon Across the Way (1925), or San Martín Copybook (1929)—perhaps because at this time Borges the poet feels more at home in his city than he does later, when he wishes to express some alienation from it. Might certain key images in Borges's vocabulary have undergone "labyrinthification" throughout the years, a movement from the simpler forms of an expansive spirit to the complicated shapes of an entrapped one? In this movement, Borges's texts register, among other things, the transformation of Buenos Aires. As the city expands from the large town whose streets allow glimpses of the Pampa to the metropolis whose paths become ever more intricate, Borges's texts change from poetry describing the still rather primitive city to prose works whose linguistic limpidity encloses labyrinthine convolutions of thought. Let us attempt to chart this change for a moment. The garden in the poem "The Garden," where "the whole garden is a peaceful light / that illuminates the afternoon," and "the little garden [which] is a fiesta day / in the eternity of the earth" becomes the infinitely complicated "garden of forking paths."[46] The expansiveness expressed by the "infinity of the suburbs," by "my city of sunset gilded corners / and blue suburbs made out of the heavens," vistas of Buenos Aires extending out through those suburbs to the Pampa, and beyond that to the sunset, are replaced by more complicated street itineraries like those of Emma Zunz or Lönnrot, and by landscapes like those of "The House of Asterion" or "Labyrinth."[47] In the latter, we hear that the labyrinthine house encompasses the universe. And the Borges narrator in "Borges and I" laments that "I . . . went from the mythologies of the suburbs to games with time and infinity" (Labyrinths, 246–47). The sea which is "solitary like a blind man . . . impenetrable like carved stone" becomes in a later poem "the labyrinth / without walls or window, whose gray trails / Long diverted the eagerly awaited Ulysses" (Poemas, 89, 157). The sound of a guitar that is able to hide the Pampa—"the Pampa was cradled / in the depths of a brusque guitar"—becomes "the thrumming of a guitar . . . a kind of meager labyrinth infinitely winding and unwinding" (A Personal Anthology, 166). In the later poems, the sense of infinitude remains, but it connotes weariness rather than wealth.

The landscapes in Borges's earlier poems evoke a sense of spiritual expansiveness, recalling the European Romantic vision and Borges's own youth. The labyrinth is largely absent from them, appearing principally in the prose after 1940. One might have predicted its disappearance again at the end of Borges's life, when he returns to writing poetry, when he says that he prefers to be remembered as a poet, that he is tired of labyrinths, that he wishes to write simple stories. But though it appears less frequently, less centrally, than in his earlier stories, the pattern has not entirely vanished; the labyrinthification of the city and its reflection in the text are here to stay.[48]

Borges's own statements about labyrinths in interviews provide an informative accompaniment to his use of the image in his work. The statements, like some of the texts themselves, often reveal a certain detachment from the design, but in typically Borgesian fashion, that detachment coexists with a fondness for it as well. At one point, for example, he says of a French edition of his stories (entitled *Labyrinthes*) that "the title *Labyrinths* is a good one. . . . Since I like the word 'labyrinth,' I think it's good. . . . Yes, it's very good, *Labyrinths*. The word is a rather mysterious word, a Greek word. The *y* [i grec], all that works well."[49] A year later, though, he shows less enthusiasm for the word, demonstrating that he may indeed be "weary of labyrinths": "I think of the world's literature as a kind of forest, I mean it's tangled and it entangles us but it's growing. Well, to come back to my inevitable image of a labyrinth, well it's a living labyrinth, no? A living maze."[50] In his reaction to the French title *Labyrinthes,* Borges's friend Ibarra comments on what he takes to be a critical tendency to identify Borges with labyrinths (here exemplified by Borges's French editor, Roger Caillois):

> It's Caillois who gives that title to a collection of Borges's stories. The volume he takes them from is called *The Aleph. Labyrinths* is a kind of judgment pronounced on Borges, a definition of Borges by Caillois. A definition of that Borges or of Borges period. I don't know if Borges concurs; I know that the word *labyrinth* is generally disliked by him. Now and then throughout his works, Borges imagines, denounces various labyrinths; Caillois collects them all in one and imprisons Borges there. [As if to say,] That'll teach you![51]

Caillois has said (in his introduction to a later series of three stories by Borges) that "Borges appears equally haunted by the relations of the finite and the infinite. Whence comes the explicit or latent obsession with the symbol of the labyrinth."[52]

Borges appears to have recognized this obsession, and—explicitly or latently in the texts and interviews—to attempt to exorcise it through a strange mixture of acceptance and rejection. In a sense, with his return near the end of his life to poetry, from which the symbol was originally absent, and to somewhat simpler stories, he "deconstructs" part of his literary identity, the part associated with labyrinths as signs of intricate fabulation. Thus Borges's texts and interviews indicate that although he is fascinated by labyrinths he is aware of their aura. He occasionally associates the labyrinth pattern with his criticism of a restricted perspective on the world, or man, or the divine. Frequently this contrast corresponds to a parallel opposition between dry rationality and emotional sensitivity. This is of course not to say that Borges's many labyrinthine patterns are devoid of emotion. We have already discussed the quotients of fear and anguish he expresses by his frequent use of the symbol in his stories. At this point I wish to investigate Borges's distrust of labyrinthine literary activity as it represents an overemphasis on intellectual complications.

I have argued that some of Borges's most forceful (and well-received) stories end by confronting the reader with an unnerving and strong emotion.[53] And furthermore that the impact of this raw emotion of the narrator depends in part for its impact on its suddenness, on its contrast with the foregoing ingenious mental complications, and with the reader's previous perception of the story as primarily an intellectual exercise. Finally, then, these stories suggest the danger of too much labyrinthine activity, of becoming so lost in mental calculations as to risk emotional desiccation. In this context, labyrinths may contrast with majestic natural phenomena like the desert or the Pampa. In "The Immortal," for example, the labyrinth, which has a recognizable purpose—to confuse man—is contrasted with the more terrifying, more powerful, and in the end more awe-inspiring city of the immortals, which exists at the center of the labyrinth, and which has no apparent purpose.

Borges begins his poem "Baltasar Gracián" with a derogatory refrain that includes the labyrinth:

Labyrinths, quibbles, emblems,
Such bleak laborious minutiae
Were all this Jesuit knew of poetry.
Which he had reduced to strategems.

No music in his soul; but this inane
Herbarium of metaphors and punning
And a veneration of cunning
And contempt for the human and superhuman.

(*A Personal Anthology*, 84)

The charges Borges levels at the seventeenth century satirist recall criticism often made of Borges himself, and more importantly, they may represent Borges's worst fears about his own limitations. Seeing beyond the praise or blame of others for his articulate "strategems," his "metaphors," his "cunning," in this poem, particularly in the use of what has become "his" symbol, the labyrinth, Borges suggests his anxiety about becoming a twentieth-century Gracián. Here labyrinthine activity contrasts with divine power and man's ability to respond to it. A man with a narrow perspective, creating intricate designs, misses the grandest design of all, God's truth. And the repetition of the first line further emphasizes the impasse represented by Gracián's kind of "labyrinthine" art:

> What happened when the relentless
> Sun of God, The Truth, put forth its fire?
> Maybe the light of God left him blind there
> In the center of the endless heavens.
>
> I know another ending. Doped on his themes
> Infinitesimal, Gracián never noticed heaven
> And turns over in his memory as ever
> Labyrinths, quibbles, and emblems.
>
> (A Personal Anthology, 85)

A fate worse than death (or blindness in this case) is to remain unmoved by an overwhelming vision, to lose sight of implacable forces—in other words, to remain forever in the intricate paths of the labyrinth, without reaching its sacred center or comprehending its divine plan.[54]

In the poem "Of Hell and Heaven" Borges again contrasts vain labyrinths with a more brilliant and meaningful divinity. The appearance of this poem in 1942 suggests that while Borges's dissatisfaction with labyrinths is most prevalent in his middle and later works, it was not long in emerging. The speaker of the poem maintains that

> God's hell does not need
> the effulgence of fire.
> . . . .
> A hated labyrinth

of triple iron and painful fire will not
oppress the dumbfounded souls of the damned.

(*Poemas,* 152)

The trite conventionality of such visions will appear on the day of
judgment, for we will see then

> . . . a face
> sleeping, immobile, faithful, unchanging
> (perhaps a lover's, perhaps yours).
> And the contemplation of that immediate
> ceaseless face, intact, incorruptible,
> will be for the damned, hell;
> for the elect, Paradise.

The powerfully simple prevails. Both poems distrust the potentially
labyrinthine nature of the intellect. Borges gives further evidence of
this kind of distrust when his texts undermine identification with
the labyrinth symbol. In the late story "The Congress," for example, the organizers of the congress obtain reference books for their
library, "from Pliny's *Natural History* and Beauvais' *Speculum*
down to the pleasant mazes (I reread these words with Fernández
Irala's voice) of the illustrious French Encylopedists, of the Britan-
nica, of Pierre Larousse" (*The Book of Sand,* 37). Note the distance
the narrator establishes between himself and the labyrinth of schol-
arly activity through the parenthetical remark immediately following it; just after he has pronounced the word *maze,* he quickly endows himself with another voice. The original Spanish uses the
word *labyrinth,* but perhaps the translator, working in collaboration
with Borges, has reflected the degradation the image suffers here by
translating it as *maze,* for Borges "not very much of a labyrinth, a
kind of a toy labyrinth."[55]

I have suggested that "The Two Kings and Their Two Labyrinths" also includes a similar attack on the labyrinth as it represents ingenuity that has overextended itself. The king with the
majestically simple desert wins over the king with the fussy labyrinth. The narrator proposes here that only gods, not men, should
build labyrinths; this is, of course, only *one* of Borges's many reflections on labyrinths, but as we have been seeing here, one that per-

vades his work. It remains true even when we consider the story's extratextual frame; Borges informs us in a note that "The Two Kings and Their Two Labyrinths" served as the rector's example of sinful pride in "Ibn Hakkan al-Bokhari," in a sermon meant principally to chasten Ibn Hakkan as he built his enormous labyrinth. The labyrinth of the king of Babylonia is "a blasphemy, for confusion and marvels belong to God alone and not to man" (*Aleph*, 89). Furthermore, the king of Babylonia thinks he will make fun of the "simplicity" of the Arabian king, but in the end he himself is made fun of by a different kind of majesterial simplicity, orchestrated by his "simple" former guest. Significantly, the Arabian guest requests divine assistance and hence escapes from the manmade labyrinth; not so the Babylonian. In this story, the Gracián-like mentality is overcome by the grandeur of nature and those who appreciate it. Likewise, "The Two Kings and Their Two Labyrinths" moves us more by its elegantly spare and grand resolution than the complicated story of "Ibn hakkan al-Bokhari" that serves as its frame. Rodríguez Monegal has suggested that Borges's admiration for the tiger and the old warrior represents a regret for action he has missed. Similarly, the narrator in "The Immortal" speculates that his being deprived of military action may have caused him to set out in search of the labyrinthine city of the immortals, through "fearful and diffuse deserts" (*Labyrinths*, 106). The simple and yet powerful life of the tiger or the warrior contrasts poignantly with the labyrinthine intellect of the librarian and the labyrinthine imagination of the storyteller. Like Jacques Revel and Ambrose M——, those labyrinth-makers long for, yet in the end might not be able to live, a life without labyrinths. In Borges's labyrinths, then, as in many others, the shapes of ambiguity prevail.

6 / Symbolic Landscapes

Two groups of texts that employ the laby-
rinth as a symbolic landscape illustrate the two predominant meanings of labyrinthine journeys in modern literature. The category of
the voyage toward the self includes novels by André Gide, Lawrence Durrell and Anaïs Nin; the rubric of the voyage toward the
text encompasses an essay by Albert Camus, and novels by Julio
Cortázar, José Donoso, and Umberto Eco. It is easy to predict, however, that while the first category is more psychologically oriented,
the second of a more metafictional nature, the lines of these two
journeys—toward the integrated self and toward the artistic text—
will tend not only to intersect but to converge. In any case, in their
employment of the labyrinth as symbolic landscape, both groups
should be imagined as falling under the general heading of the
world-as-labyrinth that permeates all uses of the image. Furthermore, the works resist even the categorization of two kinds of voyages for a more general reason; this is because, as I have suggested,
the labyrinth's greatest strength is its polyvalence, its capacity to represent different areas of experience and thus to suggest the interdependence of diverse phenomena. This quality of semiotic indeter-

minacy is itself conceptually a labyrinth, one path of interpretation leading inevitably to another.

The first four narratives I will discuss—by Gide, Durrell, Nin, and Camus—use the labyrinth in such a way that it forms part of the geography of romance. The voyage in the labyrinth is accomplished in a realm that is more primitive than the habitual dwelling place of the explorer, and at some distance from it. In the last three narratives—by Cortázar, Donoso, and Eco—the labyrinths of city, house and library are explored daily by their occupants. The first group of explorers returns with some sense of renewal, of discovery, or of growth. The second does not. The first group's narrative use of the labyrinth thus remains closer to the old initiation pattern of a single ordeal, endured and left behind. In the second case, the process of renewal suggested by the labyrinth pattern, though desired, is not completed, for in them the labyrinth expands into all time and space.

As in Ovid's original description of the labyrinth, and in other symbolic uses of the design, during the journeys in these modern texts the labyrinth mediates between natural and constructed forms and spaces, and between man's different imaginative capacities. Similarly, symbolic treatments of the labyrinth in the twentieth century, as earlier in its history, often set the pattern in opposition to another image. In Camus's "The Minotaur or the Stop in Oran," Oran as labyrinth is contrasted with the sea beyond it, and also with European towns. In Nin's *Seduction of the Minotaur,* two labyrinths—city and jungle—oppose each other. In Cortázar's *Hopscotch* the labyrinth contrasts with heaven. This kind of opposition frequently establishes an interplay between two concepts, between a labyrinthine space and a nonlabyrinthine space, between a real or imagined journey and a subsequent place of rest, between postponed and satisfied desire. It thus suggests the possibility, or the problematic nature, of movement between them.

In all cases, the image of the labyrinth in the twentieth century reflects man's confrontation with a world no longer perceived as mapped out by God. It still functions as a structure of quest, though of course the object of the quest differs from work to work. As I have just suggested, most frequently the quest represented by the labyrinth is a journey of self-discovery; ostensibly a voyage out, it is symbolically a voyage within. In developing the correlation between labyrinthine physical environments and labyrinthine thoughts, and between setting and psychological and artistic development, these texts, like those examined at greater length in the previous sections, point up the complex and puzzling interdependence of the world and the mind, the perceived and the perceiver. The labyrinth in these works thus suggests a parallel with modern physics, where the medium of perception alters the entities perceived, and vice versa. Finally, considered as a group, these texts attest to the variety of manifestations and the persistent attraction of the labyrinth as a significant figure of thought in modern literature.

André Gide: Theseus

Each is led on by the complexities implicit in his own mind to lose himself, if I may so put it, in a labyrinth of his own devising.

Theseus stands out from other uses of the labyrinth pattern in our times because it is an explicit retelling of the classical story. However, within this classical framework, Gide departs in significant ways from the original narratives. George Painter traces Gide's interest in Theseus and his adventure in the labyrinth back to a passage in *Fruits of the Earth:* "The memory of the past had only such power over me as was needed to give unity to my life; it was like the mysterious thread that held Theseus to his past love, yet did not prevent him from travelling through the newest of landscapes." He also records Gide's later notes in his journal that lead toward his interpretation of the myth in *Theseus:* "Ariadne, after he has slain the minotaur, makes Theseus return to the point from which he set out. . . . In the Theseus this must be brought out—to put it vulgarly, the thread is . . . the apron-string" ("le fil à la patte").[1] We see here that the labyrinth serves Gide as a model for the integration of past and present selves, of old and new experiences, but also—in the discrepancy between the statements, the first from 1897 and the second from 1927 and 1940—for the problems involved in achieving such an integration. Gide's version of the myth thus engages the labyrinth as a symbol for the mind, and builds imaginatively and explicitly on that idea.[2] It can serve therefore as an introduction to the texts by Durrell, Camus, Nin, Cortázar, Donoso, and Eco, who develop that idea in different ways. It is possible also that Gide's treatment of the myth, written late in his life, when he was already an influential voice, brought it to the attention of the other writers, and may have encouraged them to use the literary tradition of the labyrinth for their own differing narrative purposes; at the same time, however, his retention of the plot and characters of the original myth may have deterred them from undertaking a similar retelling.

Gide retains the familiar resonances of youthful initiation in his labyrinth, for the Theseus who journeys to Crete is clearly a young man. Yet we hear of his exploits from the mature Theseus, and so the diachronic/synchronic duality of the image, the difference between the wanderer and the designer or the surveyor, is thus inherent in the narrative technique itself, for we continually sense the distance between the young Theseus as actor, exploring the labyrinth of his own youthful desires, and the mature Theseus as narrator, placing, explaining, surveying, and designing his discourse about those desires.

In contrast to this distinction between wanderer and designer, Gide also prefigures a modern tendency to merge Daedalus and Theseus, the artisan and the explorer, a concept more explicitly developed in the texts of Butor, Robbe-Grillet, Cortázar, and Donoso, by having the two men meet to discuss the labyrinth. Daedalus tells Theseus that he has planned the labyrinth around the individual's consciousness rather than around exterior forces. Since he believes that desire is the essential factor in controlling a man, or the minotaur, the jailer must work on his captive's desires. As a result, he calculates that the best way of keeping someone in a labyrinth is to make it so that he doesn't want to leave; therefore he has constructed a labyrinth that the minotaur will enjoy. In this labyrinth, then, heavy vapours put the will to sleep and induce "a delicious intoxication, rich in flattering delusions, and provoke the mind, filled as this is with voluptuous mirages, to a certain pointless activity," devoid of logic or substance.[3] Daedalus has converted the task of building the labyrinth into the construction of an entire aesthetic universe, which subverts rational, purposeful activity. The labyrinth is art for art's sake rather than art that leads to or away from anything. It is Gide's version of Daedalian ingenuity overextending itself, ingenious artistry gone wild. Although its pleasurable environment appears as a reversal of the fear usually associated with winding corridors and unknown egress, this labyrinth is dangerous precisely because it is so pleasant. It works like a drug. The aesthetic world of Gide's labyrinth is magical and chameleon-like, for it lures and entraps people in many ways, according to their various desires and designs: "Each is led on by the complexities implicit in his own mind to lose himself, if I may so put it, in a labyrinth of his own devising" (76). (The original French uses the anatomical word *cervelle—brain,* recalling that a labyrinth has the same convoluted shape as the brain.) In this clear and cogent interiorization of the myth, it is evident that it is not only the minotaur's desires that must be satisfied, but also those of his pursuers.

Theseus is saved, as usual, by Ariadne's thread, but the thread here represents not love but reality, duty, an antidote to the pure and pleasurable art of the labyrinth itself. For Theseus and his youthful companions, the sensual labyrinth embodies the danger of forgetting themselves; escape from this labyrinth therefore represents an affirmation of individual identity.

The sexual dimensions of achieving this identity provide intriguing complications for Gide's labyrinth. Here let us recall first that early labyrinths in the form of ritual dances sometimes served to symbolize a process of amorous initiation; in psychological interpretations the maturity to love someone other than the suffocating mother is often the goal of a labyrinthine journey, the achievement of which is signaled by the rescuing of a youthful female partner.[4] R. F. Willetts reminds us that "the youths and maidens who accompanied Theseus underwent an ordeal" and that after this ordeal Theseus married the king's daughter. He concludes that the labyrinthine "Knossian dance in her honour was part of the ritual of collective marriage, following on the graduation of the initiates: it was a love dance."[5] In his interpretation of the myth, Gide takes on these resonances and turns them about, presenting Ariadne's love as an additional danger, a constraining force. Theseus is cooped up by Ariadne as he might have been in the labyrinth, both temptations of the flesh. Her holding of the thread is distinct from the thread itself, which is a thread of practicality, "the tangible symbol of duty [,] . . . your link with the past. Go back to it. Go back to yourself. For nothing can begin from nothing, and it is from your past, and from what you are at this moment, that what you are going to be must spring" (77).[6] As the thread represents responsible integration of his past, it is constructive; as it transmits Ariadne's powers of sensuality and coercion, it is simply entangling, taking on qualities of the labyrinth it is intended to conquer. In a half-comic, half-serious bit of misogyny, Gide explictly rejects the idea that a man's rite of passage toward his adult self requires a woman's aid. He conflates the enveloping mother and the liberating anima figures, working against the tradition that sees the latter as a help-mate and a reward for differentiating oneself from the former. Gaston Bachelard detects a similar fear of female power in the novel *Philae's Death* by Pierre Loti. There the narrator explores the crypt of an Egyptian temple whose corridors, which seem about to close in and bury him, are filled with a thousand sculptures of a large-breasted goddess, which the explorer must brush as he passes. Bachelard asks if it is not "symptomatic that the fear of brushing a breast and the fear of being buried are united on the same page."[7] Here it is also useful to recall that the church emphasized Ariadne's string as a symbol of grace, of the help man required to extricate himself from the labyrinth of worldly entanglements. Again, Gide recognizes the dangers of remaining in the labyrinth, but he rejects both this symbolic force of Ariadne and the feminine form it takes, advocating instead man's independent strength. The labyrinth of this particular life does not lead to the paradise of the female heart or to God but rather to individual force.

The battle at the center of Gide's labyrinth is never revealed, for as Theseus has told us, the labyrinth's mystery is different for each individual; the vapours will cause him to create his own particular prison and his own minotaur as well. Theseus's brain is his labyrinth and ours is ours. Although Gide leaves us to imagine exactly how the conquest takes place, we do get a few hints. After his return, Theseus says that the monster even appeared beautiful— another reversal of traditional visions of terror at the center of the labyrinth and an indication that Theseus's victory over the minotaur may have been sexual. These hints about the struggle at the heart of the labyrinth indicate that in addition to his rejection of the feminine, Gide also distances himself a bit from his own youthful sexual exploits, for in making Theseus express a preference for young men and in having him tell us on his return from the labyrinth that the minotaur was a young man, and beautiful, we realize that this dream of voluptuousness—this minotaur—was the one the vapours caused Theseus to imagine for himself, the one most dangerous for him, the one that he must finally subdue if he is to return to the world.

In the philosophy the narrator expresses, Gide integrates the classical ideal of the middle way into his treatment of the labyrinth, emphasizing that the task of conquering this particular labyrinth, representative of youthful excesses, requires a steady, reasonable man. This labyrinthine trial, narrated by an older man, represents less a coming of age that is a break with the past than an initiation into consciousness of continuity with the past.[8] Ariadne's thread in this context represents the line of Theseus's life story, a line which is to remain unbroken and inclusive. Nevertheless, in addition to his responsibility, Theseus is also "disponible," or open to all kinds of experience. In addition to praising him for devotion to the task at hand, Daedalus also commends him for audacity and temerity, and finally says that what he loves in him is his joy. Theseus is able to conquer the minotaur and the labyrinth because he meets them on their own terms, even uses their own weapons against them. At the same time that Theseus holds onto the string of reality, of rational perspective, he conquers the minotaur in a manner consistent with his sensual surroundings. As we shall see shortly, in this idea Gide anticipates a symbolic resonance utilized also by Nin and Camus— the idea that in order to defeat the labyrinth or the minotaur we must first learn to accept them.

In contrast to Theseus, of course, Icarus represents a defeated sensibility.[9] As with Theseus, Icarus's labyrinth is located within himself, but he cannot free himself from it—from the danger of too much abstract reasoning, but also of too much poetry: "Icarus was . . . the image of man's disquiet, of the impulse to discovery, the soaring flight of poetry" (82). Icarus represents extremes, Theseus the middle way. Icarus describes from the grave the prelude to his flight and fall in a parodic résumé of what appear to be some of Gide's own intellectual stages. He reveals his attraction to God, whose kingdom "is peace. All is absorbed, all is reconciled in the Unique Being"; his discontent with the merely horizontal plane of logic where he is tired of wandering: "Ah, how sick I am [therefore] of 'therefore,' and 'since,' and 'because'! Sick of inference, sick of deduction"; and his attraction to pure poetry: "to lose my shadow, to lose the filth of my body, to throw off the weight of the past! The infinite calls me!" (80–81).[10] The ignominious nature of his death clashes with the high-flown quality of his rhetoric. His failure and Theseus's success demonstrate that the world of the sensual imagination, of the vaporous labyrinth, must be tempered with the heavier weight of one's past, one's duty, and an aesthetic based on a rational as well as an intuitive relation to the world; in literary terms, poetic flight is to be combined with prosaic exploration.

Near the end of the *récit,* Theseus confronts Oedipus at Colonnus. The confrontation, through the contrast of the two men, further defines Theseus's character and the nature of Gide's labyrinthine space. Theseus pays homage to the older man's spirit as he tells of their meeting, saying that he recognized his own achievements to be merely human, whereas Oedipus had "stood man upright before the riddle of life, and dared to oppose him to the gods" (105).[11] Theseus knows that his conquest of the labyrinth has required steady labor, and his victory constitutes not flight into a higher realm but passage through the vapours into another stage of life on earth. It stands for action in the world and confrontation with a dangerous part of the self, whereas Oedipus's activity figures an opposing side of man's activity, his union with the divine. This meeting of Theseus with Oedipus after Theseus has conquered the labyrinth exemplifies Eliade's distinction between two kinds of initiations, the normal human variety and the shamanic or esoteric one. The first is often symbolized by a labyrinthine structure, on the ground, and represents exploration of the earth and the human mind; the second is frequently symbolized by a pole or a tree that rises toward the heavens, and represents assumption of superhuman powers.

Typical of the twentieth century in his use of the labyrinth, Gide both recalls and denies allegiance to the ancient religious resonances of the pattern. On the one hand, with his imaginary vaporous labyrinth that represents every person's psyche, Gide, like Durrell and Nin, transfers the traditionally sacred space at the center of the labyrinth and the knowledge it represents to the psychological domain, and also locates the heroic myth in human experience. The labyrinth is thus divested of religious overtones; Oedipus and the superhuman realm are located outside it. On the other hand, Gide's use of this part of the classical plot, where Theseus confronts

Oedipus's supernatural realm after narrating his own ordeal in the labyrinth, preserves the traditional kind of labyrinthine path that leads to a sacred center.

Lawrence Durrell: The Dark Labyrinth

. . . an outward symbol of an inward march upon reality. Resembling Gide and Camus in his fondness for the Hellenic world, and in his sense of the continuing relevance of classical forms and conceptions, Durrell creates a distinctly Mediterranean version of the labyrinth. He sets part of *The Dark Labyrinth* on the island of Crete, thus clearly exploiting the historical resonances of the myth. But like the vaporous labyrinth in *Theseus* and the tangled forests and cities that we will encounter in Nin's *Seduction of the Minotaur,* this Cretan labyrinth becomes a metaphor for the mind, and more specifically, for self-exploration. *The Dark Labyrinth* comprises the personal histories of a group of people who, like the original Athenians, unite for a cruise to Crete. There they visit the Caverns of Gortyna, the "labyrinth" of the book's title. Some of the passengers do not enter the caverns; some enter and find their way out; some disappear in the labyrinth after a rockfall traps them inside. (Durrell's concrete historical orientation is evident here since Cretan civilization is thought to have been ended by a colossal earthquake.)

Early on, the narrator expresses his fascination with the very word *labyrinth,* which suggests to him "something at once terrifying and enticing."[12] Durrell's text illustrates that ambiguity well, for the characters are eager to examine the labyrinth, but they also fear what they may find inside. As the story progresses, the physical labyrinth on the island of Crete becomes increasingly mirror-like, reflecting the personalities of its explorers; before this process is complete, and the enigmas of the labyrinth are explained and dispelled, they have left their mark on the characters. The bull's bellow, for example, which terrifies the explorers in the labyrinth, turns out to be a horn blown by the tour company's hireling; the seemingly inexplicable disappearance of a body is later explained by someone's having carried it away. In this process of systematic demystification, the mystery of the physical labyrinth is thus slowly relocated within the characters; their psyches are the true dark labyrinths: "Each is led . . . to lose himself . . . in a labyrinth of his own devising." Like Gide and Nin, Durrell adopts the sign of the Cretan labyrinth, empties it of some of its ancient mysteries, and provides it with a new referent. Furthermore, in its creation of several personal labyrinths, the story resembles the multiplication of labyrinths that characterizes the exploitation of the pattern as a structural design for narrative in Joyce, Butor, and Robbe-Grillet, a multiplication that highlights our entrapment within the labyrinths of self and world.

The inhabitants of the dark psychic labyrinths in Durrell's novel frequently discuss their personal philosophies, and the cruise they take seems to be a continuation of previous voyages of self-discovery. An aura of inevitability surrounds the trip, suggesting that an exploration of such interior labyrinths represents a necessary confrontation. Each character in turn uses or is associated with images that imply the exploration of the self-as-labyrinth, and their statements often prefigure their experiences in the Cretan labyrinth at the end of the novel. Fearmax, Baird, and the Trumans are the best examples of this process.

Fearmax announces that he expects to find confirmation of his spiritualist theories in the pyramid he plans to visit. He also predicts an accident that "would assist him in the discovery of 'the Absolute'" (82). Baird thinks Fearmax's idea "a fine medieval conception" (83). Though Baird simply means that Fearmax thinks anachronistically, Fearmax here reflects the medieval conception, as evidenced by mosaic church labyrinths, to find the absolute or God at the heart of the labyrinth. A modern man is more likely to find a mirror there. Fearmax can hope to find both God and mirror, for he seeks the reflection of his own pet theories, which in turn reflect medieval religious doctrine. The last image of Fearmax after the rock fall is his own: he feels himself being picked up, or so he says, in the warm soft mouth of a gigantic being, and thinking about what is happening to him:

> Or was this whole place merely a mad exteriorization of his inner confusion; his feet walking slowly down metaphoric corridors of his own subconscious—in which only the roar of the sleeping monster gave him a clue to his primal guilt? It was a pretty fancy. If he ever got out he

would have the pleasure of sharing it with Hogarth. The work of Rank on the symbolic significance of labyrinths, and their connexion with divination by entrails. Olaf's observations upon the corridors of the Great Pyramid; was it possible that the place he was traversing had been hollowed by the hands of men to suit some occult purpose? (176)

Durrell is obviously aware of the symbolic and historical associations of ancient labyrinths and wishes to include them in his text. Like Gide, he also wishes to focus attention on their modern psychological resonances without completely sacrificing the magical air of ancient myths. The introduction of these associations through the ridiculous Fearmax allows Durrell the opportunity to satirize the invasion of the English tourists into the Mediterranean world; their careless remarks about minotaurs and their irresponsible desire for an adventure, like Fearmax's egotistical desire for self-indulgent confirmation of his theories, suggest an inability to confront either their own repressed emotions or hidden telluric violence. So Durrell takes his distance from modern claims to reinterpret and understand ancient myths while at the same time paying homage to the continuing force of myth as a repository of ancient wisdom.

The one member of the party who does not join the tour of the labyrinth is Baird. He had penetrated it before, during wartime activity there with a small band of anti-Germans led by "the Abbot," a priest who lived in Crete. At that time they had been forced to kill a captured German and flee into the labyrinth. The murder of the German has since haunted Baird's dreams, and he has gone to a psychoanalyst. His not exploring the labyrinth at the time of the cruise suggests that his analysis has already acted as a self-revealing journey, allowing him to piece together the labyrinth of his own psyche. His analysis is described as a voyage in a tunnel: "It was hard and cruel work, he was reflecting, to bore down through the carapace of pride, self-esteem, apathy" (64). And the analyst's "completely female and immoral" intuition reflects the traditional idea that a man entering a labyrinth traverses female territory. When, back in Crete at last, he actually attempts to dig up the German at the entrance to the labyrinth, "somewhere, in the depths of his mind, [Baird] felt that a corner had been turned" (159). This is because Baird and his analyst have already explored the labyrinth of his psyche, and together have "disinterred Böcklin from his unceremonious grave." Characteristically, in this labyrinth, as in others we have explored, the sense of an underlying if unknown pattern mitigates the prevailing experience of confusion; while Baird felt that the explanations the analyst gave him regarding his condition "were not always comprehensible," yet "behind it all, Baird felt, there was a design and purpose in what he said" (66). Further tying this labyrinth to primitive rituals, Baird's analyst describes the general existential crisis facing Baird's generation as a puberty rite.

An idyllic couple, the Trumans, say halfway through the novel that they would like to stay in Crete forever. Once again, the labyrinth offers fulfillment of the characters' wishes. At the end of the book the Trumans go calmly and lovingly through the labyrinth until they emerge in a meadow on top of a high plateau where they seem likely to remain forever, since there is no evident means of escape. When they emerge, as if in recognition of the labyrinth as an initiation into a new state of being, Mrs. Truman exclaims, "It's like being reborn" (206). Durrell also uses Mrs. Truman in another context to imply that the voyage through this labyrinth is to be understood as a metaphor for the process of self-discovery. As the party approaches the hill of caverns in Crete, Mrs. Truman remembers how the painter Campion, in a moment of annoyance, has thrown overboard the portrait of her he was painting:

> It was as if there had been something valuable to be learned from the painting: as if the act of destruction were a wanton and wasteful refusal to let her learn about herself.
>
> The cars rumbled down the hill towards the village of Cefalû and the labyrinth. (141)

The juxtaposition of Mrs. Truman's desire for self-knowledge with the collective voyage toward the labyrinth once again transforms that labyrinth metaphorically into the several interior labyrinths of the characters and their individual self-explorations. The fact that several of them have been psychoanalyzed confirms this idea. As Baird says to himself, "travel was only a sort of metaphorical journey—an outward symbol of an inward march upon reality" (48).

Before Sir Arthur Evans discovered the palace at Knossos, it was often thought that the Caverns of Gortyna comprised the famous Cretan labyrinth. This assumption manifests a certain evolutionary truth, since labyrinthine palaces and tombs, and eventually the symbol of the labyrinth itself, seem to have evolved from caverns. In his narrative transformation of the caves into a symbol for self-exploration, then, Durrell reenacts the development of the labyrinth from physical structure to symbol, from practical to metaphorical utility, as it occurred in the ancient world. In doing this, however, particularly in making his Cretan labyrinth respond to the invasion of the English tourists with the physical force of an earthquake rather than with the picturesque mystery they have anticipated, he has in a sense also reversed this very progression from nature to culture, from thing to sign, preserving the physical dimensions of experience in the Mediterranean that characterize much of his better-known fiction.

Anaïs Nin: Seduction of the Minotaur

The brain of man is filled with passageways like the contours and multiple crossroads of the labyrinth.

Anaïs Nin has written that the image of the labyrinth is her favorite symbol.[13] Perhaps she is so fond of it because it serves her as a sign of introspection, but introspection not detached from the world around her. Like Gide and Durrell, Nin specifically exploits the labyrinth as a symbol for the exploration of unfamiliar mental territory. And like theirs, the physical labyrinths she describes serve as symbolic landscapes of the interior, settings for a voyage into the self.

At the beginning of *Seduction of the Minotaur,* Lillian lands in Golconda, Mexico, where she hopes to free herself from her complicated past and perhaps from her marriage. The "simple" tropical life that so appeals to her is joyous at first, but memories intrude. And the one person in the town with whom Lillian genuinely sympathizes is an introspective doctor who returns her to her problems. The doctor tells Lillian that she may wish to use Golconda as a drug for forgetting, but that finally we cannot escape from the design that comes from within us. Immediately after this, Lillian expresses her sadness at having made friends with "a man intent on penetrating the mysteries of the human labyrinth from which she was a fugitive."[14] Here, the first time Lillian uses the word *labyrinth,* she qualifies it as human. But in later invocations of the symbol Lillian merely says "the labyrinth" and assumes it will be understood as referring to the human psyche—either individually or collectively.

The most significant exploitations of the labyrinth symbol occur near the end of the novel. In this passage, the Mexican doctor has just been shot; Lillian reflects that it is not the bullet that killed him, but rather his propensity to put himself in dangerous situations. Lillian continues, in the same vein, to muse about her relationship with her husband:

> She knew that by similar detours of the labyrinth, it was not the absence of love or the death of it which had estranged her from Larry, but the absence of communication between all the parts of themselves, the side of their character which each one feared to uncover in the other. The channels of emotion were just the passageways running through our physical body which some illness congests. . . . The passageways of their communication with each other had shrunk. (102)

The generalized labyrinth at the beginning of the paragraph is later particularized to mean "channels" of feeling, "passageways" of communication. Here, as in Durrell, the adventure-seeker in the foreign labyrinth is refocused, the outer voyage in the labyrinth transposed into an interior journey of self-exploration and self-discovery. As in *Ulysses,* the longest way 'round is a way home in the end.

The same process occurs in the next passage. Here Lillian is flying home from Golconda:

> Lillian was journeying homeward. The detours of the labyrinth did not expose disillusion, but unexplored dimensions. Archeologists of the soul never returned empty handed. Lillian had felt the existence of the labyrinth beneath her feet like the excavated passageways under Mexico City, but she had feared entering it and meeting the Minotaur who would devour her.
>
> Yet now that she had come face to face with it, the Minotaur resembled someone she knew. It was not a monster. It was a reflection upon a mirror, a masked woman, Lillian herself, the hidden masked part of herself unknown to her, who had ruled her acts. (111)

The labyrinth symbolizes the soul, and the minotaur represents the danger of not fully knowing one's own soul, or the soul of one's lover. Lillian keeps trying to escape from her inner labyrinth instead of exploring it, preferring exotic exterior labyrinths in faraway places, but she finally realizes that she must confront—even seduce—the minotaur of the unknown parts of her self, which waits at its center: "The farther she traveled into unknown places, unfamiliar places, the more precisely she could find within herself a map showing only the cities of the interior" (80). She comes to believe that she and her husband need and support each other, that she has internalized his traits, and truly loves him. Now that she has understood her own hidden fears and faults, which hindered their communication, she can better understand him and rebuild their relationship.

The minotaur of the title is thus first of all symbolic of Lillian's hidden or unconscious self; her voyage enables her to fathom certain suppressed desires—for security, for a rich interior life of self-reflection, for example—and thus to integrate them into her personality rather than to flee them. Through acceptance of her fears, her doubts, her past, she has seduced them and thus reduced their power over her. At the end, the labyrinth image occurs again; her husband becomes another labyrinth for Lillian to explore. The minotaur is then also symbolic of the insecurity at the heart of the husband's apparently cold labyrinth; Lillian must seduce this minotaur in order for his hidden self to emerge. Both cases develop the archetypal pattern of a labyrinthine journey toward personal fulfillment, and in doing so, they activate resonances associated with the labyrinth of love. As in *Theseus,* here the seduction is not a primary goal, but rather the means to a more complete personality; and here, as in Gide's novel, in order to triumph over the minotaur the explorer in the labyrinth accepts him first.

The labyrinth symbols throughout Nin's novel constitute the medium through which Lillian reaches her conclusions about her life, providing a symbolic landscape for the novel's development. The simple existence Lillian seeks in Golconda, for example, is often symbolized by the clear waters of the sea or the hotel's swimming pool. The labyrinth images form small but persistent intrusions into this other element, suggesting the complications of self-reflexive thought that Lillian is unable to escape. The principal labyrinth Lillian explores is her own mind, and later the mind of her husband, but her internal labyrinth is projected back onto the world, which has in turn of course contributed to the internal pattern in the first place. In the world described by Lillian, many things appear labyrinthine. Here again, as in many of Borges's stories, labyrinths of the world and labyrinths of the imagination reverberate back and forth. The external labyrinths throughout Nin's novel foreshadow Lillian's final acceptance of her inner labyrinth with its necessary yet often disturbing complications. By explicitly describing correspondences between interior configurations and exterior realities, Nin delineates the interdependence of inner and outer worlds, the interactions of modes of thought and the physical environment—ultimately, as we shall see more clearly in the context of the labyrinthine fictions we have examined earlier, the interdependence of subject and object.

The physical labyrinth Lillian mentions most frequently is the city—particularly Mexico City, where she grew up. Her memories of its intricacies intrude on the seaside pastoral she attempts to live in Golconda. Early on, she takes a canoe trip with the doctor; that "flowing journey" contrasts with a recurrent dream which the canoe trip brings to Lillian's mind and from which she seeks to liberate herself. She dreams that she is in a boat, but caught in a "waterless place," sometimes even in a city street, where she would get down from the boat and attempt vainly to push it toward some water. The sexual implications of the image, of a woman caught high and dry in the city, seeking satisfaction in what she perceives as a more flowing environment, which would, presumably, loosen and moisten her both emotionally and physically, again conflate interior and exterior realities. Later, in the middle of the book, there is a proliferation of these city-labyrinths. They help Lillian recognize the power of her past, and the nature of her own mind with which she associates the same labyrinthine form. Lillian describes how she and her childhood friends played in "a city beneath the city, which had been partly excavated to build a subway like the American subway, and then abandoned" (71). These children act out the simultaneous fear and fascination of the labyrinth, for even though it was their favorite play spot, "they were fearful of getting lost" (71). Lillian does get lost in these underground passageways one night, and before she is rescued she feels she knows the meaning of death. Lillian subsequently asks herself whether everyone lives thus in two cities simultaneously, "one, above the ground, in the sun of Golconda, and one underground?" (74). She realizes that she is still in that "underground city" of her childhood, in the "subterranean chambers of memory" that she has recognized earlier in someone else (88, 77), implying that only by confronting the minotaur of the unknown parts of her psyche will she be able to live comfortably in the sunlit labyrinth of the world and the conscious and unconscious labryinths of the self.

Imperceptibly, Lillian associates her labyrinthine "cities of the interior" with caves and prisons; describing the interior journey of self-exploration she wishes her friend Dr. Hernandez had taken, and which she believes might have prevented his death, she modulates from "ancient cities within ourselves" to "isolation cells" to "caverns of the soul," and "geological depths where lay hidden the imprisoned self" (94–95). Earlier, she asks herself why her true self should hide so far below the surface, and says that she feels as if she were descending far into the earth to explore "ancient caves covered with paintings and carvings"(89). Here Nin obviously creates an analogue for the exploration of the unconscious—presumably the Jungian collective unconscious as it expresses itself through art. But beyond this, we can see that in a Lawrentian attempt to recover a more earth-centered existence and to reverse in her own history the general historical development of the labyrinth from a natural to an increasingly artificial construct, Lillian tends to pass from "civilized" manmade labyrinths to more primitive natural ones. This kind of natural form is what she seeks in her flight toward the jungle of Golconda, away from the city of her childhood, and of her married life:

> Lillian could feel as they [the Mexicans] did at times. There were states of being which resembled the time before the beginning of the world, unformed, undesigned, unseparated. Chaos. Mountains, sea and earth undifferentiated, nebulous, intertwined. . . . Dense, invisible, inaccessible to articulate people. She would live here, would be lost. (83)

Lillian *is* articulate, though, and the doctor has earlier used the word *design* to characterize her interior geography. She describes her past: "All this was painful, like a jungle in which I was constantly lost. A chaos" (29). But these images of chaotic jungle laby-

rinths picture her misguided desires; she is wrong to want to identify herself with them. The doctor perceptively observes that
"chaos is a convenient hiding place for fugitives. You are a fugitive
from the truth. . . . So you will plunge back into chaos, and this
chaos is like the jungle we saw from the boat. It is also your smoke
screen"(29). If she lived here, as she says, in the jungle, she would indeed be lost, but in a different way than she imagines; she would be
lost from herself. Lillian's nature is closely linked to the complicated labyrinths of her past—the city and her own and her
husband's thoughts. She cannot reverse history, but only confirm
its progress. She has traveled through her primitive labyrinthine jungle to find herself, and to accept her own civilized labyrinthine
mind. This duality of city and jungle suggests the dangers not only
of psychological dead ends and personal monsters but also of erroneous paths of inquiry. It thus reveals the desire for exploration
allied with the potential for self-deception. Like Gide's Theseus
and Durrell's Baird, Nin's character takes a voyage into a labyrinth
that reaffirms her past, though during the journey she develops a
new attitude toward it. And like Camus's narrator, for whom being
spared by the minotaur will require having previously accepted
him, Lillian exits from her inner labyrinth by affirming it. In these
texts, then, we witness the incorporation into the present of the labyrinthine realm of the past and of the mind with their undiscovered
and perhaps formerly unconscious potential, rather than an escape
out of their coiled enclosures into a fresh and restful place.

In contrast to Gide and Durrell, who speak as male explorers entering a female domain, Nin here utilizes the labyrinth to figure the
development of female consciousness. In doing this, she reverses
the sexual identities of Theseus and Ariadne, for when Lillian journeys away from her home and her husband (whom she nevertheless
remembers from time to time as a kind of thread) through a labyrinthine learning environment, and back again, she as the woman
explorer/hero encounters the male guide figure of Dr. Hernandez.[15]
Nin thus invests what has traditionally been articulated as a sign of
implicitly male sexual maturity and civic leadership with explicitly
female desire and power.

Albert Camus: "The Minotaur or the Stop in Oran"

In order to be spared, one must say Unlike Gide's mental labyrinth
"yes" to the Minotaur. in *Theseus,* the metaphoric labyrinth Camus draws from the
Algerian city of Oran in his essay on "The Minotaur or the Stop in
Oran" is closely tied to physical reality. This urban labyrinth differs
from the common modern embodiment of the design as a large city
with a confusing grid of streets, which we have encountered in
Joyce, Butor, and Robbe-Grillet, for it is a small city in the desert.
The inhabitants of Oran, like the explorers of Durrell's "dark labyrinth," are not so much lost in the world as lost to it:

> One expects to find a city open to the sea, washed and refreshed by the
> evening breeze. And aside from the Spanish quarter, one finds a walled
> town that turns its back to the sea, that has been built up by turning
> back on itself like a snail. Oran is a great circular yellow wall covered
> over with a leaden sky. In the beginning you wander in the labyrinth,
> seeking the sea like the sign of Ariadne. But you turn round and round
> in pale and oppressive streets, and eventually the Minotaur devours the
> people of Oran: the Minotaur is boredom. For some time the citizens of
> Oran have given up wandering. They have accepted being eaten.[16]

The hyperactivity that is often represented as the cause of modern
man's exhaustion is replaced by the lack of any activity beyond a
small initial gesture. The passivity of the Oranians suggests that of
the Athenian victims in the years before Theseus comes to lead
them; they accept their fate, but, strangely enough, in that very acceptance, they gain a certain dignity in the eyes of the visitor who
narrates the essay.

There is a difference, however, between the Oranians' passivity
vis-à-vis their world and the writer's receptivity to that world. At
the beginning of the essay the narrator seeks solitude for meditation away from the charged atmosphere of his urban European surroundings. That atmosphere motivates the essay's initial poetic
description of intimacy between a city and its inhabitants. The narrator describes moments (which he has experienced overlooking
the historically charged city of Paris), moments when the atmos-

phere seems to feel, and the universe to respond, which indicate that poetry frequently depends on this sense of a humanized world. But the poet also needs a place of retreat. Even if there are not more deserts or islands, we still need them: "In order to understand the world, one has to turn away from it on occasion. . . . But where can one find the solitude necessary to vigor? . . . In order to flee poetry and yet recapture the peace of stones, other deserts are needed, other spots without soul and without reprieve. Oran is one of these" (115–16). In Oran man is "proscrit" ("outlawed" or "banished") and the town seems otherworldly. The word points up the characteristic duality of labyrinthine space in Oran with its meaning of outside the law and outside society. The irony is that Oran as labyrinth both encloses upon man and excludes him from the wider social world. Camus's essay records the experience of a voluntary exile to the other world that is Oran and concurs with a general modern refusal to associate the labyrinth pattern with poetic or divine inspiration, though, as we have seen in Gide's interpretation of Theseus's journey, it may lead there. Camus's Oran is a profoundly prosaic place. Like Borges, whose labyrinths question whether the world is orderly or chaotic, Camus uses the image to translate his ambivalence about Oran into an ambiguous portrait of the town. The labyrinth of Oran is both sought after by the poet and maligned by him as it also seeks him out and ensnares him "without reprieve" in its spectacular mediocrity. It is an island/desert that isolates and integrates the poet, providing a spatial metaphor for the writer's journey toward his text.

"The Minotaur or the Stop in Oran," included in Camus's collection *Summer,* is one of a number of essays that assert the primacy of present reality and rejoice in natural splendor. The narrator of "The Minotaur" maintains that Oran's mediocrity—its insignificance, its solidity—makes its force felt every day and holds no promise of eternity. Oran compels people to pay attention to what is not important. Statues and buildings are ugly and anonymous, but solid; they are not the stuff of poetry. The true monuments of Oran are its stones, most notably the rocks piled up for a long jetty in the harbor; perhaps they form part of the "peace of the stones" the poet needs to recapture in order to write later on. The various uses of stone in the labyrinthine city contrast with the freer stone outside in the desert, and with the sea: "The opposition here is between magnificent human anarchy and the permanence of an unchanging sea. This is enough to make a staggering scent of life rise toward the mountainside road" (121).

The essay alternates between ennui and glory in nature. In Oran itself ennui is pervasive, but near the end, for instance, the narrator endows Oran with the significance and life he attributes to European cities at the beginning of the essay. Nevertheless, the poetic significance in Oran arises out of an oppressive sense of immanence—"emptiness, boredom, an indifferent sky"—rather than out of "a certain spiritual hunger whose bread is memory" (121).

The habitual fear of entrapment in the labyrinth here takes the form of removal from the rejuvenating forces of nature. Yet the successful explorer manages to make his encounter with that sterile enclosure a prelude to opening outward. He structures his own initiation rite. Most of us dread boredom and would prefer to say no to that minotaur. But Camus suggests that we must occasionally seek him out in order to progress:

> This, perhaps, is the Ariadne's thread of this somnambulist and frantic city. Here one learns the virtues, provisional to be sure, of a certain kind of boredom. In order to be spared, one must say "yes" to the Minotaur. This is an old and fecund wisdom. . . . In the puffing water far out bathed in radiant light, is distinctly heard the muffled call of inhuman and glittering forces: it is the Minotaur's farewell. (133)

The passage concludes with the traveler at the end of his ritual stay in labyrinthine Oran, picking up a small, smooth stone from a cliff, the sign of his liberation.

The narrator differentiates himself from the Oranians to be sure, but at a certain point he also identifies temporarily with them so that he may profit from their way of life. He may—indeed must—accept and participate in the boredom of Oran while he is there; this kind of emotional void is what he has been seeking in his return to the city of stone. It is this acceptance that seems magically to elicit the poetic perception of the minotaur's farewell. The writer adopts the stance of Theseus; he penetrates a foreign and potentially enervating realm, and emerges strengthened. He is strikingly close to Gide's Theseus in that he conquers the minotaur by accepting the premises and conditions of the atmosphere inhabited by the beast. Gide's hero temporarily succumbs to the sensual vapors, but is able to turn them to his own advantage, for his victory is reportedly voluptuous. Similarly, Camus's poet/traveler accepts temporarily the reign of boredom in Oran. In neither case is the adventurer's exact method of victory over his allotted minotaur spelled out for the reader; each individual must lay down his own thread, which traces the labyrinth of his own life, and must slay his own minotaur within it.

At the center of the Oranian labyrinth, however, there is a specific and commonly watched battle referred to as a rite with sacrifices, which we need to examine for a moment. This is the boxing match. The excitement surrounding the match is the product of the rivalry between Oran and Algiers, but the scenario nonetheless recalls the original myth of the labyrinth, particularly Theseus's fight with the minotaur. At this point the narrator is just that—a narrator, not one of the combattants, nor is his minotaur really in the ring. This ironic revision of the myth suggests that the Oranians have displaced their hostilities; the brutal game represents their failure to recognize and confront the minotaur of boredom and their achievement of only temporary release from repressed tensions through vicarious violence.

The labyrinth, in addition to serving as a multifarious symbol for life in a city such as Oran, provides a background for the narrator's self-education. Much as it does in Nin's novel, the pattern illustrates a learning process. By passing through this labyrinth, whose center is boredom, the narrator comes to accept boredom in the world and in himself. Oran functions as a rite of passage to a new stage of awareness and artistry. Rather than representing a work of art itself, the labyrinth here symbolizes the phase of withdrawal, solitude, and even boredom that precedes creation. Camus entitles the last section of the essay "Ariadne's Stone." The reward for liberation from Oran is the stone he picks up, but this token of freedom is made of the same material as the prison, as if to suggest that spiritual deliverance grows out of close confrontation with the given environment. Camus activates the labyrinth's dual implications of prison and adventure in this attitude toward the town, tempering its initially hostile aura. The stones of Oran that offer no promises of eternity are mercifully solid; the force of their presence is not lost on Camus, who (in *The*

Myth of Sisyphus) will propose the fruitful absurd as the opposite of vain hope, as a passion without a tomorrow.

Camus's ambivalent portrait of stone here, sometimes the sign of deliverance, at other times an imprisoning structure, recalls the most ancient substratum of belief that associates the labyrinth with the earth mother. The inward-turning labyrinth of Oran can be seen to represent the dangerously enveloping side of the feminine from which the young man needs to differentiate himself before he matures. Alain Costes maintains that in Camus's work, defenses against the ambivalent images of nature as the mother often fail because they cannot encompass the negative images of incest in order to neutralize them. He cites as an example of the attempt to counteract this failure a dialogue from Camus's play *Caligula,* where Caligula wishes for the moon, which, according to Costes, "will replace the missing sister; it will combat the darkness of death, the terrors inspired by the Phallic Mother."[17] The stone the traveler picks up on a cliff in "The Minotaur" replaces the moon as a sign of deliverance from the labyrinthine stones of Oran that turn incestuously in on themselves within the city and away from the rejuvenating forces of the sea. We might interpret this stone as the precursor of the writer's pen; thus the essayist/explorer's confrontation with and escape from the labyrinth of Oran would signal the differentiation of the narrating self from the maternal matrix. And as in early labyrinthine rituals that were often imagined as returns to the earth as the origin of life for the purpose of being reborn, for Camus the return to the North African labyrinth constitutes just such a return, a confrontation with his past in order to progress beyond it, to become a new being, a poet. The narrator's references to desert hermits and to Descartes choosing the particular desert where he will write "the greatest, perhaps, of our viril poems" point in this direction (116). So does the image of men working, building blocks of stone into a jetty. The jetty curves out into the sea from the labyrinthine town, in the same direction the essayist will take as he leaves Oran. The construction of the jetty is a spatial analogy for the narrator's construction of sentences with words. Both are Ariadne's threads that lead out of the labyrinth of stone in Oran toward the sea; they are the same stone, but transformed by men. Those works of stone, like words, "serve man in his plans" (129).

At the end of the essay the poet has satisfied his desire for a place without poetry—a labyrinth—and accepted the benefits of the boredom experienced there. The last paragraph chronicles the lyrical ascent that is made possible by the poet's self-reflective exploration of that labyrinth. The exalted tone and the transformation of heavy substances by images of light and movement carry us higher and higher into the air along with the poet and the magical coast. As he sets off, the narrator imagines that the "heavy galleons of rock and light are trembling on their keels as if they were preparing to steer for sunlit isles," and hymns ecstatically, "O mornings in the country of Oran! . . . The whole coast is ready for departure; a shiver of adventure ripples through it. Tomorrow, perhaps, we shall leave together" (133).

Like Gide, Camus ends with a symbolic ascension after the voyage in the labyrinth, recalling Eliade's two kinds of initiations, the normal and the esoteric, the human penetration of the earth and the shamanic ascension to heaven. In analogous literary terms, the essay alternates between the two poles of prosaic labyrinthine meditation in the streets of Oran and poetic inspirational flight out over the sea, between Thesean wandering in the labyrinth or Daedalian design of it and flight beyond them both. The last page is a final, though not a definitive modulation from one realm to the other. The essay thus progresses from profane labyrinth to sacred center, the narrator having journeyed through the labyrinth of the world to the paradise of his text; in that journey the labyrinth serves as a path of personal and literary initiation, characteristically both guarding its own center and enticing the explorer toward it.

Julio Cortázar: Hopscotch *and* The Kings

The labyrinth would unfold like the spring of a broken clock as it made workman's time fly off in a thousand pieces.

Like Camus, Cortázar uses the labyrinth to picture the voyage toward the text, but in a different way. In "The Minotaur or the Stop in Oran," the labyrinth represents a part of the writer's world and a stage on his journey toward poetic language. In Cortázar's early play *The Kings* and to an even greater degree in *Hopscotch* it encompasses all of language and the world; the voyage in the labyrinth never ends. Like Gide, Cortázar examines the myth of the labyrinth explicitly in *The Kings*, rewriting the original narrative as a series of dramatic dialogues. (Cortázar's familiarity with French literature makes it likely that this rewriting may have been suggested by Gide's, published a few years earlier.) Within an allegory of political power, Cortázar prefigures the labyrinth of language that will enclose the protagonist of *Hopscotch*. He also indirectly investigates the labyrinth's conceptual similarity to a mirror, thus confirming its power as an image of self-exploration, which we have seen already in the texts by Gide, Durrell, and Nin.[18]

The Cretan labyrinth is a continual presence in Cortázar's play; its curved walls preside over the action, and the stage directions mention them at the beginning of every scene. Minos introduces this labyrinth as he waits for the Athenians to arrive by calling it an "unnamable snailshell," a "resounding marble desolation," and lamenting the angry silence of its exitless entrails.[19] Right from the start, then, the labyrinth is presented as troubling the resources of language.

It is also an image of political power: since Minos's very identity is linked to his power, he claims at first that the minotaur is a "living testimony to my strength" (11). But he later reveals in his dialogue with Theseus that the minotaur can also be seen to stand for the political power of the people and the ruler's need to pacify it with sacrifices (hence the Athenian youths fed to the beast). Minos wishes to make a deal with Theseus and proposes that Theseus secretly kill the minotaur and flee with Ariadne as his reward. Minos will subsequently free the Athenians from having to pay the tribute, and pretend to feed the minotaur with Africans, thus keeping his power alive. Theseus seems to acquiesce in this scheme; however, since the play ends with the death of the minotaur the success of Minos's plan for permanently securing his power is not revealed. For Minos, the labyrinth is unnamable and terrifyingly silent because its "legitimate inhabitant," as he himself has said, is the minotaur, the voice of the people. In this context, his plan to kill the minotaur represents his refusal to confront the bestial reality at the heart of his personal labyrinth—that he is an unsuccessful ruler, that his power rests on fear, not competence—as well as the more general idea of alliance between blood sacrifice and power in primitive political systems. The minotaur himself confirms to Theseus (in words that seem to echo those of Camus's narrator) that "there is only one way to kill monsters: to accept them" (64). For Minos, unable to accomplish this, the minotaur remains a haunting presence, even though he is enclosed.

As we might expect by now, in addition to his other roles, this minotaur figures the ignored part of the self as well.[20] Rationally out of the way, still he cannot be forgotten, and enters Minos's dreams: "Yes, a prisoner and condemned forever! But my dreams enter the labyrinth, there I am alone and ungirded, sometimes with the sceptre that bends in my fist. And you go forward, huge and sweet, huge and free. Oh, dreams in which I am no longer the master!" (11). From the seashell-shaped material labyrinth at the start of his speech he has shifted to the metaphorical labyrinth of his nighttime consciousness. Like Gide's labyrinth that reflects the trap that each visitor sets for himself, this labyrinth encloses the particular fears of individual Cretans. In answer to Ariadne's question of who made the minotaur ferocious, Minos confirms this idea, associating the labyrinth with the pattern of an individual's life, the minotaur as a fearful hidden motivating force within it. Minos describes the minotaur as residing "in the heart, in the black enclosure of the will" (34), thus conflating the psychological and the political, the individual and the communal implications of the image. The minotaur, now representing the people's repressed collective will and its potential expression in words, as well as the individual's hidden fears, tells Theseus that he will overturn Minos's throne "from my final and ubiquitous freedom, my diminutive and terrible labyrinth in each man's heart" (66).

The use of mirrors in the play reinforces the self-reflexive nature of this labyrinth. Symbolically, a man's encounter with a mirror and a labyrinth resemble each other. Just as he looks in a mirror to see another face that is a reflection of his own, so he enters a labyrinth to encounter another who is often a formerly hidden or ignored part of himself. Both are explorations out of oneself, toward another, and back again. Ariadne uses the image of a mirror to describe her father's creation of his own minotaur: "He is your secret work, like the shadow of a tree is the remains of its nocturnal terror" (19). The specular import of Ariadne's remark to her father that "to speak is to speak to oneself" links the labyrinth of the self to the labyrinths of language, as do Theseus's words to the minotaur, whom Ariadne has earlier described as loving to name things:

"They already talk about you so much that you are like a vast cloud of words, a play of mirrors, a repetition of an ungraspable fable. At least such is the language of my rhetoricians" (57).

Here the image also reveals a warning that language may remain a mere play of mirrors, endlessly reflecting surfaces, never reaching the hearts of any matters, an empty rhetorical structure, a sterile labyrinth, controlled by the official orators. Ariadne describes the labyrinth her brother the minotaur inhabits as "clear and desolate, with a cold sun and central gardens, where voiceless birds fly over" (20). A genuine, responsible use of language resulting from the minotaur's symbolic rebirth in words, in the "sea of songs, the tree of murmuring," is man's recourse against this sterility (67). At the end of the play, the dying minotaur tells a cithara player that he will return through the citharist's voice. We might imagine Minos's labyrinth as an attempt to repress the force of freedom that the authentic use of language would unleash; it would represent the official *langue,* while the minotaur would embody the creative and hence disruptive *paroles* of an individual artist or an entire people. In the same way that Oliveira wishes for a less rational form of existence than his present enclosure in a conscious canefield of words, the minotaur here desires death so that he will be more himself, so that his spirit of freedom will flow undetected through men in their words.

Laying down a thread of words within the labyrinth of language is an imperfect but ultimately meaningful way to chart a course in the labyrinth of the world and of the self. This is why the minotaur makes Theseus's destiny visible to him. It is also why Theseus, portrayed by Cortázar as an unthinking man of action, cannot bear to hear the minotaur speak: "Be quiet! At least die quietly! I'm tired of words, the hungry bitches! Heroes hate words!" (68). But the hero does not get his way in this case, for, while the minotaur's triumph is certainly not complete either, he lives on in the words of the citharist that end the play.[21] The danger that the labyrinthine enclosure or the tyrant who rules it will silence the speaking voice is averted for the time being, but the threat remains, and must be vanquished with many threads of words.

The images of the labyrinth in Cortázar's *Hopscotch* resemble those that Nin describes in *Seduction of the Minotaur,* as well as the loveless labyrinths of Butor and Barth, for they portray both the correspondence between patterns of experience and imaginative configurations and the longing for freedom from self-reflexive thought. They also confirm the modern propensity to double labyrinths, to superimpose patterns of the world and structures of thought, which we have seen in the texts of Joyce, Butor, Robbe-Grillet, and Borges, and which suggest that just one labyrinth is insufficient to describe our condition. As in those works, here again the designer designs designs from which he would like to escape, and the labyrinth is doubled to better enclose its inhabitants. As the image of a labyrinth serves to describe the influence of external space on internal space, it is, as Durrell put it, "an outward symbol of an inward march upon reality," but as it describes internally conceived space in its capacity as model for visions of the external world, it is an inward symbol of an outward march upon reality as well. This process of doubling, of the reverberation of internal and external labyrinths, is suggested graphically by a charming image near the start of the novel:

> I touch your mouth, I touch the edge of your mouth with my finger, I am drawing it as if it were something my hand was sketching, as if for the first time your mouth opened a little, and all I have to do is close my eyes to erase it and start all over again, every time I can make the mouth I want appear, the mouth which my hand chooses and sketches on your face, and which by some chance that I do not seek to understand coincides exactly with your mouth which smiles beneath the one my hand is sketching on you.[22]

The passage is a clever burlesque of mimetic writing (in addition, of course, to constituting a playful celebration of love's magic): Horacio Oliveira precisely duplicates the existing reality of La Maga's mouth, imagining it to be his own invention, while at the same time implicitly realizing that it is not, as the "real" mouth's smile suggests.

In Oliveira, Cortázar achieves a balance between the whimsy of a child playing hopscotch and the anguish of a man lost in a labyrinth. Oliveira recognizes the incongruity of his comic philosophizing and his serious play. The book's power lies in this combination of serious sentiment with comic irony, and exemplifies the mixture of gaiety and fear in the ballad with which I began this whole inquiry into the nature of labyrinths. It is a combination that characterizes many literary uses of the design, as we have seen in the often playful texts of Joyce, Robbe-Grillet, and Borges; Cortázar himself recognizes his affinity with Joyce in this respect, referring to *Ulysses* in serio-comic terms as a novel that progresses like dreams "where in the margin of some trivial happening we have a presentiment of a more serious anxiety that we do not always manage to decipher" (398–99).[23]

A central image in Cortázar's novel is the game of hopscotch that provides the title. The Argentine version of this game comprises a string of boxes with the first marked earth and the last heaven, as if earth and heaven were connected by the grid of subdivided spaces in between. The pattern represents Oliveira's quest for freedom, his desire for psychological release from mental tension. Progress from earth to heaven through the squares is analogous to a voyage through a labyrinth to a divine center. Though the hopscotch pattern is not identical to the labyrinthine path, they share the essential elements of progression through an impeded route toward a desired realm. Oliveira virtually equates the labyrinth and hopscotch designs at the center of the novel, just before the division in the text that separates Oliveira's Paris existence from his life in Buenos Aires. At that point, the narrative prose reaches a crescendo of absurdity: Oliveira has been arrested for indecent behavior with Emmanuèle the bag lady and as they are driven away in a police wagon with two n'er-do-wells, Emmanuèle alternately snivels and shouts about lost love, while Oliveira indulges in playful metaphysical speculations. The passage climaxes in Oliveira's drunken vision of his paradise; if the game goes right, he says, the stone used to play hopscotch will open up the world:

> the pebble had to pass through the eye of your asshole, . . . and from Earth to Heaven the squares would be open, the labyrinth would unfold . . . and . . . you would come into the road leading to the kibbutz of desire . . . through a land of men towards the kibbutz far off there but on the same level, just as Heaven was on the same level as Earth on the dirty sidewalk where you played the game, . . . and one day someone would see the true outline of the world, patterns pretty as can be, and, perhaps, pushing the stone along, you would end up entering the kibbutz. (216)

Here interior and exterior trajectories merge, linked by the stone; inner and outer patterns of existence coincide. The hope, similar to the one we hear from another Argentine, Borges's librarian of Babel, that one day someone will be able to perceive the pattern of the world-sized labyrinth in which we wander, concludes the passage. The new and distinguishing element here is Oliveira's desire not to explore or to survey or to understand or even to design the labyrinth, but to open it out. It is tempting to see even more Borgesian shadows behind this image; Oliveira's fantasy of "straightening out" the labyrinthine world and its events recalls in particular the magnificent and holy desert labyrinth of the second king in "The Two Kings and Their Two Labyrinths" and the straight-line labyrinth Lönnrot imagines at the end of "Death and the Compass."

Oliveira refers to his desired realm of heaven as "the center," "the kibbutz of desire," "the divine rocket," "the key." These regions are opposed to Oliveira's daily round of labyrinthine trajectories — cities, games of hopscotch, literary and metaphysical discussions. And to pass into them he needs to "discover the anti-explicatory method" (36). Cortázar's alteration of the labyrinth pattern to a hopscotch game, from a continuous path interrupted by forkings to a design composed of nonconnected squares traversible by hopping over the lines, underscores the necessity of discovering a nonlinear mode of thought to reach his goal. He wants to straighten out the labyrinthine world, to experience it nonrationally, nonsequentially, not to explore it systematically; he does not accept our dichotomy of wanderer and architect or diachronic and synchronic experience. At one point his intense desire even causes him to conflate the labyrinth with its center, explaining that for him Paris is a center, a mandala that has to be explored without dialectics, a labyrinth where pragmatic formulas will only get you lost. In traversing it as he believes we should, thought will resemble breathing, nature nostalgically replacing culture.

We encounter another use of the urban labyrinth near the beginning of the novel as Oliveira describes the game he and his lover La Maga play in the streets of Paris. They wander without any particular plan through what is described as the labyrinth of streets until they encounter each other by surreal chance; at that moment, they laugh "insanely" and sense some enriching power after having found each other in the labyrinth. This is just one of many instances where Oliveira persists in his attempt to discover a method to traverse or, still better, to transform his labyrinthine existence. This existence, like its paradigm, the hopscotch game of life, is not chaotic but, rather, discouragingly ordered.[24] The game of chance encounters with La Maga represents the desire for "an interpolation of chance in the order of the world," as Borges puts it in his story "The Lottery in Babylon." That game, like Surrealism itself—a well-known influence on Cortázar's work—and like the pattern of the labyrinth, codifies the unexpected, incorporating chance into art.[25] His game with La Maga suggests that the streets of Paris are another system of communication that Oliveira wishes to overcome by his anti-explicatory method. Like the language of gliglico, which ignores grammatical rules, his and La Maga's encounters ignore the normal urban grammar by which people communicate their whereabouts to each other in the city. Cortázar does not use the word *crazily* lightly in this context. For him, as for the Surrealists, a crazy person might well be closer to the desired heavenly realm than the rest of us; at the end of the novel, we will see the potentially insane Oliveira perched god-like above the hopscotch game in the patio of the insane asylum where he and two friends live as caretakers. Not having the patience, the ability, or even the desire, to thread the labyrinth in docile Thesean fashion, such an individual might be the only one to dare the drastic solution of uncoiling or destroying it rather than exploring it.

A powerfully absurd scene where Oliveira's best friend's wife Talita attempts to traverse a plank connecting the windows of her husband Traveler's and Oliveira's apartments provides one example of the pervasive desire to bridge gaps between separate regions, to break down barriers.[26] Traveler's final attempt to reach Oliveira, who has erected a strange and complicated barrier of strings around himself in the madhouse is another. *Hopscotch* contains various separate psychophysical regions where people exist and from which they attempt to interact. These regions include countries, states of mind, rooms, streets, times, sentences—all boxes or paths in a world-sized hopscotch game.

Oliveira is not satisfied with these "normal" barriers, or with the approved systems for communication across them. He wants to destroy the boxes in the game, in the labyrinth of the world they form, and replace them with a unitary paradise of the heart. At the end of the novel we witness what may be his final attempt at this goal. There, he is poised on a windowsill, gazing down on Traveler and Talita immobilized in what he describes as hopscotch squares below him, thinking that "the best thing without any doubt at all would be to lean over just a little bit farther out and let himself go, paff the end"—as indeed it is (349). Like some of Borges's protagonists (Tzinacán, Tadeo Isidoro Cruz), Oliveira's dream of heaven, his self-fulfillment, may lie on the other side of death, or insanity. He may then have passed a barrier, but perhaps not the one he wanted to cross.

During the first half of the novel, Oliveira (like Revel in *Passing Time*) attempts to convert La Maga into an Ariadne figure, a guide to the kind of nonrational existence he craves.[27] As often before in myths about labyrinths, the secret of exit is imagined to be guarded by a woman: "Oh, let me come in, let me see some day the way your eyes see" (96). But despite Oliveira's desire, he senses that "a whole canefield of words has grown up between La Maga and me" (85).[28] Even the natural image of the canefield that Oliveira employs here, like the images of jungles and caves to which Lillian persistently returns in *Seduction of the Minotaur,* as well as his assumption of a passive stance with regard to its construction, reveal his desire for a more "natural," a less self-reflexive existence. Oliveira builds a defensive labyrinth of words around himself with La Maga outside, but a defense that turns out to be a prison.[29] Cortázar has characterized this labyrinth of language as "an obstacle between man and his own deeper being."[30] Oliveira's occasional visions of his heaven contrast with the linguistic labyrinth he has built around himself. They burst upon him, seeming to obey no rules, just as he would like them not to. As at the end of Molly Bloom's monologue, when a vision of passion amidst flowers rises poetically and magically out of the more rational and even cynical fabric of *Ulysses,* so these visions of paradise flash out from the intricate ironic texture of *Hopscotch.*[31] But powerful as they are, they are temporary. The labyrinth of self-reflexive consciousness endures. We have moved away from the labyrinths of the unconscious, of the dreamer, which we encountered in Gide and Durrell, toward an artful—even an artificial—labyrinth of language, one which is felt by its creator to separate him from the more primitive forces he wishes to encounter in the world and in himself.

In addition to these symbolic considerations, the structure of *Hopscotch*, developing the potential of its avowed predecessor, *Ulysses*, is generally labyrinthine in its convoluted and decentered design, its autogenerative mode, its indeterminacy, its options for different paths of reading provided by its "expendable chapters." Furthermore, at the very end of the novel, the reader, watching Oliveira balanced on his windowsill, is also poised at a fork in his own path of interpretation, wondering whether Oliveira jumps to his death, goes crazy, or both. As in *Ulysses* and its French successors, then, in *Hopscotch* the labyrinthine mode of choice is encoded in the text. The same will be true to a lesser degree of Donoso's *Obscene Bird of Night*. Images of labyrinths in these two novels thus clearly function as microcosmic analogues for the texts that contain them—as we have said in Gide's terms, as mises-en-abyme. The labyrinth is an appropriate model of the open novel, avowedly productive of diverse readings, for as an architectonic paradigm it is accessible, yet not unconditionally so, open yet not entirely free in form, the number of routes through it (or readings and interpretations of the text) limited by the constructed passageways of language itself and of the particular words of its author.

José Donoso: The Obscene Bird of Night

a labyrinth of solitary, decaying walls within which I'll be able to remain forever.

In *The Obscene Bird of Night* Donoso pictures the darkest labyrinth of all, the only one from which there is no exit. Within its walls, confinement eventually predominates over the freedom to explore, and in a strange process of implosion, the labyrinth seems to destroy itself. As we shall see, in addition to suggesting the interdependence of thought patterns and fictional modes, the image of this labyrinth also joins these constructions to the social fabric that engenders them.

Donoso's use of the labyrinth as a sign of social disintegration in *Obscene Bird* appears several years earlier in a scene from his novel *This Sunday*, in which it pictures a poor area of shacks in Lima where the narrator's grandmother ventures to seek out a down-and-out protégé of hers:

> On the other side, that settlement grows and grows, a net that gathers
> in the people that the city throws out as waste: a labyrinth of adobe and
> stones and debris, of tin cans and planks and blocks of chalkstone piled
> up every which way, without any order, people who arrive with some
> branches and bricks and stick them together with a bit of mud, firm it
> up with some stones and nails, and so one more cell is added to this
> cancer which grows and grows.[32]

The labyrinth erected by an anonymous and collective Daedalus-
as-bricoleur no longer duplicates the structure of a normal brain,
as suggested by Gide's imagery, but of a cancerous tissue. The narrative leaves the grandmother fallen in a faint amidst the garbage in
this urban cancer. Like the narrator of *Obscene Bird,* she is im-
mured in her chosen labyrinth, and yet before her fall she wishes
desperately to escape from it, from "this black labyrinth full of eyes
that are looking at me" (181). But there is no exit for her; in a sense
she is receiving her punishment for wishing to play with the lives of
the poor from the safety of her comfortable economic and social position. The tables are turned here when she enters their domain—
one of "the labyrinths of that life that I don't know"—and remains
trapped there (176). This labyrinth, like many others, equalizes its
explorers, reducing them all to victims of the decaying social fabric
of which it is both product and emblem. By entering the barrio, the
grandmother wants not only to find her protégé, but also to initiate
herself into a new realm of experience, perhaps a sexual as well as
a social one, so that here again the labyrinth is a structure of desire,
and serves as both protection and prison. The inhabitants are in
one sense protected from her intrusion but in another sense they
are trapped forever within the labyrinthine barrio; similarly for Mi-
sia Chepa, the barrio provides a protection against or an escape of
sorts from her barren life at home, but ultimately she remains imprisoned there against her will. The labyrinthine structures of social class are too confining; she cannot liberate either herself or her
protégé from their respective enclosures within them.

The narrator of *Obscene Bird,* one Mudito, repeatedly characterizes as labyrinthine the "Casa de Ejercicios Espirituales de la Encar-
nación de la Chimba," an old mansion turned into a poorhouse.
Mudito is himself a deaf-mute (as his name indicates) and scribbles
his novel among aging women and crumbling walls. House and narrative shelter, the fictional labyrinth contains deformed bodies and

monstrous acts; the book's title provides us with a warning about them.[33] Like the slum in *This Sunday,* the labyrinthine form of the house in *Obscene Bird* represents not a voluntary construction but the result of decay. At first Mudito, who regresses into childhood as he recounts the history of the house, usually maintains that he is master of this labyrinth: "a labyrinth of solitary, decaying walls within which I'll be able to remain forever" (98). But like the minotaur, he is trapped inside his labyrinth because he is too monstrous to go out. Theoretically in control of his surroundings, he nevertheless occasionally becomes confused, and instead of the leader he becomes the led:

> I could never hide, you always found me and made me follow you, getting me all confused in passageways I thought were a labyrinth for everyone but me, making me lose my bearings in the Casa, *my* Casa, that I know like the palm of my hand, so that when I believed I'd led you to a nook where I was going to lock you up forever, I suddenly found myself in the vestibule court. How? (59)

Again here, as in Borges's story of "Ibn Hakkan al-Bokhari, Dead in His Labyrinth," and in *This Sunday,* a labyrinthine environment equalizes its explorers by reversing their roles, confounding pursuer with pursued. In this instance, the question of sexual inversion arises as well, and Mudito, as we shall see, becomes very much the masculine intruder in the feminine domain of labyrinthine walls and words, but a masculine intruder who is not only forced to abandon the traditionally masculine role of the leader for the feminine role of the led, but in addition seems almost to assume a labyrinthine shape; his feeling of being interwoven in the passageways virtually incorporates him into the design, recalling Borges's statement in "Ibn Hakkan al-Bokhari" about the significant correspondence between monstrous labyrinthine dwellings and their inhabitants. Here, as there, the labyrinth diffuses the power of the individual, subordinating the single to the multiple, confounding interior and exterior realities, subjects and objects of the discourse.

Slowly this labyrinthine house becomes associated with the process of fabulation, of storytelling—a more voluntary activity than the physical process of decay that modifies the house itself: "Generations of Azcoitía women scheme and weave a protective net

around the Casa" (392). The net is ostensibly a protective labyrinth, but inside it the women—weavers of words—finally become
prisoners of their own imbecility. This labyrinth of feminine storytelling, often called lying in the novel, is doubled—yet again, one
labyrinth is not enough to describe the entrapment; the Casa has a
twin, a strange dwelling where human freaks are employed as caretakers for the monstrous child of the house's wealthy owners.[34]
Like the old women in the house, the dwarf mistress of this estab-
lishment is said to "weave the labyrinth of solid lies like old adobe
walls" to protect her paradise.[35] The image reiterates the metaphorical identification of storytelling with the crumbling adobe of the
decadent labyrinthine house. The women have woven protective
labyrinths that suffocate the intruder, and Mudito ends up an abandoned infant, an "imbunche," a bundle with all its orifices sewn
shut. He has regressed beyond recognition rather than progressed,
and has been swallowed back up by a maternal matrix. Having
failed to differentiate himself sufficiently from this realm, he enacts
a reversal of the maturation traditionally accomplished in the labyrinth. As we contemplate the imbunche at the end of the novel,
after having watched Mudito explore the labyrinthine house and
construct the labyrinthine novel, we experience an escalation of the
labyrinthine situation of entrapment, for Mudito completes the process of his own labyrinthification (begun earlier in his feeling of being woven into passageways) and symbolically becomes the most
terrifying kind of labyrinth, a labyrinth with no exit.

That Mudito narrates most of the novel links literary discourse
to the process of social decline; Mudito's words grow out of crumbling yet all-too-potent social structures that, like the Casa, trap
their inhabitants. Hernán Vidal analyzes Mudito's end in relation
to his social milieu. He maintains that Mudito is finally destroyed
by the social values he has absorbed. He wants to triumph over the
rich with entertaining magic—the only way the poor can—but, Vidal asserts, "in the image of the imbunche, [Mudito] unconsciously
recognizes his status as the prisoner of a social tradition that has
driven him crazy."[36] This kind of suffocating labyrinth, hermeti-
cally sealed against outside innovation, becomes a prison—a madhouse in this case, a prisonhouse of language.[37] The combination
of chaos and order that characterizes the labyrinth in general here
takes on a particular social dimension: the aristocratic owners of

the house represent a decaying order, the dispossessed inhabitants a growing chaos; together they constitute the claustrophobic labyrinth of the social world and of Mudito's text that reflects it.

Even though Mudito himself ends up in a passive state, the fictionalized scene of writing, as well as its physical and social environment, implies a challenge to bourgeois social and fictional structures. Before regressing back to infancy, Mudito claims to be one of the witchly women fable-tellers who live in the casa. And near the end of the book, which we are beginning to suspect he has written, he, like Daedalus, wanders lost in his own invention; just as he goes astray in the Casa he thought he knew, Mudito becomes entangled in his fictional description of it. According to an acquaintance,

> Yes, he started out talking about that, but later on he distorted everything. [Mudito] had no talent for simplicity. He felt the need to twist normal things around, a kind of compulsion to take revenge and destroy, and he complicated and deformed his original project so much that it's as if he'd lost himself forever in the labyrinth he invented as he went along that was filled with darkness and terrors more real than himself. (392)

The labyrinthine house and the labyrinthine novel that chronicles its decay are mirror images, Mudito lost in both. Like Oliveira's, his narrative stance, regarded in an explicitly metafictional light, symbolically narrows the distance between story and discourse, a narrowing which finds its full expression in the labyrinthine texts of Joyce, Butor and Robbe-Grillet.[38] Mudito's labyrinth, conceptually doubled in this way, becomes all the more inescapable and oppressive, narrative invention proceeding precariously in the opposite direction from individual and social development. The narrator's words are not the key to an exit from the social structure of language. The novel thus becomes a kind of anti-Bildungsroman, for the protagonist is increasingly overwhelmed and ultimately swallowed up in his labyrinthine world and his book, rather than progressing toward a mastery of the complexities of the world, the development of the self, and the construction of the text. Practically self-begetting, the novel becomes symbolically self-destroying, implicitly criticizing, as it implodes, not only itself, but the social codes that engendered it. Rather like Gide's similarly monumental *The Counterfeiters,* which provocatively links storytelling and counterfeiting, this novel questions the regenerative nature of fabulation, even suggesting its regressive tendencies. Poetically and politically, Donoso rejects the writer's comfortable installation in his house of fiction, transforming that space into a ruined and fearful labyrinth, a strangely potent sign of repression and regression.

As it does for Borges, the labyrinth thus serves his two Latin American successors, Cortázar and Donoso, to signal our capacity for invention and our entrapment within our own designs. But while Borges is for the most part content to create fictional speculations on that duality, Cortázar and Donoso, more acutely aware of its social and political consequences, chafe against it in their fiction.

Umberto Eco: The Name of the Rose

The universe of human culture must be conceived as structured like a labyrinth.

As a semiotician, Umberto Eco is well qualified to examine the predominant signs of our times. In his novel *The Name of the Rose* and its accompanying *Postscript to "The Name of the Rose,"* he confirms that the labyrinth is indeed one of these signs by proposing it as a metaphor for the process of semiosis as he conceives it. In his tripartite definition of labyrinths in *Postscript,* Eco further complicates the duality between unicursal and multicursal patterns by adding a third variety, the rhizome. But we will begin with the first.

The first kind of labyrinth, according to Eco, is the classical labyrinth, the labyrinth of Theseus. This kind of path does not allow anyone to get lost, and so there is no need of an Ariadne's thread. Here Eco seems to founder on the inherent dichotomy between unicursal and multicursal labyrinths, which may stem originally from the interaction of visual icon and verbal image, but which eventually carries over into the verbal sign. Eco has recognized the problem in the classical labyrinth, which is that the visual representation of the pattern is generally unicursal, while the myth implies a multicursal path where the explorer needs an Ariadne's thread, but he chooses to excise this ambiguity at the beginning of the design's development and save the multicursal labyrinth for later in history.

Here he illustrates (unwittingly?) his own final point in *The Name of the Rose:* that all we have is the *name* of something—the name of the rose or the name of the labyrinth—and that name may refer to different things according to the semiotic system in which it is embedded. The name of the labyrinth can imply a number of different paths, and always could. Otherwise the "classical" labyrinth as described by Eco cannot fit into the classical myth. Eco implicitly recognizes the multivalence of the image, of course, in his discussion of the three kinds of labyrinth, each defined by the cultural system of a particular period, but in the case of the classical labyrinth he seems not to apply it. The second kind of labyrinth Eco mentions, and only briefly, is the multicursal kind, or what he terms the "mannerist maze." Here one needs a thread to keep from getting lost because "this labyrinth is a model of the trial and error process."

The third, and last, kind of labyrinth Eco describes is the rhizome, or net; in it "every path can be connected with every other one" and "it has no center, no periphery, no exit, because it is potentially infinite. The space of conjecture is a rhizome space."[39] In his earlier study on *Semiotics and the Philosophy of Language,* where he first formulated these definitions, Eco adds a number of other qualities to this rhizome, one of which is that its structure changes through time; like Butor's labyrinth of Revel's days in Bleston, it deforms itself as we explore it. Furthermore, for Eco, "the universe of semiosis, that is, the universe of human culture, must be conceived as structured like a labyrinth of the third type."[40] In characterizing this labyrinth as a rhizome, Eco returns the design to an organic model, and to one which, because it grows and changes, can never be definitively described. Because of the nonartificial nature of this image, Eco's rhizome departs significantly from the large family of labyrinths as I have been considering them. He expands the term *labyrinth* so far as to make it virtually ubiquitous. This is the danger we foresaw for the image at the start of this study, and it is fitting that we re-encounter it now at the end, for this expansion is in itself an interesting phemonenon in the history of the image.[41] Eco's primary interest is not in the history of the labyrinth but in the image of semiosis that it provides. For our purposes here, however, we can turn that emphasis around, and observe that while Eco's treatment of the labyrinth as an image of the organization and pursuit of knowledge, makes use of the labyrinth as a sign problematic, and our attempts to encompass its use disturbing, in its very disruption of well-defined borders, in its impulse to take over language as the very sign of signs, his treatment confirms the importance of the labyrinth as a figure of thought in our time.[42]

In *The Name of the Rose,* as everyone knows, the scribe Adso of Melk narrates the adventures he and his mentor William of Baskerville encounter as they investigate a mysterious series of murders in an Italian abbey. The library of this monastery is the primary physical labyrinth in the novel, and the diagram of it in the text shows a rectangular tower with heptagonal turrets, each of which is divided on the inside by a series of interconnecting rooms labeled with letters that spell out the names of regions of the world. Note here how once again (as in *Passing Time*) the presence of the labyrinth as the subject of a verbal text motivates a visual map to orient the reader, highlighting the troubling inability of Daedalian designers to provide sufficient orientation for Thesean explorers from the inside, so to speak, from within one kind of language. The import of Eco's labyrinthine library as a description of language itself is implied by the naming of the rooms by letters forming words, but words articulated in a convoluted fashion, tracing a specifically labyrinthine itinerary of forward, backward, and circular paths, of alternate branches: "The system of words was eccentric. At times it proceeded in a single direction, at other times it went backward, at still others in a circle; often, as I said before, the same letter served to compose two different words."[43] Most significantly, as we have noted before, the labyrinth pictures the multifarious nature of language as a semiotic system — as a system in which the same sign can denote two different referents or participate in two different codes. In addition, in his metaphoric description of the library, Eco continues and exploits the interchange between visual and verbal structures that has characterized the sign of the labyrinth since ancient times. As we shall see in a moment, the avowedly labyrinthine spatial structure of the library, whose center is forever sought and ultimately inaccessible, corresponds to the labyrinthine temporal mystery of the sequence of murders in the abbey, whose central motivation is similarly elusive. Both of these specific decentered labyrinths made of words are analogous to the all-encompassing and yet ultimately indeterminate labyrinth of language itself by which they are articulated. They are "second degree" labyrinths, so to speak, constructed out of the "first degree" labyrinth of language itself.

Eco explains that "the labyrinth of my library [In *The Name of the Rose*] is still a mannerist labyrinth, but the world in which William realizes he is living already has a rhizome structure: that is, it can be structured but is never structured definitively."[44] The burden of being Daedalus, as we have observed in Butor, Borges, and Barth, rather than the desire for it, motivates man's acceptance of the church's potentially comprehensible mannerist labyrinth where God or his delegated authority the abbot knows the plan. The reverse side of the burden of being Daedalus is the attraction of his power, and here, even more than for the other labyrinths we have examined (with the exception of Minos's labyrinth in *The Kings*), the issue of power is crucial. Thus the true beast at the heart of this labyrinthine library (which symbolizes language and the systems of knowledge it enables) is he who would control it. The most controllable labyrinth of all, of course, is Eco's classical one, and he implicitly gives that to the Devil, who "is grim because he knows where he is going, and, in moving, he always returns whence he came," as one does in a unicursal labyrinth, with no possibility for growth or discovery (581). In their different ways, both Jorge of Burgos and the abbot hunger for control over the labyrinth of the library, and, by extension, of language itself. Jorge sits at the center of the library literally consuming Aristotle's treatise on laughter, the book he fears would cause what has been marginal to leap to the center of the world—indeed, to cause "every trace of the center" to be lost; the abbot rules the community of the abbey absolutely, stifling any marginal heresies (578). Because it embodies an essentially static view of verbal truth, their hunger for control threatens to suck the life blood out of the living labyrinth that is language. Even William and Adso participate momentarily in that bestiality at the heart of that labyrinth when they "could have taken [Jorge of Burgos] calmly, but we fell on him with violence" in their eagerness to preserve Aristotle's treatise; that violence, a desire for possession of a text, of knowledge, is what starts the fire that destroys the library. It is not good in itself, but, as William says in another context, it is useful only as it is surpassed, for the library had to go, and William, with his pluralistic philosophies, is a fitting agent of its destruction—even more fitting in that he accomplishes it inadvertently.

In Eco's system, the mannerist model of knowledge that the unchanging labyrinth of the library embodies cannot endure for long, because in his view, the static view of culture it represents would ultimately put an end to writing itself, which is a process of constant reinterpretation, just as language itself depends on constant change. We see a graphic illustration of this danger when Adso tells us that the abbot commanded him to forget all he had seen and we realize that in obeying the abbot's command (a command fortunately sidetracked by William), Adso would never have produced this very book, the one that we are reading at this moment. As we have seen, Eco's redefinition of the labyrinth itself participates in the very process of linguistic change he uses it to describe, showing us that the name is all that remains of the thing. It is similar in this respect to the ending of the novel as it is written in Latin: the words are all we have left, but most of us can no longer read them, proof again—rather discouraging proof this time—of the profoundly temporal nature of the rhizome of language, which changes to such an extent that men may eventually be unable to decipher its earlier formulations, the linguistic codes of the past.

According to Eco, the theory of the organization of knowledge as a rhizomic labyrinth means that any one system of knowledge must be recognized as local and transitory, and that "every attempt to recognize these local organizations as unique and 'global'—ignoring their partiality—produces an *ideological* bias." Eco's "Porphyrian tree tried to tame the labyrinth. It did not succeed because it could not, but many contemporary theories of language are still trying to revive this impossible dream."[45] As *The Name of the Rose* is on one level the story of Christianity's attempt to close its hand over the proliferating heresies at the end of the Middle Ages, it is in part the story of the attempt to realize this dream, an attempt that goes up in smoke as the library burns. For those who cling to a centered, mannerist view of the world, then, the monster at the heart of the rhizomic labyrinth that is superseding theirs is that there isn't one—no center, no ultimate cause or explanation of existence, just pathways to be explored.

Just as the centered mannerist labyrinth of the library is a misguided spatial model for human knowledge, so the same pattern does not fit the temporal sequence of events in the world as Eco describes them.[46] As William first tries to unravel the labyrinth of the murders in the abbey, he thinks there is a divine plan directing them, and a central revelation that will explain them. And so do we, for a while. But pathways of events lead to unexpected places, inevitably forming designs as they evolve, but not preconceived designs; furthermore, there is no central cause, no one murderer.

In conclusion, we can place Eco in the company of two other eminent labyrinth makers whose works span the twentieth century. That Eco has written a study of Joyce conveniently joins the symbolic landscapes in his work (with which we are ending) to the narrative design in *Ulysses* (with which we began). Though they are of course very different works, several generally labyrinthine aspects of *Ulysses* that Eco includes in his study of Joyce make it in some sense a distant precursor of his own novel. Eco says in the introduction to the English translation of his essay that "to me Joyce was the node where the Middle Ages and the avant-garde meet." Note the labyrinthine term *node*, both signaling the ability of one figure to belong to and mediate two systems, and designating an ideal position of a particular text in the labyrinthine progress of knowledge, a position that Eco might well imagine for *The Name of the Rose* as well. If, as Eco says, his book on Joyce "is the story and the historical-theoretical foundation of such a paradoxical meeting," then perhaps *The Name of the Rose* is the fictional embodiment of that meeting, drawing on both ancient traditions and avant-garde theories of language. For one thing, the rhizome structure is already inherent in Eco's claim that the Proteus chapter of *Ulysses* is a declaration of poetics picturing not chaos, but a universe in which new connections between things are perceived and which introduces a world of metamorphoses that constantly produce new centers of relations.[47] Even the title of Eco's book, *The Aesthetics of Chaosmos,* is appropriate in joining his labyrinths to Joyce's, for it inherently asks a central question posed by labyrinths—the question of chaos or order in the world and the work of art, a question that continually perplexes William and Adso during their inquiry into the abbey murders. Finally, in his reading of Joyce, Eco extends the labyrinth of language to the experience of the reader, playing on the ambiguity of the labyrinth as threshold and barrier, as both open and closed. *Ulysses* is "a labyrinthine territory where it is possible to move in many directions and to discover an infinite series of choices; but it is at the same time a closed universe, a cosmos beyond which there is nothing."[48] This is because, according to Eco, the scholastic order in which Joyce was schooled encloses the book in a net of signs and yet also leaves it open, presumably because these signs are not gathered into an order. Similarly, in *The Name of the Rose* medieval signs and doctrines proliferate and we can take our choice between them, but in the end no global perspective obtains. On a more microcosmic level, already in connection with Joyce, Eco describes the destruction of the unitary medieval symbol, a process that is central in *The Name of the Rose,* maintaining that in *Ulysses* Joyce is recording "all the symbolic possibilities that criss-cross one another in all dimensions of the contemporary cultural universe."[49] Clearly, this idea of crossroads of meaning and choices of interpretation, which Eco discerns in Joyce, also motivates Eco's use of the labyrinth as a sign of modern writing in his theories and his novel.

That Eco alludes to Borges, a writer known for his labyrinths, in this novel where the labyrinth figures so prominently, confirms once again the existence of a labyrinthine tradition in postmodern literature, a tradition in which the labyrinth serves as a sign of language itself, of the fabulator, of the unfolding of human history in the world. A complete comparison of Eco's novel and Borges's stories will have to wait, but a few parallels will illustrate how Eco can be seen to expand on Borges's labyrinths. First of all, Adso recalls Borges's labyrinths of art that correspond in some way to the labyrinth of the world when he asks William if "the plan of the library reproduces the map of the world" and gets a Borgesian answer: "That's probable." As in many of Borges's stories where allusions to the world-sized labyrinth in which we wander pervade the text, the labyrinth raises this eternal question of design or disorder in the world. And as if to give this question concrete dimensions, in the same way that in "The Garden of Forking Paths" Yu Tsun's actual path toward the labyrinthine book of his ancestor forks, here William and Adso encounter a main path divided into three as they ascend the mountain toward the abbey with its labyrinthine library.

Secondly, the medieval view of the world to which the majority of the monks in the abbey subscribe corresponds to the kind of labyrinth Borges describes in "The Immortal," a labyrinth "compounded to confuse men," "its architecture, rich in symmetries, . . . subordinated to that end," a labyrinth with a plan, even if the plan is completely conceivable by God alone. The city of the immortals does not conform to this plan, and neither does William's investigation. He says of his inquiry, "There was no plot . . . and I discovered it by mistake" (599). At this point, William goes one step farther than Borges does in questioning cosmic order, starting with the figure of Jorge as Daedalus, "overcome by his own initial design." From that point on, "there began a sequence of causes, and concauses, and of causes contradicting one another, which proceeded on their own, creating relations that did not stem from any plan" (599). Thus William realizes that he can never exit from the labyrinths of events and languages or fathom their plans, but he has undergone an initiation of sorts in the labyrinthine structures he has explored, an initiation into this very knowledge—that he never can and never will completely understand or control them. And unlike the narrator at the end of "The Library of Babel," he doesn't even hold out the "elegant hope" of doing so one day. Adso, on the other hand, at the end of the novel, perhaps fearing death and thus less receptive than he had been to his mentor's iconoclastic views, returns us momentarily to the Borgesian position; he poses the question of order or chaos in the world, rather than asserting that chance and chaos reign, by wondering if the string of words he has written (as Theseus) forms a design with "some hidden meaning" (perceptible to some Daedalian God), "or more than one, or none at all" (610). Characteristically, the features of this labyrinth of events in the world are analogous to those in the labyrinth of language by which they are known and recorded; Adso asks himself essentially the same Borgesian question about language that he has about events, the question of whether he has been speaking of the fragments he has gathered from the burned library or whether they have spoken through his mouth, whether he is designer or designed.

Thirdly, Eco's mannerist maze seems to be prefigured by the labyrinth in "The Garden of Forking Paths" as it exists in the form of Ts'ui Pên's book with choices of alternate paths and with a finite structure; but as the idea of this book is brought forth and actualized as a description of life in the world, which continually changes, and hence is potentially infinite, it disconcertingly takes on a rhizomic shape. The progression is the same one Eco illustrates in the shift from mannerist to modern labyrinth in *The Name of the Rose*. However, the way Eco defines the labyrinth he considers most important, the rhizome, and leads up to it with the various labyrinthine images in his novel, indicates the continuing development of the image in the direction of decentering and indeterminacy. Many of Borges's labyrinths do seem to have centers, while Eco's rhizome does not. He shows a centered view of the world to be wrong, even to cause literally its own destruction in the form of the library, a library that recalls Borges's library of Babel, and that consumes Jorge of Burgos in its inferno.

Lastly, what about Jorge himself—echoes of Borges in this Burgos of Eco? In that character Eco presents an indeterminate sign: he is Borges and he isn't. We might see, for example, the monstrous figure of Jorge—like Borges, blind, like Borges, the temporary master of a library—hastily devouring a manuscript, as a parody of Borges's literary technique of pastiche, of textual absorption.[50] But Jorge's view of unitary truth, his unwillingness to relinquish his power over the library, his lack of humor, all distance him from Borges as we know him. In the final analysis, then, Borges is present as an eminent and enigmatic precursor, source of numerous ideas and techniques, not the least of which involves an initially misleading and in the end a mistaken identity; Borges appears here, in his own style, as everyone and no one, like the labyrinth itself in Eco's text and elsewhere, both a nostalgic and a prophetic figure. Appropriately, more enduring than his individual figure is his symbol of the labyrinth, which Eco refashions in his own way, as Borges would have approved, to embody our systems of knowledge—decentered, everchanging, complex. Once again, the design is multiplied, and once again it serves as a sign of the interdependence of the world of things and the world of thoughts, and of the languages with which we attempt to explore and encompass them.

7 / Metafiction and Mimesis

The Labyrinth of Art: Narrative Structure

THE LABYRINTHIFICATION OF NARRATIVE DIS-
course in the twentieth century that we have been examining in the
works of Joyce, Butor, and Robbe-Grillet serves both a metafictional and a mimetic function; the labyrinth of language concerns
both the text and the world. The writer's exploration of the labyrinth of the world leads him to create a mirroring labyrinth—the
work of art—that builds its own complexities at the same time that
it reflects the complexity of the world. In this respect, the labyrinth
is a powerful spatial model, which, in Juri Lotman's terms, "act[s]
as a kind of metalanguage" to describe a given culture's view of a
world order. The labyrinthine fictions we have examined illustrate
clearly and even explicitly Lotman's contention that "the structure
of the space of a text becomes a model of the structure of the space
of the universe."[1] In using the labyrinth pattern to portray the
shape of writing itself, the twentieth-century texts I have analyzed
represent a compelling verbal reconstruction of the ancient labyrinthine temple or palace, which duplicated the convolutions of
sacred caves or grottos: a writer signals the importance of his

enterprise by locating it in a traditionally significant space. And because both events and landscapes in the story and the discourse that presents them take on the shape of a labyrinth, as does the act of narrating that transforms one into the other, the reader experiences an initiation into the scene of writing; the convoluted prose, like other initiatory labyrinths, teaches perseverance.

Moreover, the circling and recircling around the subject in the city that these texts perform—the dance they lead the reader— reactivates yet another ancient resonance of the labyrinth pattern. Whether it signals a fertility ritual or the founding of a city, the common aim of many labyrinthine dances, which function according to the principle of conditional penetration, is the symbolic exclusion of hostile beings, or of those not fit to take part in the ritual inside the labyrinth.[2] What the dance of the discourse in these novels protects and thus in some strange way sanctifies is the apprehension of the text itself by the reader, the very act of reading, and since, in addition, the reader participates in the creation of the text, it protects and sanctifies the act of writing as well. It also celebrates the fertility of language—particularly its self-generative properties. In doing all of this, however, it signals a problematic aspect of much modernist and postmodernist writing—its elitist nature. The labyrinth of the text excludes not only hostile but dull beings, hence the literally academic nature of these texts, many of them hardly read outside of universities. In following the labyrinthine convolutions of the prose, the reader really re-enacts in the secular realm the sacred convolutions of the Christian "roads to Jerusalem," the labyrinths on cathedral floors that served as substitute penitential pilgrimages for those unable to make the trek to Jerusalem itself. In the case of these textual itineraries, what sin are we expiating? Perhaps our assumptions of easy access to the literary text fostered by the popularization of the novel in the nineteenth century.

The use of the labyrinth as a design for narrative constitutes the structural counterpart of the renewed tendency to regard the labyrinth as a symbol for literary art, which we noted in the texts of Borges, Gide, Camus, Cortázar, Donoso, and Eco. As we have seen, the labyrinth pattern dictates a number of fictional strategies in *Passing Time* and *In the Labyrinth*. In them the reader is often bewildered, though he senses the presence of a design. Similarly, the repetition of a series of images in the same order suggests an already explored passage in a labyrinth; contradictory statements suggest bifurcations in a path; narrative sequences cut off abruptly represent dead ends. A comparison of the avowedly labyrinthine structures of *Passing Time* and *In the Labyrinth* with the design of *Ulysses* reveals several important similarities. These texts, together with other selected uses of the labyrinth symbol, illustrate the force of its presence as a significant figure of modern literary discourse.[3]

The design of the labyrinth implies both a journey through time and a form in space. In this simultaneous designation of progression and stasis, the labyrinth as a symbol for reading—and, by extension, for interpretation—represents the twofold process of experiencing a text: the initial diachronic or Thesean reading and the subsequent synchronic or Daedalian reflection.[4] In this application of the design to the reading process, an important change occurs. As I have suggested, particularly with regard to the texts by Joyce and Robbe-Grillet, the reader as an explorer seeks not only to triumph and to escape, as did the mythic Theseus, but also to become Daedalus, to comprehend the plan of the labyrinth. In the sense that the writer will always design and the reader will always explore, the Daedalus/Theseus, synchronic/diachronic duality will always exist, even when the labyrinth serves as a linguistic and structural design for fiction. Yet the tendency we have noted in Joyce and his French successors and in much modern fiction that does not recall the labyrinth specifically, for the narrator to expose his journey toward a story, and for the reader to participate in determining the final form of the text, works toward conflating these traditionally separate activities.[5] These narrative labyrinths embody the experience of all readers of fiction who must constantly juggle their Thesean and Daedalian roles, their diachronic explorations with their synchronic interpretations. This tendency to collapse symbolically the distinction between reader and narrator is made explicit in an essay by Butor. His discussion of alchemical texts in code reads almost like an allegory of the reader's progress through *Ulysses, Passing Time,* or *In the Labyrinth:*

> These are coded documents, but ones which invite the reader to figure out the code. They are labyrinths covered with locks, but which must provide their own keys. . . .

The alchemist considers this difficulty of access essential, for it's a question of transforming the mind of the reader in order to make him capable of perceiving the meaning of the sections described. . . . The code is not conventional, but it springs naturally from the reality it hides.[6]

The labyrinthine experience of error and backtracking in a text is most clearly developed in the structure of *In the Labyrinth*. We have seen that passages or scenes nearly identical to preceding ones suggest the trials and errors of narrative discourse as it articulates a story. Likewise, the reader's trials involve the interpretation of these trajectories. The same situation characterizes *Passing Time*, though there the reader's choices regarding events are fewer, and the narrator's backtrackings do not appear as repetitions of entire passages or scenes but rather as his remembering various events over and over again. In both cases, however, the effect is to conflate the shapes of story and discourse. Retraversed paths are less easily recognized in *Ulysses* than in *In the Labyrinth* and *Passing Time*; they consist principally of image and thought patterns that the reader encounters throughout the novel or revisions of ideas and interpretations. And though the process is less formalized than in Butor's or Robbe-Grillet's texts, the text of *Ulysses* often suggests the need to pass a series of associated objects or ideas before emerging into a new branch of the labyrinth. As Stuart Gilbert has pointed out, "ideas, once they have formed an association in Stephen's mind, ever after reappear together."[7] Within this design, the reader makes choices of syntactic and semantic meaning from one word to the next, and so, as we have seen, language itself becomes a labyrinth and the process of reading an attempt to chart and navigate its various courses. In *Passing Time* and *In the Labyrinth*, the choice regarding syntax and semantics concerns the larger narrative units of objects and events and their interpretation rather than alternate linguistic possibilities.

The reader's journey through these labyrinthine novels, whether they branch syntactically or semantically, emphasizes the meanders rather than a structural, or even a thematic center. Revel, the narrator of *In the Labyrinth*, and Bloom return from their mental and physical journeys to a central place. Revel's room and that of Robbe-Grillet's narrator serve mainly as physical *points de repère*, whereas Bloom's house provides a spiritual anchor as well, although he returns to his house less often than do they to theirs. All three places are central, but they do not constitute centers for their respective fictional labyrinths. Unlike the classical labyrinth where Theseus kills the minotaur, nothing conclusive happens in these central spaces. Furthermore, we return to them several times as we do to other locations or images. In their lack of a precise center, these modern labyrinthine novels reflect the decentered self and the disorderly world, but they retain traces of the old, more formal order. "The center cannot hold," though a sense of pattern still prevails.[8]

Jacques Derrida's discussion of the problematic concept of centered structure as it figures origin through presence and the subsequent "decentering" and "structurality of structure" in recent thought extends these implications, and suggests that the development of the labyrinth from centered to decentered textual pattern reflects a more general movement of thought. Derrida opposes the Rousseauistic nostalgia for a lost origin, a centered world, to the Nietzschean affirmation of freeplay. That "affirmation then determines the non-center otherwise than as a loss of the center." Derrida's discussion of centering and interpretation that follows this statement sheds light on the use of the labyrinth as a sign for writing and interpretation:

> There are thus two interpretations of interpretation, of structure, of sign, of freeplay. The one seeks to decipher, dreams of deciphering, a truth or an origin which is free from freeplay and from the order of the sign, and lives like an exile the necessity of interpretation. The other, which is no longer turned toward the origin, affirms freeplay and tries to pass beyond man and humanism, the name man being the name of that being who, . . . through the history of all of his history has dreamed of full presence, the reassuring foundation, the origin and the end of the game.[9]

I think this second model of the total affirmation of freeplay is no longer possible once the sign of the labyrinth is invoked as a paradigm for writing and knowledge. We might then see the labyrinth of language as it exists in post-Joycean fiction as mediating between Derrida's two positions, because even decentered varieties of labyrinths necessarily recall their centered precursors, even if they deny them in the end. Derrida himself acknowledges the impossibility of expunging entirely the notion of center, claiming that it is a function, not a being: "I refuse to approach an idea of the 'non-center' which would no longer be the tragedy of the loss of center—this sadness is classical."[10] A classical sadness is what these decentered fictional labyrinths often evoke for readers in the western tradition. And yet sadness is not despair. In considering the labyrinth as an embodiment of the ins and outs of narrative discourse and of its problematic nature, it is also important to recall that the labyrinthine path is commonly an unbroken line: even though it is a perilous journey, it continues; it represents danger, but danger surmounted; it is often imagined as progressing from life to death and back to life again. Similarly, the twistings and turnings of the text are difficult, even dangerous, but not impossible to create or to decipher.

The literary implications of decentered labyrinthine texts are further illuminated by a brief consideration of quest structures in literature. In his discussion of grail stories, Tzvetan Todorov opposes the uncertainty of the outcome of the ordeals and obstacles in profane narrative logic to the foretold conclusion of ritual, religious logic, opposing, we could say, decentered to centered narrative labyrinths.[11] In his consideration of a similar set of stories, Northrop Frye maintains that the central myth of literature in its narrative aspect is the quest myth.[12] The novels I have been discussing here adopt the labyrinth—a frequent obstacle in many quests, as well as an emblem of the quest per se—to portray the problematic nature of reading and writing. In the text as explicit temporal puzzle, we experience a quest made of language itself. And as I have suggested, the reader's passage through the text represents a quest for narrative competence, a rite of passage toward understanding the processes of literary construction. Successful traversal of the pattern constitutes a kind of initiation. To undergo such an initiation through traversing these labyrinthine novels is to choose between various paths of interpretation, or to choose not to choose, for, according to Robbe-Grillet, "the function of art is never to illustrate a truth—or even a question—known in advance, but rather to put forth questions . . . which don't even know themselves yet."[13] The reader's freedom, or burden, of choice as he explores these labyrinths is counterbalanced by the self-reflexive nature of the texts, which compel him to focus on the narrative process. Decentered and directed toward itself, the act of reading is thus invested with a new quotient of anxiety.

Butor and Borges express the self-reflexive narcissism of such labyrinthine activity with similar images. Recall that near the end of *Passing Time*, Revel describes the pages of his diary-novel as mirrors covered with white paint. As he writes, and scratches off the paint, the pages reveal to him his own face, and the city of Bleston behind it. Similarly, as we have noted, Borges's writer in *The Maker*, who proposes to picture the world through his works, discovers just before his death that the labyrinth of lines he has created composes the features of his own face.

Robbe-Grillet discusses a complementary aspect of curtailed freedom, one which provides a link between his own work and that of Borges. His discussion concerns the notion of inadvertent intertextuality that the labyrinth often suggests—the metaphysical fear, or hope, that the world mirrored by the writer in his text may have been "written" first by a larger hand. In a recent discussion of his work, Robbe-Grillet describes Frank Robinson's science fiction story "The Labyrinth," which he remembers as "In the Labyrinth" when it appeared in *Les Temps Modernes*. Robinson's narrator claims that he has constructed a labyrinth to test extraterrestrial beings, but, comments Robbe-Grillet, "one ended up realizing that it was he, the narrator, who was in the labyrinth from the start. He had been captured by beings from another planet who had invaded earth and who were trying to understand the working of the human brain. It's an astonishing story. I have rarely encountered something as astonishing in a work of science fiction, unless it was the texts of Borges."[14] Here Robbe-Grillet may have in mind Borges's story "The Circular Ruins," where one man dreams another before discovering that he himself is a dream. In addition, it is entirely possible that the statement also recalls the labyrinth/novel Borges imagines in his modified detective story, "The Garden of Forking Paths"; if this is so, we might see that story as a prefiguration of or a directive for Robbe-Grillet's own *In the Labyrinth*, which presents just the kind of alternative events in fiction that Borges describes in the labyrinthine novel of Ts'ui Pên. The French edition of *Ficciones*, which includes "The Garden of Forking Paths," was published in France (by Gallimard) in 1951, several years before Robbe-Grillet's novel.

In this context of narcissistic narrative, I would like to consider briefly the labyrinth as a problematic figure of desire in language. In a general way, the form of the labyrinth with its ins and outs, its errors and backtracking, its combination of form and chaos, control and bewilderment really embodies the spatial structure of desire itself. I am using desire here in its general sense of arousal and anticipation of pleasure, as a metaphor that, like the resonances of the labyrinth I am evoking now, is grounded in but not confined to the sexual domain—the kind of desire that Peter Brooks maintains is the motive of narrative.[15] This narrative structuring of desire can be seen as a continuation in a twentieth-century mode of the tendency, as Ross Chambers and others have described it, for narrative to propose the metaphor of seduction as a description of itself, "mobilizing" in this way the "forces of desire."[16]

There are really two parts to this discussion: the first is the linking of literary and erotic desire; the second is the place of desire as it relates to fulfillment. To begin with the first, for Barthes, for example, "there is no other primary *significatum* in literary works than a certain desire: to write [and, I would add, to read] is a mode of Eros."[17] At the starting point of critical activity, according to Julia Kristeva (following Barthes), "the text is an object of pleasure," "the terrain of the reading subject's desire."[18] As I have suggested, actual labyrinthine bowers in hedge mazes and literary labyrinths of love where amorous intrigues are straightened out at the end of a text implicitly associate the processes of desire and decoding. Indeed, the continuing popularity of the labyrinth as a sign for writing and reading may result in part from the way in which it denotes both the quest for narrative, even the quest for meaning in a text, and the journey toward sexual initiation or sexual satisfaction. With its simultaneous evocations of amorous intrigue and literary invention, it pictures the sense in which the reader in quest of meaning resembles the lover in search of the beloved.[19]

Secondly, to recall very early uses of labyrinths in rituals of sexual initiation reinforces our sense of literary labyrinths as structures of desire in its sense of postponed gratification, ritual couplings taking place after the detours in a labyrinth of one kind or another have been negotiated. In this context, we could say that labyrinthine narrative discourse balances the impulse to arrive at a desired meaning and the impulse to tarry.[20] It encodes in the very structure of the text the same ambiguities present in that ultimate premodernist moment of self-conscious desire, the moment when Swann, about to kiss Odette for the first time, holds her cheek away from him for a few seconds, to prolong his about-to-be-satisfied desire, fearful that consummation will kill his passion. Wolfgang Iser confronts some of these problems of readerly desire as he concentrates on the search for meaning that is thematized in Henry James's *The Figure in the Carpet,* suggesting that in James, as in much twentieth-century literature, "meaning is no longer an object to be defined, but is an effect to be experienced."[21] Linguistic meanings, like other objects of desire, begin to be understood as things we seek and never possess. For Iser, the position of the reader of James is in conflict between the nineteenth-century desire to extract a clear meaning from the text and the willingness to abandon that project for the less definitive perception of an image. In the ambiguity of his desire, that reader corresponds to Swann, hesitating at the beginning of the twentieth century before kissing Odette's cheek. Just as the cheek represents a goal Swann would reach and yet an end point that may ruin his desire, the Jamesian image as described by Iser suggests something that we wish to define and possess at the same time we realize we cannot. It is clear by now that this issue of desire in narrative gets us quickly into the question of closure. Brooks, among others, takes up this problem in terms of desire, maintaining, after Lacan, that "desire must be considered [not only the motive but also] the very motor of narrative," and, after Barthes, that "the passion that animates us as readers of narrative is the passion for (of) meaning."[22] Furthermore, since "meaning plotted through time depends on the anticipated structuring force of the ending," Brooks concludes that "the desire of the text (the desire of reading) is hence desire for the end, but desire for the end reached only through the at least minimally complicated detour, the intentional deviance, in tension, which is the plot of narrative," a detour whose importance for narrative is made more and more explicit in the structure of recent labyrinthine fictions, which are filled with detours and deviances.[23] Indeed, that awareness of the necessity for postponing closure is why the labyrinth with its excessive meanders is such an apt embodiment of modern narrative desire.

On one hand, the labyrinths of language I have been describing serve as distancing mechanisms, as frustrations of desire carefully encoded in the texts. They propose their own centers, or for our purpose now, their own possibilities for gratified desire, embodied in the successful quest for linguistic meaning, only to subvert and annul them. The convolutions of the discourse remove the quester/lover/reader from the object of his desire. The lack of a single central point denies the satisfaction of a climactic possession of meaning, or at least postpones it, requiring it to take place in the realm of interpretation. On the other hand, if we continue with the metaphor of desire, in a labyrinthine narrative mode the erotic paradigm of penetration and satisfaction shifts in part to the act of reading, locates itself in the realm of discourse rather than in that of story. Linda Hutcheon recognizes a similar duality in her discussion of "narcissistic narratives." According to her, in metafiction "the life-art connection" is "reforged, on a new level—on that of the imaginative process (of storytelling), instead of on that of the product (the story told). And it is the new role of the reader that is the vehicle of this change." In what she terms "process mimesis" we encounter not art versus life but art as part of life.[24] From this viewpoint the distancing effect of labyrinthine prose is reduced, for the reader is engaged in the generative processes of the text. Thus the object of desire is changed, or rather, it is doubled, for the referential function of the discourse never entirely disappears. Furthermore, since the words of Joyce, Butor, and Robbe-Grillet constitute decentered and inescapable labyrinthine structures, they are affirmations of entrapment in language rather than escapes from it, but entrapments that in their erasure of definite goals provide some of the delights of leisure.

Before concluding this discussion of the theoretical implications of labyrinthine literary icons, I would like to insert them briefly into the broadest historical spectrum via a formulation by Derrida. In *Of Grammatology* Derrida explores (after Rousseau) the phenomenon of "writing by furrows," that is, "writing by *the turning of the ox*—boustrophedon": proceeding "economically," the ploughman, "arrived at the end of the furrow, . . . does not return to the point of departure. He turns ox and plows around. And proceeds in the opposite direction." Derrida then asks why writing in similar fashion, from left to right and back again from right to left was abandoned. "Why did the economy of the writer break with that of the ploughman? Why is the space of the one not the space of the other? Derrida, still following Rousseau, explains this rupture by the fact that "it is more convenient to read than to write by furrows," and so script developed from left to right, in deference to the movement of the hand.[25] Interestingly enough, now that we no longer always write by hand, this rupture has been healed somewhat by computer printers, which do proceed in the ancient economical pattern of the plowman. But be that as it may, the turn of the ox that Derrida describes and the way he makes it question the identity of the two kinds of cultivation, of text and terrain, is conceptually similar to the impulse toward the conflation of terrestrial and scriptural itineraries made explicit in recent labyrinthine fictions, which thus represent a newly conceived kind of "chthonization" of writing.[26] Could we consider these fictions as attempts to recover in part that original spatial coincidence of ground and text, reversing its economic imperative in favor of an aesthetic and philosophical one? These textual labyrinths represent traces of exploration rather than cultivation, made not to bear fruits but to pose questions, their proliferation of linguistic possibilities offering a pluralistic view of literary discourse and contrasting with Flaubert's statement (as reported by Maupassant) that "whatever you want to say, there is only one word to express it, one verb to animate it, and one adjective to qualify it."[27] These modernist and postmodernist urban narratives, as they propose the suspension of choice in a multicursal labyrinth, might also be seen to defy the imperative implied in that locus classicus of pastoral American poetry, Robert Frost's "Stopping by Woods on a Snowy Evening," where the speaker feels compelled to choose one road to take, leaving the alternative fork of his labyrinth unexplored.

I have just discussed at some length the metafictional implications of the labyrinth pattern as narrative structure, of how labyrinth-shaped texts function as iconic signs for writing itself, commenting implicitly on its nature. Before concluding, it remains to consider the related mimetic functions of the labyrinth as a symbol for the world and for thought, and to speculate on the sexual dynamics of labyrinthine narrative design.

The Labyrinth of the World: Urban Landscapes

The labyrinth as a symbol for the world is dramatized graphically in Fernando Arrabal's play, *The Labyrinth,* in which a "labyrinth" of sheets hung out to dry in the park of a chateau covers the stage. Here again, the labyrinth poses the question of whether order inheres in the world or whether chaos is the only ruling principle. Talking to a stranger who has wandered into the park, the daughter of the house says that "things here may appear to be in some disorder, but it is an apparent disorder which only throws into relief the existence of a superior order which is much more complex and exigent than any we can imagine."[28] In contrast to the earlier Christian concept of the labyrinth of the world parodied here by Arrabal—present even when the labyrinth was used as a secular love symbol—which assumed that disorientation within a labyrinth was temporary because God knew its plan and would help us out of it, modern texts suggest permanent convolutions. The problem is not how to escape from the labyrinth of the world, but how to live in it. Nevertheless, although it symbolizes the daunting complications of the world in its suggestion of a possible voyage, the labyrinth remains a structure of initiation and hence generally proposes a challenge to the explorer, holding out some hope of progress. This challenge, however, carries the germ of its own defeat, because progress within the world, when the world is pictured as a labyrinth, is necessarily limited and overdetermined, particularly since this world is so clearly a function of the individual mind that perceives it.[29]

Disorientation within a formal pattern has always characterized urban life; as cities have grown larger and larger, obviously the problem is compounded. Literary portraits of cities thus frequently present the labyrinthine experience of the world in concentrated form; they suggest the tension of feeling oneself lost within a complicated environment and yet forced to follow a prescribed pattern. A cartoon in the *New Yorker* of a minotaur contemplating a subway map, for example, illustrates the problem well.[30] Whether or not streets are logically planned, or even form a grid, their very number is confusing, as is their similar appearance—sameness and difference are confounded. The literary heroes who survive in such cities need a tenacious strength or a native guide. In the opening story of his volume of city fiction, the Argentine writer Eduardo Mallea characterizes the port area of Buenos Aires as an antechamber to the labyrinthine metropolis, a sorting room that separates those strong enough to undertake the urban adventure from those too weak to try: "The strongest ones entered the city afterwards, but the weak ones remained mired in that barrio, people who would never enter the labyrinth, pale ones despised by Ariadne."[31]

It is not accidental that the three novels I have discussed in detail concern city life, for the labyrinth has always been primarily an urban image, even in its earliest manifestations as city defense, dance floor, or burial site. Particularly in the cases of Butor and Robbe-Grillet—and in European literature generally since the Renaissance—the model of the hedge maze can be seen as an intermediary between the architecture of cities and the construction of verbal labyrinths. The similarities between them are numerous and significant. The garden labyrinth cleverly combines both nature and art, abstracting its form from the paths in forest and town, similar to urban writing in both reflecting and transforming its referent. Just as a maze differs from other kinds of formal gardens in inviting the spectator to become a participant, so labyrinthine fictions similarly invite the reader to become their active explorer and cocreator. Like cities themselves and the texts they engender, the hedge maze with its formalized and avowedly ludic form of living script continually threatens to overflow its prescribed boundaries. Present in many parks and grand gardens, it prefigures labyrinths constructed for readers to wander in. In the labyrinth at Versailles, the prefiguration is virtually explicit, for statues placed throughout it originally illustrated several of Aesop's fables. That labyrinth, very likely known to Butor and Robbe-Grillet, and perhaps even to Joyce as well, contained several focal points rather than a single central enclosure, anticipating the decentered nature of modern labyrinths of language.

Butor's statement that he walks around in books as he does in houses—and (I would add) as he does in cities—encapsulates the sense in which the cognitive maps of the walker in the city resemble the decoding strategies of the reader in the text. They are both repertories for the competent traversal of a given space. This complex interdependence of urban and textual construction suggests that we take seriously the pun of "architexture" as a metaphorical description of much urban writing. In addition, because the design of the labyrinth simultaneously represents a puzzle and a solution, a journey and an arrival, it embodies the way in which urban texts can be seen as both maps and routes, as descriptions and projects, portraits of streets and guides within them. Fictional urban labyrinths—symbolic or iconic—duplicate man's experience of the city as diachronic wandering and synchronic mapping. The labyrinth signals this duality well because it figures both time and space, becoming and being. The paradoxical dichotomy between the confusion the labyrinth has come to symbolize and the formalized visual pattern the image calls up enables it to suggest this aspect of cities and their texts. Nevertheless, unlike earlier uses of the labyrinth pattern, recent texts reflect the decentered configuration of the modern city. The labyrinth of the world does not open into the paradise of the heart just as many modern cities are no longer centered by their cathedrals and the textual enigmas of *Ulysses* are not unraveled at its end.

The narrative mode in these novels, derived in part from the trajectory of the wanderer in the city, illustrates the movement Burton Pike perceives in literature from the Renaissance ideal of the city as consisting of "fixed spatial relationships embodying an ideal cosmic order" to "the dynamic modern city," which is "presented in terms of action in time."[32] Still, the image of the labyrinth as it "schleps, trains, drags, trascines" its load of ancient symbolic resonances, can never be rid of that dream of cosmic order.[33] As I have suggested earlier, it gains in poetic force because it implies the existence of a sacred space or order within the surrounding profane chaos. It is thus a nostalgic, not a futuristic image of the city, however many times we may see the labyrinth-as-computer-chip (with its complicated patterns of circuitry). This may be one reason why it appears so persistently in literary portraits of cities—a tribute to the archeology of thought.

In an indirect way, the narrators of *Ulysses, Passing Time, In the Labyrinth, Hopscotch,* and *The Obscene Bird of Night* all express a fear that the mobile labyrinthine city will soon cover the world, just as city suburbs spread over the landscape. Revel pictures Bleston as interlocking with other similar cities so that he cannot reach clear countryside. *In the Labyrinth* ends when the narrator leaves the city, a city whose characteristics suggest those of Everycity. It seems unlikely that Bloom will ever leave Dublin to relocate in the country cottage of his dreams or that Oliveira will reach a heaven outside his urban labyrinth. And Mudito ends up as a piece of trash in a decidedly urban wasteland. Furthermore, in modern cities man often becomes minotaur. Old labyrinthine city defenses were designed to repel invaders; modern inhabitants are frequently trapped inside cities described as labyrinths. Instead of castle or town protected *by* a labyrinth, we have the city *as* labyrinth. The convolutions have moved within, and are threatening rather than protective. In these urban labyrinthine texts, then, we see another important change from classical times, one that is heralded of course by medieval and Renaissance labyrinths. The labyrinth is no longer a special dwelling constructed for a particular monster, but rather a house where everyone lives.

We have seen that the labyrinths of the city are duplicated in labyrinths of language, which in turn have modeled those visions of the city. The canefield of words that Oliveira erects between himself and La Maga, the complicated funhouses that Ambrose builds for *other* people to play in, Revel's rampart of written lines that separates him from the Bailey girls, all subvert what we might see as the communicative purpose of language. But beyond these realms of referent or story, the labyrinths of discourse—what I have termed the iconic verbal designs—reflect these problems of communication, and thus begin to counteract them. The labyrinths *of* the novels reinstate the expressive powers of language frustrated by the labyrinths *in* the novels, recalling the labyrinth's ancient ritual functions of protection and renewal of life. When discussing "the maze factor" in cities, Peter Smith maintains that "the labyrinth was a sign of citizenship in cities; to know its secret conferred both status and the freedom enjoyed by burghers." Furthermore, he maintains that "inscrutable urban space holds a fascination for people" and that "when the key to the labyrinth has been discovered, or, in psychological terms, a cognitive map or model has been constructed, the relationship between the individual and the environment aspires to a new level. Once a place has yielded its secrets it facilitates empathy between mind and artefact. Man and buildings become symbolically bound together."[34] This comprehension and subsequent appropriation of a form, the symbolic binding of man and his dwelling places, describes in a different domain the process that has taken place as Joyce, Butor, and Robbe-Grillet— and Borges as well—explore the modern urban environment and create their cities of words in a mirroring shape, facilitating empathy between mind and artifact for their readers. Those fictions are verbal equivalents of Smith's cognitive maps and models, but they often achieve the empathetic connection between mind and matter by not always yielding their own secrets or those of their places. In foregrounding the problematic nature of writing and reading, and in linking them symbolically and iconically to the designs of cities, they function as powerful and multivalent signs of the unity of city, text, and thought. Here again, as from its very inception as the formalization of a sacred cave, through its incorporation into church architecture and doctrine as a representation of worldly entanglements, and generally, in its emblematic capacity as a microcosm of the world, the sign of the labyrinth represents the correspondence not only between man's actual and scriptural itineraries, but also between those itineraries and the cosmos in which they take place.

One particular kind of visual text that demonstrates our preoccupation with labyrinthine urban space, further emphasizing the continuing fascination of the labyrinth pattern, is the three-dimensional labyrinth. A number of contemporary artists have constructed labyrinth sculptures of various kinds: furrows in the earth, stones on the ground, walls of cement, plexiglass, wood, bales of hay, table models of diverse materials. These works, in addition to those of an English architectural firm called Minotaur Designs, which specializes in building private labyrinths, continue in our time the ancient traditions of cathedral floor labyrinths and turf and hedge mazes. Now, as before, such a sculpture, like the urban texts we have analyzed, joins spatial and temporal modes, for in constructing an actual labyrinth, the artist achieves a static form, but one that directs movement—of either bodies or eyes. And again, like those texts, which suggest the interdependence of words and the world, through their symbolic resonances and their invitations to active participation, these labyrinths implicitly propose the interaction of art and environment.

Noncanonic Texts

While I have focused this study on the appearances of labyrinths in texts that belong in large part to the modernist and postmodernist literary canon, its attraction as a figure of thought in our time extends to all kinds of discourses, both "high" and popular, thus lessening the gap between them. Borges's labyrinth-filled story of "The Garden of Forking Paths," for example, really a modified detective fiction, and by now a classic postmodern text, won a prize years ago as a spy story. It is not possible to be inclusive here, of course, but a brief discussion of two distinctly popular discourses will demonstrate that the literary texts we have examined are grounded in widespread cultural constructs.

In its use of different interpretations that branch out from one or more clues, and in its emphasis on linear progression through a complicated and confusing but nonetheless predetermined itinerary, the structure of the detective story is analogous to that of a labyrinth. (It is a question here of degree rather than kind, of course, all fiction functioning as a series of events and choices in time.) In this context it is helpful to recall Butor's idea of fictional railway switches, of a linguistic labyrinth of nodes with alternate possible itineraries extending from them. The activity of the detective, especially, as he attempts to trace (and in the end to solve, or arrive at the center of) a labyrinthine puzzle of events, is analogous to the movements of an explorer in a multicursal labyrinth where choices of direction are needed in order to proceed forward. The combination in detective fiction of mystery-filled and complicated search preceding final and total revelation and comprehension exploits with particular intensity the labyrinth's characteristic duality of diachronic and synchronic forms of perception. In addition, the double fictions of detective stories that narrate both crime and solution resemble all of our labyrinth patterns, which we have created and in which we can also become lost; both kinds of structures shuttle us back and forth between the stances of control and bewilderment, between knowledge and ignorance.

As if to confirm this sense of affinity between labyrinths and detective stories, Borges, the most obsessive labyrinth maker, is an aficionado of detective fiction, and he, as well as Butor, Robbe-Grillet, and Eco, incorporates its elements into his work.[35] Butor also implies the connection between detective fiction and his own when he has George Burton explain to Revel that detective fiction superimposes two temporal narratives, the story of the crime and the account of its investigation, and then shows Revel's own narrative in *Passing Time* to superimpose at first two and then more and more time sequences, which are then compared to a labyrinth. But Revel's sequences become much more confused in this postmodern use of the form, and so his story becomes a more confusing labyrinth than the traditional kind that Burton describes.

The difference, of course, then, between traditional detective fiction and the postmodern novels inspired by it is that the former is finally comprehensible in the end; the path is traced to a central raised narrative platform from which detective and reader survey the labyrinthine course of events they have uncovered, while the latter may often leave choices between alternate events or interpretations unmade, abandoning the reader inside the convolutions of the narrative labyrinth. We never ascertain, for example, a fully comprehensible plan behind Burton's car accident in *Passing Time* or the murders in the abbey in *The Name of the Rose*. Similarly, as David Grossvogel has pointed out, Borges's modified detective stories really preserve the mysteries at the hearts of his labyrinths— God's name, or the unknown—rather than revealing them to us as a detective story would do. The center of perfect comprehension is never reached. Here again, in modern verbal texts the central chamber of the traditional labyrinth is an erased possibility, a nostalgic presence.

My second example of the presence of the labyrinth in popular culture is the labyrinth cartoon. It continues the interplay of visual and verbal forms that has frequently characterized the labyrinth's appearance. Cartoons that compare contemporary life to entrapment in a labyrinth appear frequently in a wide variety of media, from the newspaper to the *New Yorker*. Reagan in a labyrinth labeled "Hostage Crisis" reads on one of its walls a graffito attesting that "Jimmy Carter was here"; guests shown arriving at a house preceded by what looks like an enormous hedge maze—either of city streets or of their hosts's own making (it's not clear which)— congratulate the host on his perfect instructions for finding him. In addition to the clear resonances of bewilderment, of entrapment in someone else's design, these drawings also play inherently with the idea that we are still enmeshed in ancient forms, however modern we may think we are. To put a map of the labyrinth in the minotaur's hands, as several cartoons do, is a new twist, and plays on the duality of synchronic and diachronic forms of perception that the pattern encodes. It reveals an ironic awareness that even though we may know all about the kind of pattern we live in, we cannot control it or get out of it.

Often a creature in a labyrinth is watched by one outside it, a situation that exploits the dichotomy of designer and prisoner, or at least of comprehensive seer and uncomprehending seen, which operates throughout the history of the image. This is the assumption, of course, behind the situation of the mouse in the maze. However, the cartoons on that theme—really a whole subgenre of labyrinth cartoons—often play havoc with that pattern to achieve the humor of the unexpected. One such cartoon portrays a huge scientist contemplating another, smaller, scientist in a maze-like suite of offices, who is watching a mouse in a maze. Such a drawing reveals the Orwellian fear of "Big Brother" watching us and the Borgesian sense that even though we may recognize that our dreams are dreams, we may not recognize that we may form a dream for a grand dreamer.

Some of the mice in these cartoons seem to have accustomed themselves to their labyrinthine environment in one way or another—pushing a supermarket basket through a labyrinth, visiting a labyrinthine picture gallery—confirming that contemporary labyrinths are seen as permanent dwelling places rather than extraordinary adventures. To portray mice in this relatively relaxed role disrupts in another way the dichotomy of designer and designed, or torturer and victim, because if the victim no longer feels victimized, and is leading a normal life in his labyrinth, what's the difference? The same feeling motivates the cartoon of an ecstatic and rather sportif-looking rat exiting with thumbs up from a maze, to the apparent incredulity of two codgerly white-coated experimenters with clipboards—another version of the ancient comedic paradigm where youth triumphs over age. But characteristically, the opposite, darker tone of frightening entrapment also appears; in several cases a mouse explores a maze, where, unbeknownst to him, lurks a minotaur—in one case with complacently and sinisterly crossed arms.

The best cartoon of all for my purposes here is the one I have chosen as a frontispiece, where an enormous labyrinth design extends
from a small and portly yet jaunty-looking man's mouth. Even at
first glance, the scale in the drawing asks implicitly whether the
man exists as a function of his discourse or vice versa. It also suggests that the perplexing nature of our world is created in large part
by our own words. If we follow the line out of the man's mouth, we
return there again, a process which reaffirms that sense of puzzled
responsibility. The little man is thus a kind of rhetorical Daedalus,
astonished at and perhaps about to be lost in his own creation, because once the labyrinth of his own words exists, he is instantly
transformed from its creator to its potential explorer. Appropriately, in keeping with the labyrinth's characteristic oscillation between light and dark emotional resonances, this cartoon can be
either festive or foreboding, depending on the viewer's mood, on
whether we perceive the labyrinth as intriguing or threatening. It
suggests not only that we produce labyrinthine discourses and that
they are asymmetrical and have no single center, but that we may be
either proud of them or overshadowed by them—or both at once.

The Labyrinth of Thought

The labyrinth as it symbolizes the mind is bound closely to the labyrinth as an image for art and for the world, since both art and the
world reflect and are reflected by the mind that shapes them. For
this reason Borges's image of the writer whose fictions duplicate the
labyrinth of his face is such an apt expression of the labyrinth's
presence in modern literature. In recent texts, the symbolic equation of mind and labyrinth implies a certain narcissism, an uneasy
narcissism. That a man usually explores the labyrinth of the world
and of his mind by himself suggests a measure of confidence in his
intellectual powers. This confidence leads him to depend increasingly on those powers, but then, in turn, to fear either their malfunc-
tioning or their usurpation of emotional faculties. Thus modern
representations of the mind as a labyrinth express loneliness and
the anxiety that comes from the labyrinth's conflicting functions of
protection and imprisonment. It is this same duality that Octavio
Paz highlights in his discussion of masks in Mexican society in *The*

Labyrinth of Solitude, masks that, like labyrinths, may simultaneously protect and imprison their wearers. Proust's Marcel, and his descendant Revel, along with Oliveira, Mudito, Ambrose, and Bloom, are both protected and isolated by their labyrinthine thoughts.

The labyrinth in literature reflects the importance of psychoanalytic thought in both its manifestations, as symbolic landscape and as narrative design. The exploration of unknown regions that the labyrinth represents in the texts by Gide, Durrell, and Nin clearly associates it with the analytic uncovering of unconscious events and processes in the self; the principle of associative thinking that produces the labyrinthine narrative structure of the texts by Joyce, Butor, and Robbe-Grillet coincides with the primary technique of psychoanalysis. Nevertheless, as I have suggested earlier in my discussion of *Passing Time* and "Lost in the Funhouse," unconscious longing may assert itself *against* the self-reflexive and labyrinthine complexities of fabulation, which means that in contemporary literature, the labyrinth is frequently associated with consciousness, or even with overly self-reflexive thought, rather than with the unconscious, and its use in some cases implies a protest against the increasingly self-reflexive nature of modern thought and its embodiment in words. Even so, if we reflect on this phenomenon for a moment, we might wonder if the transformation of this sign of the unconscious into an emblem of meticulous fabulation and a design for fiction may also represent the desire of modernist stream-of-consciousness narratives to picture the unconscious undercurrents of the mind and of autogenerative postmodernist narratives to embody the unconscious workings of the text—of the desire of texts to go beyond themselves in a sense, to comprehend their own origins even as they deny the very concept of origin.

Gaston Bachelard's discussion of the image illustrates the situation prior to this last trend, for he classifies the labyrinth as a structure of the unconscious rather than of the conscious mind: "All these images . . . propose to us . . . the same movement toward the sources of rest. The house, the womb, the cave, for example, carry the same grand imprint of the return to the mother. From this point of view, the unconscious commands, the unconscious directs."[36] Bachelard situates the labyrinth in the domain of rest rather than in that of action, examining it in the volume called *La*

Terre et les rêveries du repos (*Earth and the Reveries of Rest*), rather than in the companion essay *La Terre et les rêveries de la volonté* (*Earth and the Reveries of the Will*). Because it forms part of his oneiric optic, he traces the contours of an archetypal night-time labyrinth as it manifests itself through a large assortment of texts. Bachelard's statements about the pattern, though written in the 1940s, are influenced by the nineteenth- and early twentieth-century literature he discusses—Hugo's *Les Misérables*, Huysman's *En rade*, Nerval's *Aurélia*, Sand's *La Comtesse de Rudolstadt*, and others which, like the novels of Durrell and Nin, describe dark, often underground, mysterious, and dream-like labyrinthine structures such as caves or cellars.[37] A recent literary labyrinth that resembles Bachelard's oneiric cave labyrinths of the unconscious appears near the end of Walker Percy's *The Second Coming*. Will Barrett decides to enter a cave and wait for some kind of a sign from God; if he doesn't receive one, he'll die there. Appropriately enough, the cave he has entered, unbeknownst to him, connects with the greenhouse where his true love lives. Following an invisible Ariadne's thread, he literally falls out of the labyrinth onto her floor—and shortly into her arms. As often before, but increasingly rarely now, the labyrinth has led to the sacred space of love.

The novels Bachelard describes differ in their use of the labyrinth pattern from the self-reflexive texts of Joyce, Butor, and Robbe-Grillet. In discussing them, however, Bachelard introduces an ingenious variation of the labyrinth that highlights an important aspect of the labyrinthine narrative structure that we have been investigating. This is the idea of the worm that eats earth to make a path for itself that Count Hermann von Keyserling includes in his *South American Meditations*.[38] Bachelard's comment on this image is especially pertinent to the labyrinthine design of the novels I have been discussing here: "If we think a bit about this image, we see that it corresponds to a kind of doubled labyrinth. The eaten earth advances inside the worm at the same time the worm advances in the earth."[39] Joyce, Butor, and Robbe-Grillet similarly double their labyrinths by designing the shapes of their discourses to duplicate the forms of its referents and the process of narrating itself. Indeed the texts of these writers can be said to triple the labyrinth: the reader of *Ulysses* experiences the labyrinthine language and structure of the novel while Bloom and Stephen explore the labyrinths of

Dublin and of their own thoughts; while the reader of Revel's diary traverses the labyrinth of the text, Revel traverses the labyrinths of Bleston and of his own thoughts in order to create the diary-novel; in *In the Labyrinth* the reader experiences the labyrinth of the story-making process, which in turn reflects the narrator's mental journeys, within which the soldier traverses the labyrinthine town. These three labyrinths really comprise the three times that Butor claims are superimposed in the novel: the time of adventure, the time of writing, and the time of reading.[40] The tripling of the labyrinthine pattern and its consequent compression of narrative times increases the power of the labyrinth as an image of intricate disorientation, of entrapment in self-reflexive designs.[41] This multiplication has a precedent in the classical myth, for after arriving on Crete, Theseus is reported (by Plutarch) to have danced the "dance of the cranes," which duplicated symbolically the twistings and turnings of the labyrinth. The difference is that there the duplication celebrated difference, or escape from the labyrinth's coils; here, the doubling being created from the inside, so to speak, it represents continual entrapment in them. Even so, that sense of repetition of the pattern as liberation lingers, for it still embodies a minute difference, a distance from the labyrinthine enclosure that permits us to speak it, we might say, if not to escape from it.

As we have begun to see briefly, the presence of the labyrinth as a significant figure of thought extends beyond literature to other areas of culture, as Umberto Eco has suggested by describing all thought as a labyrinth. Pierre Rosenstiehl explains this extension by maintaining that since the labyrinth is an image whose meaning is different for everyone who sees it (as Gide proposed with his adaptable vaporous labyrinth), it cannot have an official function, and that "its role is [rather] to provide a receptive geometry for the spatial visions of the workings of the mind"—a useful formulation of the labyrinth's cultural function.[42]

The receptive geometry of the labyrinth is demonstrated in a recent article in *Science* magazine, which claims that our mouse in his maze is the most common form of scientific joke, and thus suggests that our current multicursal, decentered spatial vision of the labyrinth encompasses the process of scientific inquiry as well.[43] This is because it really encodes the design of inquiry itself, of the routes of exploration and error, the experience of taking a wrong turn and correcting it before proceeding forward. Similarly, the structure of computer systems that rely on binary oppositions, on impulses that travel a continually forking path, requiring choices at given nodes, is generally labyrinthine and contributes to the contemporary fascination with the metaphor of the labyrinth. There is an important distinction to be made, however, between the labyrinths of scientific inquiry and the labyrinths of language we have examined here, and that is the value accorded efficiency in the scientific varieties. Rosenstiehl maintains that the mathematical solution to a labyrinth consists of never taking the road already traveled except as a last resort, when there is no other way.[44] But the repetitions, backtrackings, and alternate paths that intrigue the voyager in literary labyrinths distinguish his journey from the mathematical one, for they induce him to value the journey equally with arrival at its end.[45] We can see that in representing these two intellectual tendencies, the search for the solution and the willingness to explore, in combining the contrasting impulses of control and bewilderment, the labyrinth as a spatial metaphor for modern thought really exists, as we do, between "the will to power" and "the will to chance."[46]

The labyrinth's appeal as a metaphor for thought stems from its capacity to encompass the chaotic and the formal, the surprising and the planned. For Kristeva, "discovering a new object through a metalanguage elaborated halfway between chance and necessity seems to be the rule today in all the sciences."[47] The sign of the labyrinth belongs to that current metalanguage because a pursuit of knowledge that operates between chance and necessity, recognizing the claims of both, traces a labyrinthine path, which incorporates both freedom and regulation in its complex and convoluted form.[48]

Sexual Dynamics

According to many recent feminist reinterpretations of cultural history, the unitary nature of many of our discourses and the logocentrism of our culture are essentially masculine phenomena and represent a suppression of earlier, more polyvalent, feminine forms of speech and social order, forms that are also often associated with postmodernism. The interesting question, finally unanswerable in this case as with postmodernism generally but certainly worth considering, is whether the decentered quality of recent labyrinths, and even the popularity of the labyrinth itself, have any sexual connotations, whether they constitute a resurgence of feminine power in the world and in the text, or whether they are simply, as I have maintained for the most part, modern and postmodern events, independent of sexual issues.[49]

From one perspective, nevertheless, the history of the labyrinth's development from prehistoric to modern times, its progression from nature to culture, from cave to palace, out of the earth to the city, and more recently, out of the unconscious to the overly conscious, represents the masculinization of a feminine form, the male covering up the female, as Minos's labyrinth hides Pasiphae's minotaur.[50] Carolyn Merchant chronicles a similar development in the natural sciences, claiming that during the scientific revolution of the seventeenth century the qualities of nurturing mother and mystical force were taken away from nature, and mother earth was envisioned as passive and chaotic rather than peaceful and serene because she threatened the growing masculine virtues of scientific objectivity.[51]

In this context, the formal structure of the labyrinth represents the world of conscious articulation, the traditionally masculine world of order and intellect. This labyrinth corresponds to Eco's classical and Mannerist varieties of centered designs, associated with the One and the Father, and it retains this sexual identity even in contemporary self-conscious texts that conform to Eco's decentered rhizomic structure of thought. (Eco's own novel is a striking illustration of this tendency, since all of its labyrinths of knowledge are presided over by men, in a monastery no less; in Butor and Barth too, masculine labyrinth makers are alienated from women and from their own desires as well.) One might even regard the denial of center and origin in recent labyrinths as the desperate erasure of feminine desire (which used to be present in the minotaur engendered by the passion of Pasiphae) from the labyrinth of language. Along these lines, examine, for instance, Marcel Brion's interpretation of the labyrinth myth, which, in emphasizing the conquest of the minotaur rather than foregrounding the exploration of the labyrinth, highlights the triumph of the masculine hero of consciousness and reason; he sees the death of the minotaur as a victory of "spirit over matter, and, at the same time, of the eternal over the perishable, of intelligence over instinct, of knowledge over blind violence."[52]

But what if we do not kill the minotaur, or what if he is not even in the labyrinth anymore? Then we might investigate how the recent decentering of the labyrinth could pull us in the opposite direction. Patriarchal labyrinths have buried the originary feminine, changed it into a beast to be killed by a male hero, but it—"we the labyrinths" of Hélène Cixous—survives as a continuing presence of the feminine in literary discourse, a principle that is becoming stronger as time passes.[53] Thus from another perspective, the patriarchal labyrinth reveals the one it covers up, because the decentered rhizome can also be imagined as the entity Kristeva calls the "semiotic," the *chora,* or receptacle, which is "unnamable, improbable, hybrid, anterior to meaning, to the One, to the father, and consequently, maternally connoted to such an extent that it merits 'not even the rank of syllable.'"[54] (Here we need to recall that even the highly formalized labyrinth at Versailles, like Henry II's Bower of Rosamond, was apparently known after its reconstruction in 1775 with a feminine designation as the "Wood of the Queen"—"le Bosquet de la Reine."[55]) Thus defined, it represents—borrowing Luce Irigaray's terms—a language that is not one, that is, a language that is not officially recognized and also a language that is not unitary but multiple, or bifurcating, in its assigning of signs to referents.

Irigaray's feminist reinterpretation of Plato's *Hystera* as womb confirms my speculations here about a traditionally male labyrinth of cultural discourses covering over another traditionally female one. Irigaray claims that the cave, the original place of habitation, place of dream "has been covered over for all useful purposes by the language of reason." She thinks that "the dream space remains, but it is projected infinitely far ahead. Excess of logos, which one no longer reaches by returning into the mother but by trusting in the ex-sistence of the Father. Fantasies would be chased away from 'the mother's body,' and sent into an infinitely external world."[56] Bataille presents us with a similar image that also opposes labyrinth and logos; he identifies himself with his acephalic god—the incarnation of anti-platonic, a-theistic thought—and imagines that "his abdomen is the Daedalus in which he himself loses the way, misleads me along with him, and within which I rediscover myself as him, that is to say as a monster." Allen Weiss glosses that passage in this way: "Such monstrosity is a radical break with the rationalist tradition; it is a sign of the excessive, the incommunicable, the different. . . . This monster is the self which must be sacrificed within the labyrinth. Is it, perhaps, identifiable with the overman?"[57] With Kristeva's and Irigaray's ideas in mind, might we identify this break with rationalist tradition, this sign of excess, of difference, not only with the overman but also with woman?

The heterogeneous, rhizomic labyrinths of language we have been examining, considered as a return of the repressed female body and its decentered, polymorphous desires, as constituting part of Kristeva's semiotic code, a code that underlies and challenges the symbolic codes also present in the texts, return us in part to Bachelard's idea of the labyrinth as a sign of the unconscious, but a verbal unconscious, the unconscious of language itself. For Kristeva, "language as symbolic function constitutes itself at the cost of repressing instinctual drive and continuous relation to the mother."[58] Even so, she argues, with Freud and Lacan we have the reinstatement of the semiotic in the form of heterogeneity, which is known as the unconscious, and which shapes the signifying function. In this context, perhaps modern and postmodern labyrinths constitute a kind of return of the repressed, yet as they are appropriated by Daedalian artist figures, their feminine power, their radical otherness, is somewhat diminished, though not entirely erased.

If, as Kristeva maintains, the other is always the other sex, then the labyrinth as the feminine domain has provided the other for the self-definition of masculine exploration and writing. As Alice Jardine says, "the space 'outside of' the conscious subject has always connoted the feminine in the history of Western thought—and any movement into alterity is a movement into that female space; any attempt to give a place to that alterity within discourse involves a putting into discourse of 'woman.'"[59] As we enter the modern period, then, the linguistic view from inside the labyrinth that we experience in the texts of Joyce and his French successors can be taken as a preliminary to what we might foresee as a switching of alterities prefatory to the growth of a conscious feminine subject.

Finally, however, these labyrinths of language, which, as I have suggested, also belong in significant ways to the world of the One and the Father, achieve an integration of feminine and masculine codes through their dual sexual identities.[60] That integration corresponds to what for Kristeva is a "reinstatement of maternal territory into the very economy of language, [and which nevertheless] does not lead its questioned subject-in-process to repudiate its [paternal] symbolic disposition."[61] The two perspectives, desperate erasure of the feminine by the masculine, and integration of the two modes, are not mutually exclusive, for they can be seen as taking place simultaneously, in reaction to each other; fear and consequent erasure of the feminine are generated by its increasing strength, but that very strength also assures that the erasure will be incomplete, the integration of the two forms constituting a continuing project. Michel Foucault gives us an image of modern literature as achieving just such a synthesis in his analysis of the works of Roussel, for in comparing caverns and brains—both labyrinthine forges—Foucault joins the two realms of earth mother and sky father as the smithy of the artist's soul, from which he "sees a whole language arise . . . forged by untiring workers on the high ground where opens the mouth of the mine," "ready to solidify into . . . the gold thread of a sanctified fabric," the fabric of language itself.[62]

Continuity and Change

In conclusion, it will be useful to trace in very general fashion the historical development of the labyrinth, to make some final distinctions between the early and the modern symbol, and to observe its semiotic continuity. This overview will serve to shed further light on the labyrinth's persistence as a literary image and to summarize in this context some of the reasons for its prominence in modern and contemporary texts. If we survey the history of the sign, we might see the labyrinth as designating, among other things, the cultural space of greatest fascination for a given period. It marks the imagined locus of the source and the end of knowledge, even, in Virginia Woolf's words, of the "meaning of life." The labyrinthine space is the realm that is always beyond our reach and therefore the object of our desire, our curiosity, our investigation, and it is also, paradoxically, the trace of that very investigation. In a sense, then, it figures both the Heideggerian understanding, or the forward motion of the mind, and the anteriority that is the opposite of that forward motion, but which is often its object; it represents both quest for knowledge and origin of life.[63]

With this in mind, we can see the earliest manifestations of the labyrinth—cut into the earth as tombs or traced along it as turf mazes—and the Greek stories of Theseus and the minotaur that reflect them as forming part of ancient earth-centered religions, which included rituals and divinations in caves.[64] Mysterious forces are imagined to inhabit the earth; an individual threads the labyrinth to draw strength from those forces. During the Christian era, from the Middle Ages to the Renaissance (and even up through the nineteenth century), the labyrinth is associated generally with the physical world, either forest or town, and comes to suggest especially man's place in the complex, fallen social world. In addition to representing the universe, it symbolizes the human condition. This condition is tortuous, and divine grace is the Ariadne's thread necessary for escape. Salvation comes from above, not from within, but in any case escape from the labyrinth of the world to the paradise of the heart is an imaginative possibility. Later on, during the Reformation and the Enlightenment, the emphasis on man's capabilities endows him with ever greater responsibility for threading the complicated paths of the world's labyrinth.

That self-reliance prepares the way for developments in the twentieth century, when the labyrinth pattern is frequently symbolic of interior journeys; the fascinating space is subjectively constituted. This resonance may have been implicit in much earlier symbolism, but it becomes explicit in the modern period, where the labyrinth (in the words of the poet Francis Thompson) represents "the labyrinthine ways of my own mind."[65] Consequently, twentieth-century texts portray figures who, like Dostoyevsky's precocious Underground Man, cannot escape from the labyrinths of their own thoughts. These figures are isolated by the inward focus and the elaborate nature of these thoughts more than by troubled exterior personal relations, which comprised earlier labyrinths of love.[66] In maintaining that "a labyrinthine man never seeks the truth, but only his Ariadne," Nietzsche reflects this shift from objective overview to subjective exploration.[67] Most recently, as we have seen in detail, the mystery associated with the labyrinth and its attendant

complications enter the domain of textuality, of writing and reading; the mysterious or problematic space is the space of the articulation of discourse itself. In brief, the sign of the labyrinth shifts
from designating the interior of the earth to portraying its natural
and social surface, and then from picturing man's interior to structuring the texts he produces—from telluric to territorial to textual—
but always conserving traces of where it has been. It thus argues si-
lently for cultural continuity even as it registers the power of disjunctive forces in its less and less regular form.

Lotman's discussion of spatial modeling is helpful here in further
understanding the literary geometry of these changes. Lotman distinguishes two basic spaces in cultural texts, the external and the
internal, which are divided by various kinds of boundaries. In this
schema, the labyrinth demonstrates its characteristic duality, for it
can play either the role of spatial realm or boundary; for the moment, however, I will limit it to the former. As spatial realm, the labyrinth has traditionally represented the external, what was out
there, or other—forest, desert, ocean, a testing ground for self-
realization. According to Lotman, since the most typical plot design is movement across the spatial boundary, "the scheme of the
plot appears as a struggle against the structure of the world."[68] He
distinguishes in this context between "plot collision," where the
hero penetrates across the boundary of space, from "nonplot collision," where there is a battle between the internal space seeking to
strengthen the boundary and the external space seeking to invade
it. In the literary history I have been charting, plot collision characterizes early stories of labyrinths, nonplot collision the later ones.
In the first type, Plutarch's Theseus explores the labyrinth, kills the
minotaur at its center, and returns, using his wits, his courage, and
Ariadne's string in the process. Self and other, internal and external, are portrayed as quite distinct. In Gide's version of the myth,
Theseus ostensibly accomplishes the same thing, but in this case
Gide makes it clear that the external has invaded the internal; the
complications of the labyrinth are imagined as vapours that have invaded the mind. As we have seen, this kind of modeling continues
in many recent texts: the labyrinthine qualities of external space—
forest outside the town, city outside the mind, compositional process outside, or at least previous to, the text—invade the internal
space, blurring the distinctions between internal and external, self

and other, reader and writer. If we consider the labyrinth as boundary rather than as space, we might see this change as a process whereby the boundary encompasses the realms it formerly joined. In any case, the interchange of interior and exterior spaces that I have been describing joins these elaborate verbal labyrinths to ancient visual manifestations of the design, which are often spatial analogues for the psychological phenomenon of the merging of self and other. In describing the labyrinth designs associated with initiation rituals in the New Hebrides islands, for example, where young men trace those designs to reach their future wives, John Layard mentions specifically that in some cases the complication of the designs disturbs the distinction between outside and inside—a confusion that seems appropriate in a marriage ceremony where people are symbolically joined, shifting in some ways the boundaries of selves and others.[69]

The recent tendency of the labyrinth to serve as a sign for the complicated workings of the imagination as it reflects and transforms the world continues the development of the image, begun in ancient times, from a natural to a constructed form. Similarly, the foregrounding of labyrinthine language, and of labyrinthine narrative structure in Passing Time and In the Labyrinth constitute our contemporary structuralist awareness that the language we may have assumed to be natural is more correctly characterized as culturally constructed. That the labyrinth now constitutes a sign of intricate artistry is prefigured not only in the classical myth of Daedalus but also in medieval times when it may have served as an emblem representing the masons who built the cathedrals.[70] Even so, recent texts often portray sensibilities that mistrust the aridity of formal labyrinthine convolutions as much as their complexity; the harsh regularity of a city, for instance, or a subway, threatens to engulf a modern explorer, whereas the narrator of an early Renaissance text like Comenius's The Labyrinth of the World and the Paradise of the Heart feared the chaos of cities.[71] In the Christian context, order in the world was imagined to originate in divine providence; in contemporary literature, however, the labyrinth may evoke paranoid visions of an overordered world, of patterns, plots, conspiracies intuited beneath the concretions of reality. The value of order per se is thus called into question.

In the geometry of culture, modern decentered labyrinths can be seen to figure the shift in modern times from the logocentric to the liminal, following the increasing valuation of marginality in twentieth-century thought.[72] Similarly, whereas earlier rites and literary symbols often suggested voyages with definite goals, modern labyrinths may lack such directionality. Because of this change, the modern use of the sign emphasizes labyrinthine paths themselves rather than the regions that they connect or the center to which they lead. Renaissance religious treatises, for example, placed great importance on the two realms joined by a labyrinth, as did rituals of initiation. For many contemporary writers, however, it is the journey, not the arrival, that matters. The process of labyrinthine movement is its product as well. In the text as in the world, the plaza has become an intersection. Thus Santarcangeli's distinction between the two directions of movement in traditional labyrinths, between the centripetal journey involving the conquest of a hidden center and the centrifugal movement toward new horizons, is blurred though not entirely erased. For Dante-the-pilgrim more clearly than for Bloom in *Ulysses,* the descent to a central point precedes the vision of the stars—though Bloom's and Stephen's stargazing near the end of their labyrinthine text echoes the earlier trope. The duality of directions persists, though in recent times the lack of a precise center for the labyrinth and the sense of permanent enclosure in it mean that the two distinct movements are often present as nostalgic rather than actual itineraries.

In discussing the labyrinths in Borges's work, Nicolás Rosa develops a related idea. He argues that while in earlier times the labyrinth guarded a larger sign, such as God, salvation, the temple, it is now a symbol of hiding, of the secret. Like characters in fictions who find themselves the subjects of other fictions and plays within plays, "the labyrinth has suffered a semiotic obliteration that forces it to symbolize itself."[73] The self-referential nature of modern and contemporary literary labyrinths, particularly as they symbolize or simulate the processes of thought, writing, and reading, certainly distinguishes them from earlier manifestations of the design. Still, the labyrinth's literary past remains strong, resonating through its presence in recent texts. This resonance, together with its frequent appearance as an interior or exterior symbolic landscape, means that the labyrinth's mimetic functions have not entirely disappeared. The labyrinths I have described here serve as emblems of both the self-reflexive and the mimetic impulses in modern fiction, of the modern literary imagination as it reflects and transforms itself and the world, and of the reader's perception of these visions.

The appeal of the labyrinth as a literary image derives from its adaptability to modern literary concerns, many of which involve the fusion of contraries within an individual work of art. The labyrinth pictures simultaneously the modern city and a character's thoughts as he traverses it, or a narrator's journeys as he constructs a novel that mirrors the world, and thereby demonstrates the interdependence of the world, the mind, and the text. Because one may lose one's way in a confusing labyrinth, even though it is constructed in a formal pattern, the design implicitly poses the question of whether the world is orderly or chaotic. Through its whimsical and frightening resonances, the labyrinth also suggests the combination of playful, intellectual mazemaking with fear of entrapment in mental complications; the labyrinth of language both protects and imprisons. Like the original Daedalus, the designer of fictional labyrinths creates ingenious structures in which he himself may remain lost. But behind these uncertainties—these labyrinths with no centers—stand echoes of the classical myth, echoes that reflect our longing for a restful sacred center and for the artistic security of myth itself.[74] The power of the labyrinth rests in its capacity to absorb these contradictions, to portray questions rather than answers, and thus to represent simultaneously the adventures of living, writing, and reading in the modern world.

Notes

Chapter 1. Introduction

1. Cited in Ross Lockridge, *The Labyrinth of New Harmony, Indiana* (New Harmony: New Harmony Memorial Commission, 1941), p. 40.

2. Before proceeding further, a rough definition of the visual design of the labyrinth will be useful. It consists of a regularly patterned path that frequently forms concentric circles or squares about a central enclosure, and is often divided in half or in quarters by lines that shift direction along one or two axes. The meanders of the design impede progress toward the central enclosure. The inadequacy of this description, however, illustrates the specific culturally determined nature of the image. The reader must have seen diagrams in order to visualize the patterns of labyrinths; this spatial model forms part of our cultural codes. The reappearance of the image in a modern text thus constitutes a broad kind of intertextuality, a partial rewriting of the original myth.

English dictionaries often give *maze* as a synonym for *labyrinth*. The same pattern may be called by both names, but the tone differs; the words imply different experiences. The word *labyrinth* evokes something darker than a maze: a labyrinth, which suggests Crete and the minotaur, is more mysterious, more frightening, more likely to be underground. A maze is of a lighter color, so to speak, less serious in connotation, and usually implies a game, a puzzle, or a garden amusement. Shakespeare seems to have recorded the dichotomy between *maze* and *labyrinth* in his use of the image:

> The quaint mazes in the wanton green
> For lack of threading are undistinguishable.
> > *Midsummer Night's Dream*, 2.2
>
> . . . here's a maze trod indeed
> Through forthrights and meanders.
> > *Tempest*, 3.3
>
> I have thrust myself into this maze
> Haply to wive and thrive as best I may.
> > *Taming of the Shrew*, 1.4
>
> Thou mayst not wander in that labyrinth;
> There minotaur and ugly treason lurk.
> > *King Henry IV*, 5.3
>
> Here no, Thersites! What, lost in this labyrinth of thy fury.
> > *Troilus and Cressida*, 2.3
> > Cited in Lockridge, *The Labyrinth of New Harmony*, pp. 39–40

More recently, Jorge Luis Borges has suggested the same distinction in an interview:

> *Borges:* Perhaps the word *labyrinth* is more mysterious than the world [sic] maze.
> *Burgin:* Maze is almost too mechanical a word.
> *Borges:* Yes, and you feel the 'amazement' in the word. With labyrinth you think of Crete and you think of the Greeks. While in maze you may think of Hampton Court, well, not very much of a labyrinth, a kind of toy labyrinth
> > Richard Burgin, *Conversations with Jorge Luis Borges, 1968* (New York: Avon Books, 1970), p. 38.

3. See the introduction to Gaston Bachelard, *La Poétique de l'espace* (Paris: Presses Universitaires de France, 1957).

4. Georges Matoré, *L'Espace humain: L'Expérience de l'espace dans la vie, la pensée et l'art contemporains* (Paris: La Colombe, 1962), p. 33.

5. Jacques Derrida, "Structure, Sign, and Play in the Discourse of the Human Sciences," in Richard Macksey and Eugenio B. Donato, eds., *The Structuralist Controversy* (Baltimore: Johns Hopkins Press, 1972), p. 271.

6. Robert Alter suggests that this is the result of our contemporary sense that everything has already happened, of our consciousness of all

that has gone before us. Alter quotes Claude Mauriac's description in his novel *The Marquise Went Out at Five* of "a novelist animated by a novelist whom I (myself a novelist) have put into a novel in which, however, nothing was invented, a labyrinth of mirrors capturing some of life's sensations, feelings and thoughts." Alter then adds that "Cervantes' emblematic image of the mirror . . . is complicated in Borgesian fashion by a labyrinth not because the old quixotic probing of reality through fiction has changed in nature, only because the complexity of the enterprise has been many times multiplied by both historical and literary experience"; Robert Alter, *Partial Magic: The Novel as a Self-Conscious Genre* (Berkeley and Los Angeles: University of California Press, 1975), p. 240.

7. Peter Brooks: *Reading for the Plot: Design and Intention in Narrative* (New York: Random House, 1985), p. 319.

8. Roland Barthes recognized the problems involved in *speaking* of the labyrinth pattern, in transferring its force from the visual to the verbal domain, problems that are both entrancing and daunting in our attempts to define its meaning: "The labyrinth is so well-conceived a form that what can be said about it easily falls short of the form itself. Which is to say that the case in point is finally richer than the generality, the denotation richer than the connotation, the letter richer than the symbol." Reported by Pierre Rosenstiehl in "The *Dodécadédale,* or In Praise of Heuristics," *October* 26 (Fall, 1983): 19.

9. Paolo Santarcangeli, *Le Livre des labyrinthes: Histoire d'un mythe et d'un symbole,* trans. Monique Lacau (Paris: Gallimard, 1974), p. 401.

10. In their study of our lived labyrinths, Abraham Moles and Elisabeth Rohmer confirm the strange "conjunction of freedom and constraint" the design embodies; *Labyrinthes du vécu: L'Espace, matière d'actions* (Paris: Librairie des Méridiens, 1982), p. 83.

11. Michel Foucault, *Death and the Labyrinth: The World of Raymond Roussel,* trans. Charles Ruas (New York: Doubleday, 1986), p. 94.

12. Philip West, "The Redundant Labyrinth," *Salmagundi* 46 (1979): 64.

13. The interconnectedness of these roles in the myth of the labyrinth is taken up by Robert Rawdon Wilson, who defines the labyrinth as a variety of "Godgame." The victim of a Godgame "finds himself in the bewildering necessity of having to think himself out of a context he cannot understand." An effective narrative labyrinth thus must have "a character within it trying to get somewhere," a player who is actually played upon since he is not the artificer himself. This last qualification would seem to exclude an important component of many modern fictional labyrinths, which, as we shall see, play masterfully on just this duality of wanderer and artificer. At the end of his essay, however, Wilson seems to blur his earlier distinction by

writing that "perhaps the game of labyrinths, making the player both passive and active, played and playing, caught within a game-structure even while creating it, underlies all other modes of literary game"; Robert Rawdon Wilson, "Godgames and Labyrinths: The Logic of Entrapment," *Mosaic* 15, no. 4 (1982): 1–22.

14. Ovid. *Metamorphoses,* trans. Frank J. Miller, Loeb Classical Library (Cambridge: Harvard University Press, 1951), I Book VIII, ll. 152–68.

15. For a more complete discussion of the labyrinth's place in the Christian way, see Edith Schnapper, *The Inward Odyssey: The Concept of "The Way" in the Great Religions of the World* (London: Allen and Unwin, 1965), pp. 5–27.

16. I might note here that recently, since most of us do not have access to topiary labyrinths (though those also are enjoying something of a renaissance, especially in England), the irrepressible attraction to labyrinthine paths has inspired a quantity of playbooks. See the booklet by Adrian Fisher, Randoll Coate and Graham Burgess, *A Celebration of Mazes* (Saint Alban's, Herts.: Minotaur Designs, 1984), which documents this resurgence of interest in the construction of mazes and predicts that it will reach even greater heights in 1991, which has been designated the Year of the Maze. A review by Martin Gardner (*New York Times Book Review,* July 27, 1975), entitled "Labyrinthian Way," describes several of what he reports were about thirty paperback books of mazes on sale at the time he wrote. Gardner speculates about "why children and adults in the United States should develop a sudden hankering for mazes. . . . Is it because millions feel trapped in various kinds of labyrinths—religious, moral, economic, political—and finding a way out of a paper maze somehow helps relieve anxiety? . . . Perhaps it is just a case of publishers discovering an interest that children have had all along."

17. W. F. Jackson Knight, *Cumaean Gates,* in *Vergil: Epic and Anthropology* (New York: Barnes and Noble, 1967), p. 67.

18. Mircea Eliade, *Mythes, rêves, et mystères* (Paris: Gallimard, 1957), p. 228.

19. For a discussion of the labyrinth interpreted in this manner, see Erich Neumann, *The Origins and History of Consciousness* (New York: Pantheon Books, 1965).

20. Pierre Rosenstiehl implicitly suggests a similar interpretation when he proposes to abandon the nightmare of the minotaur and to substitute for him, faithful in this to the "genealogy of the myth, the seduction . . . of the bull, . . . the seduction omnipresent in all labyrinths[, the] call to exploration, the fascination with the space of the quest"; Pierre Rosenstiehl, "Les mots du labyrinth," in *Cartes et Figures de la Terre* (Paris: Centre Culturel Georges Pompidou, 1980), p. 95.

21. Gaston Bachelard, *La Terre et les rêveries du repos* (Paris: Corti, 1948), p. 257.

22. Angus Fletcher, *The Prophetic Moment: An Essay on Spenser* (Chicago: University of Chicago Press, 1971), p. 45. Michel Foucault makes a similar distinction in his discussion of the works of Raymond Roussel, distinguishing the labyrinth, "the line to infinity, the other, the lost," from the metamorphosis, "the circle, the return to the same, the triumph of the identical," the one the space of enigma, the other the space of theatre (Foucault, *Death and the Labyrinth,* p. 96).

23. Cf. Fletcher: "Because the labyrinth comes to be [Spenser's] dominant image for the profane space lying outside the temple, the labyrinth becomes the largest image for faerieland as a whole. Logically then, if we except the final apocalypse of the New Jerusalem, the heavenly City, the sacred temple space will always be found *inside* the labyrinth. The human temple assumes the existence of the labyrinth, where it finds itself" (Fletcher, *The Prophetic Moment,* p. 31).

24. Santarcangeli, *Le Livre des labyrinthes,* p. 184.

25. Allen Weiss goes even farther in this direction of multiple meanings than I do, claiming that "the labyrinth . . . is an all-encompassing signifier, embracing every contradiction and possibility from the chaotic to the structured, the aleatoric to the necessary, the sacred to the profane, and from life to death. As pure difference itself, it is no longer of the symbolic register, since the absorption of all possible symbols and signifiers can offer nothing in return, nothing in exchange"; Allen Weiss, "Impossible Sovereignty: Between *The Will to Power* and *The Will to Chance,*" *October* 36 (Spring, 1986): 133.

26. See Barthes's essay on "The Death of the Author," in his *Image, Music, Text,* trans. Stephen Heath (New York: Hill and Wang, 1977), pp. 142–48.

27. In her study of the labyrinth in contemporary Latin American narrative, which I discovered after formulating my ideas on that subject, Ludmila Kapschutschenko makes a similar point: "This fusion of the architectonic labyrinth with the literary one distinguishes the most representative creations of contemporary [Latin American] narrative"; Ludmila Kapschutschenko, *El laberinto en la narrativa hispanoamericana contemporánea* (London: Tamesis Books, 1981), p. 17.

28. This forking quality is what characterizes Umberto Eco's idea of an "open work"; see his diagram in *Lector in fabula ou la coopération interprétative dans les textes narratifs,* trans. Myriem Bouzaher (Paris: Grasset, 1985), p. 157.

29. Fritz Senn, *Joyce's Dislocutions: Essays on Reading as Translation,* ed. John Paul Riquelme (Baltimore: Johns Hopkins University Press, 1984), p. 69.

30. Brooks, *Reading for the Plot,* p. 21.

31. Bachelard, *La Terre et les rêveries du repos,* pp. 211–12.

32. Eric Gould, *Mythical Intentions in Modern Literature (Princeton: Princeton University Press,* 1981), p. 240.

33. Studies of all kinds and scopes investigate this correlation between theme and form, since its existence is an assumption that underlies much critical discourse; Frank Kermode's study of endings is a prime example as is Mikhail Bakhtin's investigation of the carnivalesque elements in Rabelais, or Erich Kahler's demonstration of the disjunctive nature of much modern literature.

Chapter 2. Labyrinth of Words: James Joyce's Ulysses

1. In my examination of the labyrinth as an overarching model for the structural design of *Ulysses,* I do not intend to deny its progressive transformations in narrative mode. For a discussion of these transformations, see the study by Karen Lawrence, *The Odyssey of Style in Ulysses* (Princeton: Princeton University Press, 1981). Whether one assumes (with David Hayman) that the different stylistic experiments suggest the presence of an "arranger," or (with Lawrence) that they signal the activity of language divorced from a single consciousness, I believe that these radical shifts in style constitute Joyce's most striking innovation; after seventy years they still seem revolutionary; David Hayman, *Ulysses and the Mechanics of Meaning* (Englewood Cliffs, N.J.: Prentice Hall, 1970).

2. In her discussion of the labyrinth as a controlling image in *Portrait,* Diane Fortuna has clearly documented Joyce's interest in the myth of the labyrinth and his familiarity with the discoveries in Crete; "The Labyrinth as Controlling Image in Joyce's *A Portrait of the Artist as a Young Man,*" *Bulletin of the New York Public Library* 76 (1972).

3. James Joyce, *Letters,* vol. 2, ed. Richard Ellmann (New York: Viking, 1966), pp. 369–70.

4. Fortuna, "The Labyrinth as Controlling Image," p. 136.

5. Building on Fortuna's interpretation, George deForest Lord suggests that Joyce's use of "to err" maintains the Vergilian echoes of labyrinthine wandering in the underworld. His subsequent idea that Stephen's credo of "to live, to err, to fall, to triumph, to recreate life out of life . . . clearly establishes a link in Stephen's mind between 'error' and 'creation'" recalls the central resonance of the labyrinth as a consummate form of art and leads us toward *Ulysses* as a distinctive modern example of the pattern; George deForest Lord, *Heroic Mockery: Variations on Epic Themes from Homer to Joyce* (Newark: University of Delaware Press, 1977), p. 124.

6. James Joyce, *Ulysses* (1922; New York: Random House, 1986), p. 160. Further references to the 1986 Random House edition are given in the text.

7. C. N. Deedes, "The Labyrinth," in S. H. Hooke, ed., *The Labyrinth* (London: Society for Promoting Christian Knowledge, 1935), p. 42.

8. See W. F. Jackson Knight, *Cumaean Gates,* in *Vergil: Epic and Anthropology* (New York: Barnes and Noble, 1967), chapters 5–7.

9. For further implications of this structure in *Ulysses,* see Marilyn French, *The Book as World: James Joyce's Ulysses* (Cambridge: Harvard University Press, 1976), pp. 4–6.

10. See the discussions in A. B. Cook, *Zeus: A Study in Ancient Religion* (Cambridge: Cambridge University Press, 1940), 1:470–80; Sir James George Frazer, *The Dying God,* vol. 4, part 3 of *The Golden Bough: A Study in Magic and Religion,* 3d ed. (New York: Macmillan, 1935), pp. 75–78; and Martin P. Nilsson, *Minoan-Mycenean Religion and Its Survival in Greek Religion* (Lund: Gleerup, 1950), pp. 374–75.

11. Fortuna, "The Labyrinth as Controlling Image," p. 175.

12. Studies of *Ulysses* by Wolfgang Iser and Marilyn French both acknowledge the primary importance of the reader as explorer of the text; see French, *The Book as World,* and Iser, "Patterns of Communication in Joyce's *Ulysses,*" in his *The Implied Reader* (Baltimore: Johns Hopkins University Press, 1974), pp. 196–223.

13. Harry Levin, *James Joyce* (New York: New Directions, 1960), p. 244.

14. For detailed conjectures about the ways in which Joyce's texts actualize this epigraph, see Fritz Senn, "The Challenge: *ignotas animum,*" in *Joyce's Dislocutions: Essays on Reading as Translation,* ed. John Paul Riquelme (Baltimore: Johns Hopkins University Press, 1984), pp. 73–84.

15. Iser, *The Implied Reader,* p. 228.

16. Senn also emphasizes the experiential dimension encoded in Joyce's text: "What makes *Ulysses* different in kind [from other literature] is that the processes are not just described but integrated, acted out, and that the book seems to want to redress, emend, adjust itself continually, and that it involves the reader in these processes"; Fritz Senn, "Righting *Ulysses,*" in *James Joyce: New Perspectives,* ed. Colin McCabe (Bloomington: Indiana University Press, 1982), pp. 13–14.

17. Cf. Richard Ellmann: "After fifty years *Ulysses* still presents itself as the most difficult of entertaining novels, and the most entertaining of difficult ones. To read it is not enough, one must read it with unwonted attention, and read it again. Even then it keeps some of its mysteries"; Richard Ellmann, *Ulysses on the Liffey* (New York: Oxford University Press, 1972), p. xi.

18. Roy K. Gottfried elucidates the balance of order and freedom—even disorder—in *Ulysses* in his study of Joyce's disruption of syntax; *The Art of*

Joyce's Syntax in Ulysses (Athens: University of Georgia Press, 1980).

19. Dorrit Cohn notes the referential instability of Molly's pronouns. They are crossroads with two or more possible directions to be taken; if we take one, and then decide we wish to take another, it necessitates retracing our steps. She also explains that, as we shall see shortly, "even as Joyce creates this impression of cryptic privacy he plants just enough signposts to guard against total incomprehensibility"; Dorrit Cohn, *Transparent Minds: Narrative Modes for Presenting Consciousness in Fiction* (Princeton: Princeton University Press, 1978), p. 229.

20. Although he does not mention the labyrinth in his discussion of Joyce's method, Iser proposes a similar view of the reader's progress through *Ulysses*. His use of such terms as "link" and "gap" to describe this activity indicates the reader's need to complete a suggested design: "The manner in which the different perspectives are thrust against one another compels the reader to search for a link between them" (Iser, *The Implied Reader,* pp. 206-7).

21. Richard Kain, "Motif as Meaning: The Case of Leopold Bloom," in Thomas Staley and Bernard Benstock, eds., *Approaches to Ulysses* (Pittsburgh: Pittsburgh University Press, 1970), p. 86.

22. Clive Hart has calculated the possible errors the reader is likely to make in threading the labyrinth of this chapter; Clive Hart and David Hayman, *James Joyce's Ulysses* (Berkeley and Los Angeles: University of California Press, 1974), p. 189.

23. Samuel L. Goldberg, *The Classical Temper* (London: Chatto and Windus, 1961), p. 268.

24. See Erwin Steinberg, "Introducing the Stream-of-Consciousness Technique in *Ulysses,*" *Style* 2 (1968): 50.

25. Richard Kain points out this difference from the *Odyssey*—that *Ulysses* expands Bloom's travels to cover three-fourths of the novel: the emphasis is thus placed on the homelessness of modern man, and the final return is eloquently undramatic and anticlimactic"; Richard Kain, *Fabulous Voyager: James Joyce's Ulysses* (Chicago: University of Chicago Press, 1947), p. 37.

26. Senn extends this process of corrective unrest to Joyce's composition of *Ulysses,* "graphic writing coinciding with corrective righting," and to the reader's reception of the text as well (Senn, *Joyce's Dislocations,* pp. 59-67).

27. In my definition of the inconclusive nature of *Ulysses'* labyrinthine structure, I concur with Karen Lawrence's contention that "*Ulysses* is definitely anti-revelatory," that "Joyce presents possibilities of meaning rather than a final revelation" (Lawrence, *The Odyssey of Style in Ulysses,* p. 7).

28. Professor Benstock made this point in a critique of my manuscript.

29. See Lord's discussion of his own and Knuth's ideas in *Heroic Mockery,* pp. 124–29.

30. For a discussion of this semiotic interpretation of Freud, see Kaja Silverman, *The Subject of Semiotics* (New York: Oxford University Press, 1983), p. 90.

31. Lord investigates the relevance of the ancient labyrinthine dance movement in literature, concentrating primarily on Pope and Joyce in his chapter on "The Mazy Dance" in *Heroic Mockery,* pp. 104–49.

32. John Amos Comenius, *The Labyrinth of the World and the Paradise of the Heart,* trans. Count Lutzow (London: Swan Sonnenschein and Co., 1901).

33. Joyce thought of Molly's monologue in similar terms; he wrote to Claud Sykes: "I am glad you liked *Circe* and *Eumeus.* Struggling with the acidities of *Ithaca*—a mathematico-astronomico-mechanico-geometrico-chemico sublimation of Bloom and Stephen (devil take 'em both) to prepare for the final curvilinear episode *Penelope*"; James Joyce, *Letters,* vol. 1, ed. Stuart Gilbert (New York: Viking Press, 1957), 164.

34. Ken Frieden studies a similarly syntactical aspect of Molly's final yeses, claiming that in addition to serving as "meaningful affirmation[s]," they also function as "meaningful connective[s]," which celebrate the generative processes of language itself as it creates; Ken Frieden, *Ulysses: Genius and Monologue* (Ithaca: Cornell University Press, 1985), p. 183.

36. C. G. Jung, *Ulysses: A Monologue,* trans. W. Stanley Dell (1949; New York: Haskell House Publishers, 1977), p. 18.

37. Anthony Burgess aptly observes of the ending: "There is nothing in all literature more joyous. The book is ended, and yet we are called back, after its final period, to the memory of a weary odyssey that contains this of Bloom's, the artist's exile and wanderings, the long years of toil and disregard: Trieste-Zurich-Paris, 1914–1921"; Anthony Burgess, *Here Comes Everybody: An Introduction to James Joyce for the Ordinary Reader* (London: Faber and Faber, 1965), p. 176. Interestingly enough for this investigation of the labyrinths in *Ulysses,* near the end of Molly's monologue Joyce juxtaposes Daedalus's name with the "calle de las siete revueltas" ("the street of the seven turnings") and other "bits of streets" (p. 779). The conjunction further specifies our sense of *Ulysses* as a labyrinthine journey in the world of the text.

38. Joyce, *Letters,* 1:170.

39. Ibid., p. 180.

40. Ibid., p. 170.

41. As Joseph Voelker points out, Molly contradicts herself frequently. These contradictions operate as additional forks in the labyrinthine path of her prose, presenting the reader with alternate choices of interpretation.

Similarly, the double negatives Voelker notices as characteristic of Molly's speech require the reader to shift direction while reading; Joseph Voelker, "Molly Bloom and the Rhetorical Tradition," *Comparative Literature Studies* 16, no. 2 (1979): 155.

42. Goldberg, *The Classical Temper,* p. 288.

43. Karen Lawrence agrees that "Penelope" cannot overcome the inconclusiveness of the book it ends: "However beautifully and powerfully Joyce presented the return to a single voice in 'Penelope,' he gives us a kind of closure that the rest of the book seems to subvert" (Lawrence, *The Odyssey of Style in Ulysses,* pp. 207–8).

44. For a discussion of these contradictions, see James Van Dyck Card, *An Anatomy of Penelope* (Toronto: Associated University Presses for Fairleigh Dickinson University Press, 1984).

Chapter 3. The Labyrinth of Time and Memory in the City

1. Michel Butor, *Répertoire I* (Paris: Minuit, 1960), p. 204.

2. Mary Lydon discusses other aspects of this connection between Joyce and Butor in her book, *Perpetuum Mobile: A Study of the Novels and Aesthetics of Michel Butor* (Edmonton: University of Alberta Press, 1980), p. 127.

3. Butor, *Répertoire I,* p. 222.

4. Michel Butor, *Essais sur le roman* (Paris: Gallimard, 1969), p. 34.

5. Michel Butor, *Passing Time,* trans. Jean Stewart (1957; London: John Calder, 1965), p. 183. Further references are given in the text.

6. Butor, *Essais sur le roman,* p. 116.

7. Georges Charbonnier, *Entretiens avec Michel Butor* (Paris: Gallimard, 1967), p. 98.

8. Arnold Weinstein makes a similar distinction regarding the analysis as opposed to the perception of time sequences in *Passing Time.* "In the form of a chart, Butor's analysis of Passing Time as a progressive series of references is clear; in the reading experience of the book, these interrelations are overwhelmingly chaotic"; Arnold Weinstein, *Vision and Response in Modern Fiction* (Ithaca: Cornell University Press, 1974), p. 106.

9. George Raillard, "L'Exemple," in Michel Butor, *L'Emploi du temps* (Paris: Editions de Minuit, 1970), p. 439.

10. R. M. Albérès maintains that when the mind cannot successfully reconstruct the temporal flow, we experience "the thickness of time, the depth of existence." Our past "takes on the shape of a labyrinth where Ariadne is memory, where we are Theseus, where the minotaur may be death"; R. M. Albérès, *Michel Butor* (Paris: Editions Universitaires, 1964), p. 37.

11. Butor reactivates symbolic church architecture—of which pavement labyrinths formed a part—in other ways as well, with Revel's descriptions of the New Cathedral's elaborate plant and animal sculptures.

12. Butor, *Essais sur le roman,* pp. 115–16.

13. In several cases I have preferred to modify the English translation in order to make clear a particular resonance of the text and have enclosed my emendations in brackets.

14. Charbonnier, *Entretiens avec Michel Butor,* p. 92.

15. Lucien Dällenbach and Georges Raillard both discuss Burton's novel as a model to be surpassed by *Passing Time* itself; Dällenbach, *Le Livre et ses miroirs dans l'oeuvre romanesque de Michel Butor* (Paris: Les Lettres Modernes, 1972), p. 71; Raillard, "L'Exemple," pp. 494–96.

16. Laura Kubinyi makes the similar point that Burton's theories fail to order Revel's experience of reality and that in the same way the traditional narratives of Theseus and Cain fail to work as models for Revel's experience, because "what is important for Revel is not a 'solution,' a *thing,* but rather a recognition of the process he is going through in his journal: the way in which the journal is constructed"; Laura Kubinyi, "Defense of a Dialogue: Michel Butor's *Passing Time,*" *Boundary 2,* 4, no. 3 (1976): 895. Arnold Weinstein notes also that "Revel abuses the myths as he does the detective story"; "Order and Excess in Butor's *L'Emploi du Temps,*" *Modern Fiction Studies* 16 (1970–71): 51.

17. Butor, *L'Emploi du temps,* p. 227; my translation. The labyrinthine resonance of the words is lost in the English translation.

18. For a discussion of the ways that the New Cathedral serves as a paradigm for this novel, and for Butor's theories concerning all works of art, see Raillard, "L'Exemple," pp. 447–51.

19. Lorna Martens understands Revel's transfer of allegiance from maps to blank pages as "a symbolic abandonment of his attempts to understand objectively in favor of attempts to transform imaginatively the things that disturb him." This change contributes to the way in which the novel progresses from "unsuccessful report to successful thing," because "Revel's experience is not *like* something (e.g. Theseus' story); instead it *is* something, namely, what Revel conceives it and describes it as being"; Lorna Martens, "Empty Center and Open End: The Theme of Language in Michel Butor's *L'Emploi du temps,*" *PMLA* 96, no. 1 (1981): 55–61.

20. Butor presents a similar view of myth in *A Change of Heart.* During his train journey, Léon Delmont comes to realize that he cannot transplant the mythology of Rome—or of his love for Cécile in that city—to his daily life in Paris. In both cases, ancient myths exist, and exert a certain attraction, but they are not substitutes for contemporary realities.

21. Lorna Martens points out that this valuation of time and energy

indicates the increase of personal and subjective dimensions as opposed to objective ones in Revel's narrative (Martens, "Empty Center and Open End," p. 55).

22. Butor, *Essais sur le roman,* p. 14.

23. Butor's remarks appear in Jean Roudaut, *Michel Butor, ou le livre futur* (Paris: Gallimard, 1964), p. 19.

24. See Weinstein's excellent discussion of Revel's personal eclipse as he participates in "the collective labor of awakening Bleston." According to Weinstein, *Passing Time* is a Bildungsroman of setting, not self. I agree that this is an important component of Revel's story, but I would not go so far as to say that Revel's "personal longings are a foil" (Weinstein, *Vision and Response in Modern Fiction,* p. 212).

25. *A Change of Heart* contains a similar substitution of literary for amorous activity: "then in that hotel room, alone, you'll begin writing a book to fill the emptiness of those days in Rome deprived of Cécile, debarred from going near her"; Michel Butor, *Passing Time and A Change of Heart,* trans. Jean Stewart (New York: Simon and Schuster, 1969), p. 551. Jacques Leenhardt notices that Revel's determination to capture the past means that he loses the present, including Rose and Ann and the possibility of their love; "L'Enjeu politique de l'écriture chez Butor," *Butor: Colloque de Cérisy,* dir. Georges Raillard (Paris: U.G.E., 1974), pp. 179–82.

26. Butor, *Essais sur le roman,* p. 16.

27. See Roudaut, *Michel Butor, ou le livre futur,* p. 153.

28. Martens agrees that "the text-thread itself becomes a labyrinth *without* a center to be reached" (Martens, "Empty Center and Open End," p. 55.)

29. Leo Spitzer, "Quelques aspects de la technique des romans de Michel Butor," *Archivum Linguisticum* 12 (1961): 177, 195.

30. Henri Ronse agrees that the narrative serves as a ritual journey for Revel and for the reader, who is "induced to penetrate the secret and complex architecture of the work"; Henri Ronse, "Le Labyrinthe, espace significatif," *Cahiers Internationaux du Symbolisme* 9–10 (1965–66): 40.

31. Butor, *Essais sur le roman,* p. 79.

32. John Barth, "Lost in the Funhouse" (1967), in *Lost in the Funhouse* (New York: Bantam, 1969). Further references are given in the text.

Chapter 4. The Minimal Labyrinth

1. Ben Stoltzfus recognizes *In the Labyrinth*'s capacity to mediate between the symbolic and the autogenerative models. He claims that "in *Jealousy* and *The Voyeur* language *seems* cleansed of metaphors, but is in

fact as contaminated as ever." The *nouveaux nouveaux romans,* on the other hand, are primarily language-oriented. *In the Labyrinth,* he believes, exists in both worlds, "hence its hypnotic mood and extraordinary power. It can be read as a metaphysical allegory or as a self-referential novel"; Ben Stoltzfus, "Alain Robbe-Grillet: The Reflexive Novel and Poetry," *Symposium* 30, no. 4 (1976): 352. For a very complete discussion of *In the Labyrinth,* see Jean-Pierre Vidal, *Dans le labyrinthe de Robbe-Grillet* (Paris: Hachette, 1975).

2. For a general discussion of the prefigurative roles that mythological titles play in modern novels, see John J. White, *Mythology in the Modern Novel,* pp. 120–30.

3. The quotation forms the title of a short piece by Robbe-Grillet, "L'écrivain, par définition, ne sait où il va, et il écrit pour chercher à comprendre pourquoi il écrit," *Esprit,* n.s. 32, no. 329 (1964): 63.

4. John Vernon investigates this process in his discussion of *In the Labyrinth:* "If the labyrinth of the novel depends upon repetition, it is established by a syntax of repetition that fragments the past and future and arranges them spatially, so the act of reading becomes a labyrinth"; John Vernon, *The Garden and the Map: Schizophrenia in Twentieth-Century Literature and Criticism* (Urbana: University of Illinois Press, 1973) p. 72.

5. For a more complete discussion of this problem, see Lucien Dällenbach's essay, "Faux portraits de personne" and the discussion that follows it in Jean Ricardou, ed., *Robbe-Grillet: Analyse, théorie* (Paris: U.G.E., 1976), 1:108–30).

6. See Jean Ricardou, *Nouveau roman: hier, aujourd'hui* (Paris: U.G.E., 1972), 1:65.

7. Bruce Morrissette has argued that the repetitions in the text reflect the activities of a narrator constructing a novel. This reading is generally convincing, though it does not account for the disconcerting shift in viewpoint that appears with the "I" of the "doctor" near the end; Bruce Morrissette, *Les Romans de Robbe-Grillet* (Paris: Les Editions de Minuit, 1963).

8. Dällenbach, "Faux portraits de personne," p. 127. For further discussion of the narrative voice in *In the Labyrinth,* see also François Jost, "Le Je à la recherche de son identité." *Poétique* 6 (1975): 479–87.

9. Alain Robbe-Grillet, *In the Labyrinth,* trans. Richard Howard (New York: Grove Press, 1960), p. 29. Further references are given in the text.

10. Bruce Morrissette has noted that the image of the labyrinth motivates these transitions: "precisely, the image of the labyrinth imposes on the author the strict necessity to justify the liaison of scenes, the displacement and the shifting of events, in a word, the transitions" (Morrissette, *Les Romans de Robbe-Grillet,* p. 164).

11. I am using these terms as they are proposed by Gérard Genette in his

Narrative Discourse: An Essay in Method, trans. Jane E. Lewin (Ithaca: Cornell University Press, 1980), p. 121.

12. Genette, *Narrative Discourse,* p. 214.

13. Gérard Genette, "Vertige fixé," in *Figures I* (Paris: Seuil, 1966), p. 89.

14. Alain Robbe-Grillet, *Dans le labyrinthe* (Paris: Seuil, 1959), p. 38. Further references are given in the text.

15. Vidal claims there are two ways to build a labyrinth. The most common one consists in tracing a plan *a priori* as a trap from which the promoter—"artist and god"—is excluded. The second way is "crazier in its freedom: to fix one's own wanderings in a composition where one is caught . . . as here [in *In the Labyrinth*] the writer is in the writing" (Vidal, *Dans le labyrinthe de Robbe-Grillet,* p. 24). Arnold Weinstein presents a more oppositional interpretation, suggesting that "the narrator's freedom of creation (and, by extension, Robbe-Grillet's freedom) can be exercised only at the expense of the soldier." This leads him to notice a crucial dimension of the labyrinth pattern: "Let us not forget that a labyrinth is a human-made rational structure, an expression of human creativity; it is terrifying only to those who do not understand its design"; Arnold Weinstein, *Vision and Response in Modern Fiction* (Ithaca: Cornell University Press, 1974), pp. 253–55. Jean Alter agrees that the narrator puts his protagonist through the horrors of the labyrinth while he himself is well sheltered; the soldier is forced to follow "a blind but fatal route towards death"; Jean Alter, *La Vision du monde d'Alain Robbe-Grillet* (Geneva: Droz, 1966), p. 47.

16. In Jean Miesch, *Robbe-Grillet* (Paris: Editions Universitaires, 1965), p. 47.

17. I differ here from Garzilli, who argues that "being able to see the city behind one's shoulder means that the self has been victorious enough over the labyrinth to say with *Thésée* 'I have done my work for the good of future humanity. I have lived'" (Garzilli, *Circles without Center,* p. 117). I agree that Robbe-Grillet may be echoing Gide's *récit* at the end of *In the Labyrinth,* but I perceive a hint of irony in the echo. As I have said, the narrator's exit from his labyrinthine text does not seem to me as triumphant, or as decisive, as that of Gide's Theseus from his.

18. As Ben Stoltzfus recognizes, the lack of a center in this, as in other modern labyrinths, also reflects a "metaphysical ennui." This ennui operates less on the reader than on the figures in the story, for Stoltzfus agrees that "open" works like *In the Labyrinth* function "with the help of the reader who thus gains access to the magic of the signifier and to the pleasure of writing"; Ben Stoltzfus, "Robbe-Grillet's Labyrinths: Structure and Meaning," *Contemporary Literature* 22, no. 3 (1981): 297–304.

19. Robert Rawdon Wilson divides literary labyrinths into "strong" and

"weak," the difference being that in strong labyrinths a wanderer experiences exclusive alternatives and is forced to choose between them. Wilson first maintains that *In the Labyrinth* is a weak variety, for the alternatives are simply recorded, not chosen by the narrator. Later on, however, he argues, as I do, that "the reader is invited to become the third-order victim of Robbe-Grillet's *Dans le labyrinthe,* transforming into a strong labyrinth what had been, for both the soldier and the doctor/narrator, evidently weak. A narrative can be a labyrinth if it seeks to capture its reader in the perplexities of interpretation. As if he were confronting Ts'ui Pên's imperceptible labyrinth, the reader will be compelled to bring together the available statutes of reading (from whatever directions) in order to constitute the narrative while playing it"; Robert Rawdon Wilson, "Godgames and Labyrinths: The Logic of Entrapment," *Mosaic* 15, no. 4 (1982): 20.

20. See, for example, nearly identical passages on pages 41 and 89 of *In the Labyrinth.*

21. Cf. Vidal: "The function of all labyrinths is to abolish time in a magical space where duration is merged with a landscape and the steps that traverse it. As such, it is already the image of the work of art" (Vidal, *Dans le labyrinthe de Robbe-Grillet,* p. 23).

22. The distinction is Genette's in *Narrative Discourse,* p. 236.

23. Alain Robbe-Grillet, "Nature, humanisme, tragédie," in *Pour un nouveau roman* (Paris: Gallimard, 1963), p. 52.

24. *In the Labyrinth* thus presents a good example of what Genette calls *paratextuality,* an indication of a relation to another or other texts contained in a title, a preface, or an epilogue; Gérard Genette, *Palimpsestes: La Littérature au second degré* (Paris: Seuil, 1982), p. 9.

25. Claudette Oriol-Boyer also recognizes the interaction of cultural past and fictional present in Robbe-Grillet's use of the labyrinth: "The labyrinth is a space of mythic origin that presupposes a certain level of culture in the reader and to which the definite article confers the status of something already said. The preposition 'in' is an invitation to consider the materiality and the actuality of what without it could have remained a dead letter"; Claudette Oriol-Boyer, "*Dans le labyrinthe* et le discours social: Propositions pour une lecture," in *Robbe-Grillet: Analyse, théorie,* ed. Ricardou, 378.

26. Julio Cortázar, *Los Reyes* (Buenos Aires: Sudamericana, 1949), p. 31.

27. Philip Booth, "Cold Water Flat," in *Letter from a Distant Land* (New York: Viking, 1957).

28. Genette, *Narrative Discourse,* p. 222.

29. Because of their particular structural features, these texts problematize the process Robert Scholes calls narrativity, the active construction of a story by a reader; *Semiotics and Interpretation* (New Haven: Yale University Press, 1982), p. 60.

30. C. N. Deedes, "The Labyrinth," in S. H. Hooke, ed., *The Labyrinth* (London: Society for Promoting Christian Knowledge, 1935), p. 42.

31. John Vernon argues along the same lines that "the walls, streets, and corridors of *Dans le labyrinthe* are the structure of the novel, the externalized mental structure of Robbe-Grillet's world. . . . The labyrinth of *Dans le labyrinthe* . . . is the perceiving mind of the novel as well as what it perceives" (Vernon, *The Garden and the Map*, p. 74.)

32. Gaston Bachelard, *La Terre et les rêveries du repos* (Paris: Corti, 1948), p. 213.

33. Ibid., p. 228.

34. See Harry Levin, "Some Meanings of Myth," in his *Refractions: Essays in Comparative Literature* (New York: Oxford University Press, 1966).

35. For a discussion of the mise-en-abyme and its use in the nouveau roman, see Jean Ricardou, "L'Histoire dans l'histoire," in *Problèmes du nouveau roman* (Paris: Seuil, 1967), pp. 171–90; and also Lucien Dällenbach, *Le Récit spéculaire: Essai sur le mise en abyme* (Paris: Seuil, 1977).

36. Lucien Dällenbach studies this aspect of Butor's work in his book on *Le Livre et ses miroirs dans l'oeuvre romanesque de Michel Butor* (Paris: Les Lettres Modernes, 1972).

37. Lucien Dällenbach, "Reflexivity and Reading," *NLH* 11 (1980): 442.

Chapter 5. Too Many Labyrinths

1. The importance of labyrinths in Borges's texts has been recognized for some time. Indeed, the quantity of critical attention to the symbol may indicate, in addition to its prominence in Borges's work, a general attraction to the image in recent literature and criticism. Enrique Anderson Imbert and Emir Rodríguez Monegal, among others, long ago suggested that the labyrinth is Borges's most characteristic symbol. See Enrique Anderson Imbert, *Crítica Interna* (Madrid: Taurus, 1960), p. 256; and Emir Rodríquez Monegal, "Símbolos en la obra de Jorge Luis Borges," *Studies in Short Fiction* 7 (1971): 70.

2. Jorge Luis Borges, *Nueva antología personal* (Buenos Aires: Emecé Editores, 1968), pp. 26–27. Only the first of the poems appears in Jorge Luis Borges, *Selected Poems: 1923–1967*, ed. Norman Thomas di Giovanni (New York: Delacorte Press, 1972), p. 221. Both of them are included in *In Praise of Darkness,* trans. Norman Thomas di Giovanni (New York: Dutton, 1974), pp. 36–39.

3. Borges has commented on the two poems in an interview and confirms there the necessity of a joint reading. "Q: Has the minotaur ever come out

of the labyrinth? *A:* Well, I have written two sonnets; in the first, a man is supposed to be making his way through the dusty and stony corridors, and he hears a distant bellowing in the night. And then he makes out footprints in the sand and he know that they belong to the minotaur, that the minotaur is after him, and, in a sense, he, too, is after the minotaur. The minotaur, of course, wants to devour him, and since his only aim in life is to go on wandering and wandering he also longs for the moment. In the second sonnet, I had a still more gruesome idea—the idea that there was no minotaur—that the man would go on endlessly wandering. That may have been suggested by a phrase in one of Chesterton's Father Brown books. Chesterton said, 'What a man is really afraid of is a maze without a center.' I suppose he was thinking of a godless universe, but I was thinking of the labyrinth without a minotaur. I mean if anything is terrible, it is terrible because it is meaningless. *Q:* Yes, that's what I was driving at. . . . *A:* . . . Because the minotaur justifies the labyrinth; at least one thinks of it as being the right kind of inhabitant for that weird kind of building. *Q:* If the minotaur is in the labyrinth, the labyrinth makes sense. *A:* Yes, if there's no minotaur, then the whole thing's incredible. You have a monstrous building built round a monster, and that in a sense is logical. But if there is no monster, then the whole thing is senseless, and that would be the case for the universe, for all we know"; L. S. Dembo, "An Interview with Jorge Luis Borges," *Wisconsin Studies in Contemporary Literature* 11 (1970): 318.

4. Emir Rodríguez Monegal, *Borgès par lui-même,* trans. Françoise-Marie Rosset (Paris: Editions du Seuil, 1970), p. 71.

5. For a more detailed description of this labyrinth, see W. H. Matthews, *Mazes and Labyrinths: Their History and Development* (1922; New York: Dover, 1970), pp. 6–16.

6. Jorge Luis Borges, *Labyrinths: Selected Stories and Other Writings,* ed. Donald A. Yates and James E. Irby (New York: New Directions, 1962), p. 109. Further references are given in the text.

7. Jorge Luis Borges, *The Aleph and Other Stories,* trans. Norman Thomas di Giovanni (New York: Dutton, 1970), p. 117. Further references are given in the text.

8. W. F. Jackson Knight, *Cumaean Gates,* in *Vergil: Epic and Anthropology* (New York: Barnes and Noble, 1967), pp. 135–287.

9. For further discussion of the labyrinth's association with Troy and with defensive rites generally, see Knight, *Cumaean Gates,* chaps. 5–7.

10. Jorge Luis Borges, *A Personal Anthology,* ed. Anthony Kerrigan (New York: Grove, 1967), p. 166. Further references are given in the text.

11. Carter Wheelock makes this point in *The Mythmaker: A Study of Motif and Symbol in the Short Stories of Jorge Luis Borges* (Austin: University of Texas Press, 1969), p. 100.

12. Knight, *Cumaean Gates,* p. 67.

13. The image operates in this manner in the poem "To Israel" because it represents the narrator's ancestral lineage: "Who can say if you are in the lost / labyrinth of age-old rivers / of my blood, Israel?" (Borges, *In Praise of Darkness,* p. 67).

14. For Ernest H. Redekop, "Borges's major philosophical interest is the nature of reality and the nature of our perception of reality and so the labyrinth in its innumerable spatial, temporal, logical and psychological forms becomes in his essays an architectonic symbol for the epistemological complexities of time and space"; Ernest H. Redekop, "Labyrinths in Time and Space," *Mosaic* 13, nos. 3-4 (1980): 95. Alfred MacAdam argues that for Cortázar the labyrinth is a model of the human mind, while for Borges it represents the chaos of the universe; *El Individuo y el otro: Crítica a los cuentos de Julio Cortázar* (Buenos Aires: La Librería, 1971), p. 32. While this may be true in the majority of cases, I believe that both Cortázar and Borges use the labyrinth to portray the complex interplay between the mind and the world, between internal and external labyrinths. For a convincing discussion of ways in which the labyrinth serves Borges as a medium in the search for artistic order, see Ludmila Kapschutschenko, *El laberinto en la narrativa hispanoamericana contemporánea* (London: Tamesis Books, 1981).

15. Anderson Imbert maintains that "for Borges, the world is chaos, and within that chaos, man is lost as if in a labyrinth. Except that man in his turn is capable of constructing labyrinths of his own. Mental labyrinths with hypotheses that attempt to explain the mystery of the other labyrinth, the one within which we are lost" (Anderson Imbert, *Crítica interna,* pp. 256-57).

16. *Borges para millones* (Buenos Aires: Corregidor, 1978), pp. 41-42.

17. Jorge Luis Borges, *Discusión* (Buenos Aires: Emecé, 1957), p. 174.

18. Georges Charbonnier, *Entretiens avec Jorge Luis Borgès* (Paris: Gallimard, 1967), pp. 131-32.

19. Borges says this in a note to the stories in *The Aleph.*

20. Shlomith Rimmon-Kenan has pointed out that certain words, like "innumerable," "countless," and "endlessly," which the narrator uses to describe his own unicursal, temporally limited trajectory, recall Ts'ui Pên's novel with its multicursal treatment of time as infinite possibility; Shlomith Rimmon-Kenan, "Doubles and Counterparts: Patterns of Interchangeability in Borges's 'The Garden of Forking Paths,'" *Critical Inquiry* 6 (1980): 645.

21. James E. Irby, "Encuentro con Borges," in *The Structure of the Stories of Jorge Luis Borges* (diss., University of Michigan, 1962), p. 305.

22. Other instances where Borges uses the labyrinth briefly to suggest the

puzzling nature of human destiny in its temporal progression occur in the poem "Elvira de Alvear," which contains "time's / Meandering river (river and maze)" and the poem "Texas," which has a "continual labyrinth of days" (Borges, *Selected Poems*, 125, 153). In addition, the labyrinth of time in the poem "To a Certain Ghost, 1940" reveals a now familiar ancient resonance of the labyrinth pattern. Here Borges admonishes De Quincey to build a protective labyrinth around England to keep out her enemies: "Weave nightmare nets / as a bulwark for your island. / Let those who hate you wander without end / inside your labyrinths of time" (ibid., p. 53).

23. Rimmon-Kenan concurs implicitly with this idea in her article on the ways in which speech and action are juxtaposed and interchanged in "The Garden of Forking Paths"; she concludes that Borges refuses to choose between a world of words and a world of acts (Rimmon-Kenan, "Doubles and Counterparts," p. 647).

24. Cf. L. A. Murillo, who maintains for Borges what we have seen to be true for other writers, that the labyrinth expresses a "unity of opposites" through its presence behind the stories; "The Labyrinths of Jorge Luis Borges: An Introductory to the Stories of *The Aleph*," *Modern Language Quarterly* 20 (1959): 259.

25. Alazraki attributes Borges's view of the minotaur to his perception of an inexorable destiny, and also compares this exposition of the idea to that in "The Life of Tadeo Isidoro Cruz (1829–1874)": "The legend of the minotaur has been refracted in a prism that grants it a new dimension: an intuition absent from the myth. This intuition—the acceptance of a destiny that knows itself to be inexorable, but whose meaning escapes the intelligence (of men or beasts)—has equal validity when it interprets that fundamental night when Cruz understood his intimate destiny of a lone wolf on seeing his own face in Martín Fierro's, or when it explains the strange reaction of the minotaur in front of the sword of Theseus, 'his redeemer'"; Jaime Alazraki, *La prosa narrativa de Jorge Luis Borges* (Madrid: Gredos, 1968), p. 28.

26. For further discussion of this point, see Frank Dauster, "Notes on Borges's Labyrinths," *Hispanic Review* 30 (1962): 142–48; and Neil Isaacs, "The Labyrinth of Art in Four Ficciones of Jorge Luis Borges," *Studies in Short Fiction* 6 (1969): 383–94.

27. Nicolás Rosa, "Borges o la ficción laberíntica," in *Nueva novela latinoamericana*, ed. Jorge Lafforgue (Buenos Aires: Paidos, 1969), 2:153.

28. I should note that earlier in his study, Rosa does recognize the "initial labyrinth of the world where the Grand Labyrinth of Literature is inscribed" (ibid., p. 146).

29. According to Jaime Alazraki, "for Borges art is something added to

the world, not its reflection (*La prosa narrativa de Jorge Luis Borges*, p. 84). Irby agrees, but does not consider these two alternatives exclusive: "Man can never fully understand the labyrinth of the universe, but he can create other labyrinths (and books), which reflect the nature of the world and also offer conjectural explanations of its meaning" (Irby, *The Structure of the Stories of Jorge Luis Borges*, p. 279).

30. According to Rosa, the most significant death that takes place in Borges's labyrinthine fictions is the death of literature itself, which is a result of the complete self-reflexiveness of Borges's writing (Rosa, "Borges o la ficción laberíntica," p. 160).

31. *Borges para millones*, p. 42.

32. C. N. Deedes, "The Labyrinth," in S. H. Hooke, ed., *The Labyrinth* (London: Society for Promoting Christian Knowledge, 1935), p. 42.

33. L. A. Murillo maintains that Tzinacán's soul-shattering confrontation with the archetypal dimension of being—the transcendence he achieves in the vision of the wheel—annuls personal motives: "Overall, exact displacement of the individual by the archetypal, or impersonal" explains the success of the story; L. A. Murillo, *The Cyclical Night: Irony in James Joyce and Jorge Luis Borges* (Cambridge: Harvard University Press, 1968), pp. 212-13.

34. When Borges describes the work of other writers as "labyrinthine," the word that signals anguish in the world becomes a term of praise in a critical context where it implies the accuracy of the writer's portrait of the world. In a complimentary introduction to Bioy Casares's *The Invention of Morel*, Borges argues that the twentieth century can still create interesting plots, complimenting De Quincey for having "plunged deep into labyrinths on his nights of meticulously detailed horror"; Jorge Luis Borges, *La invención de Morel* (Buenos Aires: Losada, 1940), p. 11. Borges also describes Spinoza as "dreaming a bright labyrinth" because he was virtually oblivious to his surroundings, and calls both Henry James and the *Roman de la rose* labyrinthine (Borges, *Obra poética*, 277; *Nueva antología personal*, 219, 189).

35. Murillo, *The Cyclical Night*, p. 226.

36. See Dauster, "Notes on Borges's Labyrinths," p. 143.

37. Alazraki, *La prosa narrativa de Jorge Luis Borges*, p. 40. More specifically, he notes that "The Garden of Forking Paths" "is organized like a labyrinth whose center is Albert's name"; Jaime Alazraki, *Versiones, inversiones, reversiones: El espejo como modelo estructural del relato en los cuentos de Borges* (Madrid: Gredos, 1977), p. 103.

38. John Barth, "The Literature of Exhaustion," *Atlantic Monthly,* August, 1967, p. 34.

39. In his article on "Forking Narratives," Christ discusses this aspect of

Borges's stories, the way that they, like actual labyrinths, often present the reader with two choices for interpretation, with a fork in the path of discourse; Ronald Christ, "Forking Narratives," *Latin American Literary Review* 7, no. 4 (1979): 52–61.

40. For a discussion of this characteristic tic, see Ana María Barrenechea, *La expresión de la irrealidad en la obra de Borges* (Buenos Aires: Paidos, 1967), p. 200.

41. Ernesto Sábato, for example, believes that "the labyrinths of Borges are of the geometrical chess-like kind that produce an intellectual anguish"; "Los relatos de J. L. Borges," *Sur* 125 (1945): 71. Bioy Casares, in reviewing the collection *The Garden of Forking Paths,* says that the book creates and satisfies the need for a literature of literature and thought"; in *Sur* 92 (1942): 62. I agree with descriptions of Borges as an intellectually oriented writer; this discussion indicates a complementary tendency in his work. Ana María Barrenechea also remarks that "few have observed that alongside that intellectual rigor exists a most exalted passion" in Borges's stories; Ana María Barrenechea, *Borges the Labyrinth Maker,* trans. Robert Lima (New York: New York University Press, 1965), pp. 23–24.

42. Borges in Irby, "Encuentro con Borges," p. 305.

43. What I have noticed within these stories about their emotional endings of greater simplicity than what precedes them and the dependence of these endings on the foregoing elaborations, Irby notes in the trajectory across time of Borges's works. According to him, several recent texts (he is writing in 1962 and cites the prose works "Borges and I," "The Witness," and the poems "Limits," "The Sand Clock," and "Adrogué") "poignantly express the author's pathetic awareness of his limitations, of his mortality. Like other recent works in the same genres, they are characterized by a compression of statement which to a large degree presupposes the minutely established context of Borges's main body of essays, stories, and poems in order to gain full effect" (Irby, *The Structure of the Stories of Jorge Luis Borges,* p. 39).

44. César Fernández Moreno, "Weary of Labyrinths: An Interview with Borges," *Encounter* 32 (1969): 12.

45. Interestingly enough, Santarcangeli finds evidence of a similar antilabyrinth attitude in the nineteenth century with its love of the simple and the natural; Paolo Santarcangeli, *Le Livre des labyrinthes: Histoire d'un mythe et d'un symbole,* trans. Monique Lacau (Paris: Gallimard, 1974), pp. 355–57.

46. Jorge Luis Borges, "The Garden," *Poemas* (Buenos Aires: Emecé, 1954), p. 37. Further references are given in the text.

47. The poem "Buenos Aires" seems to describe this process; it too passes from sunsets to labyrinths:

And the city, now, is like a map
Of my humiliations and defeats;
From that door I have seen the sunsets
And in front of that marble I have waited in vain.
Here the uncertain yesterday and the clear today
Have offered me the everyday opportunities
Of every human lot; here my steps
Weave their incalculable labyrinth.
Here the ashen evening awaits
The fruit that the morning owes it;
Here my shadow in the no less vain
Final shadow will lose itself lightly.
Not love but terror unites us;
That must be why I love it so much.

Obra poética, p. 232.

48. Along these same lines, in 1962 Irby observed that "many of [Borges's] latest poems and prose pieces have a more personal focus, a greater simplicity of utterance, than his metaphysical tales" (Irby, *The Structure of the Stories of Jorge Luis Borges*, p. 39).

49. Charbonnier, *Entretiens avec Jorge Luis Borgès*, p. 9.

50. Richard Burgin, *Conversations with Jorge Luis Borges, 1968* (New York: Avon Books, 1970), p. 38.

51. Ibarra, *Borgès et Borgès* (Paris: L'Herne, 1969), pp. 92-93.

52. Roger Caillois, introduction to "Trois Labyrinthes," *Preuves* 7, no. 71 (1957): 38.

53. Christ discusses an opposing trend in Borges's work. He argues that in contrast to De Quincey, who rises from the depths of his mazes in an inexplicable magical happening, in Borges's work "the extensive labyrinth leads up to a revelation which it itself embodies. . . . Always in Borges there is, from the start or more usually at the finish, a view from above which is the clarifying device of his plot or argument" (Ronald Christ, *The Narrow Act: Borges' Art of Allusion* [New York: New York University Press, 1969], pp. 177-78).

Christ cites as evidence for this tendency different (and, I maintain, less powerful) stories than the ones I am discussing here. The endings of "Death and the Compass" and "Examination of the Works of Herbert Quain" do provide a view over their labyrinthine contents; the endings of "The Aleph," "The Garden of Forking Paths," "The Two Kings and Their Two Labyrinths," and the others contrast with theirs. Though Christ's analysis of the stories he mentions is correct, the fact that he stresses the intellectual continuity within Borges's work rather than the emotional anguish it often reflects illustrates my earlier point that criticism has tended to concentrate on Borges's intellectual rather than his emotional force.

54. John Sturrock's comments on Asterion are applicable here. Stur-

rock suggests that "rather than to death, Borges's narratives look foward to a falling silent, to an end of narration." For him, Asterion is thus "a creature who dwells in a labyrinth and looks forward to release from it. He is an author weary of invention and longing, after the effort of duplication, for a reunification with reality"; John Sturrock, *Paper Tigers: The Ideal Fictions of Jorge Luis Borges* (London: Oxford University Press, 1977), p. 188. This interpretation coincides in many ways with my point that Borges is "weary of labyrinths," but in transferring the function of narration to so many of Borges's heroes, this reading, like Rosa's, tends to narrow the focus of the stories too much.

55. Burgin, *Conversations with Jorge Luis Borges, 1968*, p. 38.

Chapter 6. Symbolic Landscapes

1. George Painter, *André Gide: A Critical Biography* (London: Weidenfeld and Nicholson, 1968), p. 127; André Gide, *Journal: 1889–1939* (Paris: Gallimard, 1948), p. 347.

2. Garzilli agrees that Gide "is suggesting in the myth that the labyrinth is not only outside of man, but that it is chiefly within him"; *Circles without Center: Paths to the Discovery of Self in Modern Literature* (Cambridge: Harvard Univ. Press, 1972), pp. 94–95.

3. André Gide, *Two Legends: Oedipus and Theseus,* trans. John Russell (1946; New York: Random House, 1950), p. 76. Further references are given in the text.

4. In Jungian terms, as I have noted, Ariadne represents the anima—the sister side of woman—who helps the hero against the sexually powerful mother. Joseph Henderson explains this stage of human development with the dream of a patient who confused Perseus and Theseus: "They both had to overcome their fear of unconscious demonic maternal powers and had to liberate from these powers a single, youthful feminine figure. . . . (In all cultures, the labyrinth has a meaning of an entangling and confusing representation of the world of matriarchal consciousness . . .). This rescue symbolizes the liberation of the anima figure from the devouring aspect of the mother image"; Joseph Henderson, "Ancient Myths and Modern Man," in C. G. Jung, ed., *Man and His Symbols* (New York: Dell, 1968), p. 117.

5. F. F. Willetts, *Cretan Cults and Festivals* (New York: Barnes and Noble, 1962), p. 193.

6. In a 1912 note in his journal, Gide again stresses the element of individual, interior faithfulness in Theseus's journey: "Theseus venturing, endangering himself in the labyrinth, steadied by the secret thread of an interior fidelity" (*Journal: 1889–1939*, p. 375).

7. Gaston Bachelard, *La Terre et les rêveries du repos* (Paris: Corti, 1948), p. 234.

8. According to Helen Watson-Williams, Theseus's adventure closes the period of his individual growth so that he can proceed to develop his social conscience; *André Gide and the Greek Myth: A Critical Study* (Oxford: Clarendon Press, 1967), p. 135.

9. Garzilli makes the point that Icarus's story of creating his own labyrinths of thought is "true to the Ovid myth in that the labyrinth is so subtle that even its creator, Daedalus, is lost within its limits" (Garzilli, *Circles without Center,* p. 96).

10. The additional "therefore" in brackets was omitted from the translation.

11. Wallace Fowlie maintains that "one of the principal themes of the work is Gide's interest in pointing out the triumph of Theseus, in the worldly sense, and the defeat of Oedipus which brings with it an elevation of the spiritual and a renunciation of worldly values"; Wallace Fowlie, *André Gide: His Life and Art* (New York: Macmillan, 1965), p. 113.

12. Lawrence Durrell, *The Dark Labyrinth* (1947; New York: Pocket Books, 1963), p. 9). Further references are given in the text.

13. Nin wrote this in a letter to Jean Normand; reprinted in Jean Normand, "Anaïs Nin ou le labyrinthe radieux," *Etudes Anglaises* 29 (1976): 486. My epigraph is from Anaïs Nin, "Sabina," *The Chicago Review* 15, no. 3 (1962): 45. In this short story, which I will not discuss here, as in *Seduction of the Minotaur,* Nin uses the image of the labyrinth to describe the protagonist's mind.

14. Anaïs Nin, *Seduction of the Minotaur* (Chicago: Swallow Press, 1961), p. 19. Further references are given in the text.

15. Dr. Hernandez is a modern medicine man, who aids Lillian in her initiation, but not having successfully completed his own, he perishes. The other men Lillian encounters are false Ariadnes; by their own unfulfilled lives, they show her which path *not* to take.

16. Albert Camus, "The Minotaur or the Stop in Oran," in *The Myth of Sisyphus and Other Essays,* trans. Justin O'Brien (1938; New York: Random House, 1955), p. 120. Further references are given in the text.

17. Alain Costes, *Albert Camus et la parole manquante: Etude psychanalytique* (Paris: Payot, 1973), pp. 41–43.

18. In his excellent article on "*Los reyes:* Cortázar's Mythology of Writing," in *Books Abroad* 50 no. 3 (1976): 548–57, Roberto González Echevarría touches on both these topics in tracing the origins of Cortázar's "deadly game of self-referentiality" to a "primal scene" in *The Kings.* According to González Echevarría, Theseus's battle with the minotaur represents the "violent birth of writing"; yet, since Theseus flees and the minotaur dies, they "cancel each other's claim for the center of the labyrinth." The nar-

rative trace of their journeys remains, however, and this "writing is the empty labyrinth from which the minotaur and Theseus have been banished."

19. Julio Cortázar, *Los reyes* (Buenos Aires: Sudamericana, 1949), p. 11. Further references are given in the text.

20. Luis Bocaz Q. recognizes this aspect of Cortázar's labyrinth: according to him, it contains "a monster like the dark part of our being. One tries to arrive at its center, which is the center of ourselves"; Luis Bocaz Q., "*Los reyes* o la irrespetuosidad ante lo real de Cortázar," in Helmy F. Giacoman, *Homenaje a Cortázar* (New York: Las Américas, 1972), p. 453. Similarly, Steven Boldy maintains that "the labyrinth and the Minotaur are . . . ultimately the unconscious of Minos"; *The Novels of Julio Cortázar* (Cambridge: Cambridge University Press, 1980), p. 12. Eduardo Romano thinks that Cortázar takes from Gide the association of the minotaur with instinct and the suggestion that mythological spaces can be interiorized, their meanings multiplied; Eduardo Romano, "Julio Cortázar frente a Borges y el grupo de la revista *Sur*," *Cuadernos Hispanoamericanos* 364–66 (1980): 136.

21. For Alfred MacAdam, the minotaur is transformed at the end from an "artistic ruler of a hidden world and a being at once magical and peaceful, into a repressed aspect of all men." According to MacAdam, this kind of transformation occurs only once again in Cortázar's work, in Horacio Oliveira, who "precipitates his own transfiguration requiring that the world recognize and restore his individual dignity"; Alfred MacAdam, *El Individuo y el otro: Crítica a los cuentos de Julio Cortázar* (Buenos Aires: La Librería, 1971).

22. Julio Cortázar, *Hopscotch,* trans. Gregory Rabassa (1963; New York: Pantheon, 1966), p. 33.

23. Similarly, José Lezama Lima says of *Hopscotch* that "this mixture of the playful and the terrible . . . is one of its most frequently repeated constants"; "Cortázar y el comienzo de la otra novela," in Giacoman, *Homenaje a Cortázar,* p. 18.

24. Ana María Barrenechea discusses *Hopscotch* as a combination of chaos and order: Cortázar mirrors the world in a chaotic structure and at the same time suggests that more orderly patterns may be discovered within novel and world; Ana María Barrenechea, "La estructura de *Rayuela* de Julio Cortázar," in Jorge Lafforgue, ed., *Nueva novela latinoamericana, II: La narrativa argentina actual* (Buenos Aires: Paidos, 1974), pp. 222–47. I have noticed that at the particular points where the labyrinth image appears, it represents an unsatisfactory order. Taken more broadly, as a symbol for the structure of *Hopscotch* itself, the labyrinth pattern also suggests a portrait of chaos containing hints of a possible order.

25. In his discussion of *Hopscotch,* Julio Ortega recognizes the coexistence of chance and design that characterizes many labyrinthine fictions:

"The pervasive presence of chance, which is the nucleus of the character, also appears to be the mechanism of the novel itself. This is why *Hopscotch* constantly breaks its geometry, its field; its formalization is fragmented by the underlying presence of chance events that do not seem to be part of any sequence"; Julio Ortega, *Poetics of Change: The New Spanish-American Narrative,* trans. Galen D. Greaser (Austin: University of Texas Press, 1984), p. 43.

26. Cortázar speaks of these "'brink situations . . . where the ordinary categories of understanding have . . . collapsed.' Bridges and boards are symbols of passage 'from one dimension into another'"; Luis Harss and Barbara Dohmann, *Into the Mainstream: Conversations with Latin American Writers* (New York: Harper and Row, 1969), p. 241.

27. Graciela de Sola points out that la Maga is a descendant of the Ariadne in *The Kings.* Each woman is hurt by her love for a beast; "*Rayuela:* Una invitación al viaje," in Noé Jitrik et al., *La vuelta a Cortázar en nueve ensayos* (Buenos Aires: Carlos Pérez, 1968), p. 76.

28. Boldy traces the adherence of Cortázar's novels to two mythic patterns: the minotaur in the labyrinth and Orpheus descending. He emphasizes the minotaur as a lost force—"natural but rebellious and dangerous"— which an Orpheus figure must descend to Hades to recover and which is embedded in female characters. The center of the labyrinth would represent "man's reconciliation with the monster within" (Boldy, *The Novels of Julio Cortázar,* p. 31). My analysis differs from his in its focus on the design of the cognitive labyrinth in *Hopscotch* as a frustration of this natural force Oliveira seeks.

29. Saul Sosnowski agrees that "faced with La Maga who lived, who existed, Oliveira thought, reduced himself to pure intellect," though he tries to adopt her mode of being; *Julio Cortázar: Una búsqueda mítica* (Buenos Aires: Noé, 1973), p. 124.

30. Cortázar in Harss and Dohmann, *Into the Mainstream,* p. 233.

31. Alejo Carpentier's statement about the Latin American baroque expresses this same dichotomy between complex labyrinthine prose and the clearer space of revelatory vision, suggesting the centrality of the labyrinth as a metaphor for modern Latin American writing, in which *Hopscotch* is a key text: "We are baroque because we lack secure truths. Baroque language in Spain or Latin America is an entanglement in a thicket, with the hope of finding a clearing, a revelation"; epigraph in Rafael Conte, *Lenguaje y violencia: Introducción a la nueva novela hispanoamericana* (Madrid: Al Borak, 1972).

32. José Donoso, *Este domingo* (1966; Barcelona: Seix Barral, 1976), p. 169. Further references are given in the text.

33. The title comes from the epigraph, which ends thus: "The natural

inheritance of everyone who is capable of spiritual life is an unsubdued forest where the wolf howls and the obscene bird of night chatters"; Henry James, Senior, writing to his sons, cited in José Donoso, *The Obscene Bird of Night,* trans. Hardie St. Martin and Leonard Mades (New York: Knopf, 1973). Further references are given in the text.

34. Alicia Borinsky situates *Obscene Bird* in a line of fictions that exemplify Borges's model of the labyrinth-novel in "The Garden of Forking Paths," where several plots are interwoven in contradiction to each other. Such a novel "assumes the complex nature of a fiction and constitutes at the same time a critical commentary on its referential values"; Alicia Borinsky, "Repeticiones y máscaras: *El obsceno pájaro de la noche,*" *MLN* 88 (1973): 281–94.

35. José Donoso, *El obsceno pájaro de la noche* (Barcelona: Seix Barral, 1970), p. 406. So far as I can tell, the passage is missing from the English translation.

36. Hernán Vidal, *José Donoso: Surrealismo y rebelión de los instintos* (Barcelona: Aubi, 1972), p. 217.

37. For Cedomil Goic as well, the essential characteristic of this labyrinth is its enclosure, a mode which he then reveals to be the mode of the narration also; "El narrador en el laberinto," in Antonio Cornejo Polar, ed., *José Donoso: La destrucción de un mundo* (Buenos Aires: Cambeiro, 1974), p. 121.

38. Alfred MacAdam notes a related conflation in *Obscene Bird:* according to him, in Donoso's text, "the conventional distinction between art and artist . . . disappears, and the narrative itself is seen as a monstrous creator, . . . creating stories in its own image." He also points out the decentered nature of Donoso's text, a characteristic it shares with those of Joyce, Butor, and Robbe-Grillet: "The peeling off of the successive layers brings the reader no closer to the center and . . . at a certain point the process reverses itself. . . . The reader finds himself again at the beginning"; Alfred MacAdam, *Modern Latin American Narratives: The Dreams of Reason* (Chicago: University of Chicago Press, 1977), pp. 115–16.

39. Umberto Eco, *Postscript to The Name of the Rose,* trans. William Weaver (San Diego: Harcourt, Brace, Jovanovich, 1984), p. 57.

40. Umberto Eco, *Semiotics and the Philosophy of Language,* ed. Thomas A. Sebeok (Bloomington: Indiana University Press, 1984), p. 83.

41. As if implicitly recognizing these difficulties, Deleuze and Guattari do not invoke the labyrinth in defining their rhizome of cultural discourses. Their distinction between the tree that imposes the verb "to be" and the rhizome whose tissue consists of "the conjunction 'and . . . and . . . and . . . ,'" which uproots the verb "to be" suggests the mutual project of radical exploration that the labyrinth and the rhizome share; Gilles Deleuze

and Felix Guattari, *Mille Plateaux: Capitalisme et Schizophrénie* (Paris: Minuit, 1980), p. 36. But their rhizome, like Eco's, is more comprehensive than the labyrinth as a model of cultural knowledge. And furthermore, it is, according to them, "a short memory, or an anti-memory" (p. 32). Thus while the rhizome is certainly related to the labyrinth in its multiple paths, its nodes of intersection, its decentered structure, the labyrinth still encodes long-term cultural memory, both a particular pattern of logocentric memory, and the structures of progression and origin—of memory per se; the rhizome as Deleuze and Guattari describe it negates this sense of temporal progression.

42. In his discussion of Bataille's headless acephalic god with labyrinthine intestines, a "contestation of the Platonic body politic," which denies the "transcendental, logocentric formulations represented by Western deities," Allen Weiss provides another twentieth-century example of the labyrinth used as an image of a decentered spatial vision of thought similar to Eco's rhizome.

43. Umberto Eco, *The Name of the Rose,* trans. William Weaver (1980; New York: Warner Books, 1984), p. 385. Further page references are given in the text.

44. Eco, *Postscript,* pp. 57–58.

45. Eco, *Semiotics and the Philosophy of Language,* p. 84.

46. For a more complete discussion of the fictional and metafictional labyrinths in Eco's work, see Jocelyn Mann, "Traversing the Labyrinth: The Structures of Discovery in Eco's *The Name of the Rose,"* in *Anatomy of a Best-Seller: Umberto Eco's* The Name of the Rose, ed. M. Thomas Inge (Westport, Conn.: Greenwood Press, 1987).

47. Umberto Eco, *The Aesthetics of Chaosmos: The Middle Ages of James Joyce,* trans. Ellen Esrock (Tulsa: University of Oklahoma Press, 1982), p. 36.

48. Ibid., p. 54.

49. Ibid., p. 45.

50. James Dauphiné points out that both Jorges represent the memory of a library that is catholic in the sense of being universal; "*Il Nome della Rosa* ou du labyrinthe culturel," *Revue de Littérature Comparée* 60, no. 1 (1986): 18.

Chapter 7. Metafiction and Mimesis

1. Juri Lotman, "On the Metalanguage of a Typological Description of Culture," *Semiotica* 14 (1975): 101.

2. For discussion of this use of the labyrinth pattern, see W. F. Jackson

Knight, *Cumaean Gates,* in *Vergil: Epic and Anthropology* (New York: Barnes and Noble, 1967), pp. 188–203.

3. Henri Ronse maintains that "the labyrinth today constitutes one of our mythologies . . . under the influence of the problematic situation of contemporary man": "Le Labyrinthe, espace significatif," *Cahiers Internationaux du Symbolisme* 9–10 (1965–66): 28.

4. As I have suggested, because it implies both a journey through time and a form in space, the pattern of the labyrinth as it appears in these novels provokes the whole question of temporal versus spatial form in literature. For a general discussion of this question, see Jeffrey R. Smitten and Ann Daghistany, *Spatial Form in Narrative* (Ithaca: Cornell University Press, 1981).

5. The ubiquity of labyrinthine or forking narratives, as well as the anxiety for the reader they induce, is attested by the start of a short piece in the *New Yorker,* which claims that "a new kind of children's book, in which the reader is invited to intervene in the story, is being published these days. Little Bunny is lost in a dark wood, far from his cozy burrow and Mother Bunny, and Felix the Fox is offering to show him the way back. The book now offers a choice: if you think Little Bunny should accompany Felix, turn to page 8; if you think he should run away in the opposite direction as fast as possible, turn to page 11. Depending on your decision, and on later decisions that you must make, Little Bunny may or may not get out of the dark wood in one piece. This literary innovation is unsettling, for if in the past there was one thing that everybody could count on about written stories it was that they would march to predestined conclusions, without any assistance or possibility of interference from the reader, who was thus accorded the pleasurable status of interested but completely uninvolved spectator. . . . But now, . . . the child reader is handed responsibility for the outcome of the story, and a degree of nervousness and uncertainty, formerly characteristic of life but not of books, enters in"; *The New Yorker,* Nov. 25, 1985, p. 35.

6. Michel Butor, *Répertoire I* (Paris: Minuit, 1960), pp. 16–19. Dällenbach notes that "the reader is always for Butor a potential novelist"; *Le Livre et ses miroirs dans l'oeuvre romanesque de Michel Butor* (Paris: Les Lettres Modernes, 1972), p. 110.

7. Stuart Gilbert, *James Joyce's Ulysses* (New York: Vintage, 1955), p. 210.

8. In discussing man's capacity to orient himself in labyrinths, Santarcangeli notes the "domo-centric" abilities of certain "primitive" peoples, who learn early on how to return to their home village no matter how many turns their route away from it may have taken. Such an ability depends on the domicile remaining stationary, and is disrupted by our mobility, a dis-

ruption which in making labyrinths more frightening for modern than for traditional societies may explain its post-Kafkan popularity as an image of urban alienation; Paolo Santarcangeli, *Le Livre des labyrinthes: Histoire d'un mythe et d'un symbole,* trans. Monique Lacau (Paris: Gallimard, 1974), p. 366.

9. Jacques Derrida, "Structure, Sign, and Play in the Discourse of the Human Sciences," in Richard Macksey and Eugenio B. Donato, eds., *The Structuralist Controversy* (Baltimore: Johns Hopkins Press, 1972), p. 264.

10. Ibid., p. 267.

11. Tzvetan Todorov, "The Quest of Narrative," in *The Poetics of Prose,* trans. Richard Howard (Ithaca: Cornell University Press, 1977), p. 132.

12. Northrop Frye, *Fables of Identity: Studies in Poetic Mythology* (New York: Harcourt, Brace, 1963), p. 17.

13. Alain Robbe-Grillet, *Pour un nouveau roman,* p. 14.

14. "Robbe-Grillet à la question," in Jean Ricardou, ed., *Robbe-Grillet: Analyse, théorie, II: Cinéma/Roman* (Paris: U.G.E., 1976), p. 420.

15. Peter Brooks, *Reading for the Plot: Design and Intention in Narrative* (New York: Random House, 1985), p. 48.

16. Chambers claims that "for narrative as a communicational act to begin to lay claim to seduction as its own *modus operandi* is likely . . . to be a relatively modern phenomenon," related to Walter Benjamin's distinction between traditional storytellers as conveyors of experience and modern novels as posing questions about the meaning of existence. A story must arouse interest rather than provide facts. I would question the historical accuracy of Chambers's interpretation, though his distinction is a valid one. As I have suggested, it is in its capacities as a structure of questioning that the labyrinth achieves much of its force in recent fiction.

17. Roland Barthes, *Critical Essays,* trans. Richard Howard (Evanston, Ill.: Northwestern University Press, 1972), p. xvi.

18. Julia Kristeva, *Desire in Language: A Semiotic Approach to Literature and Art,* ed. Leon S. Roudiez (New York: Columbia University Press, 1980), p. 119.

19. Freud is of course the seminal precursor here; he joins the two realms of sexual and literary quest in discussing how artists transform their personal daydreams into art and in believing that "the true enjoyment of literature proceeds from the release of tensions in our minds"; "The Relation of the Poet to Day-Dreaming," in *On Creativity and the Unconscious: Papers on the Psychology of Art, Literature, Love, Religion,* ed. Benjamin Nelson (New York: Harper and Row, 1958), p. 54. I am concerned here not with the subject but with the process of discourse, with what Richard Howard (in his introduction to Roland Barthes's *The Pleasure of the Text*) has characterized as an "erotics of reading."

20. Shlomith Rimmon-Kenan recognizes the dilatory tendency of all narrative when she maintains that "the text's very existence depends on maintaining the phase of the 'not yet fully known or intelligible' for as long as possible"; Shlomith Rimmon-Kenan, *Narrative Fiction: Contemporary Poetics* (New York: Methuen, 1983), p. 125.

21. Wolfgang Iser, *The Act of Reading: A Theory of Aesthetic Response* (Baltimore: Johns Hopkins University Press, 1978), p. 10.

22. Peter Brooks, "Freud's Masterplot: Questions of Narrative," in Shoshana Felman, ed., *Literature and Psychoanalysis,* pp. 281–82.

23. Ibid., pp. 283, 292. In his discussion of nineteenth-century emplotting, Brooks reproduces the arabesque, or squiggly line—really a rudimentary labyrinth of sorts—that Balzac used as an epigraph to *La Peau de chagrin,* and which Balzac claims he took from one of the arabesques in *Tristram Shandy,* arabesques "which explicitly designate the unfettered, digressive line of Tristram's narrative, the incessant detours of its plot," and which suggest "the fantastic designs drawn by narrative desire" (Brooks, *Reading for the Plot,* pp. 59–60).

24. Linda Hutcheon, *Narcissistic Narrative: The Metafictional Paradox* (Waterloo, Ontario: Wilfred Laurier University Press, 1980), pp. 3–5.

25. Jacques Derrida, *Of Grammatology,* trans. Gayatri Chakravorty Spivak (Baltimore: Johns Hopkins University Press, 1976), p. 288.

26. That the labyrinthine palace in Crete served as an explicit connection to chthonian forces is suggested, as Santarcangeli has pointed out, by the specifically cave-like design of the central chamber known as Minos's throne room (Santarcangeli, *Le Livre des labyrinthes,* p. 112.)

27. Cited in Harry Levin, *The Gates of Horn: A Study of Five French Realists* (New York: Oxford University Press, 1966), p. 238.

28. Fernando Arrabal, *The Labyrinth,* in *Guernica and Other Plays,* trans. Barbara Wright (New York: Grove, 1969), p. 38.

29. For a more complete discussion of the labyrinth as a metaphor for the spatial arrangement of our daily lives, see Abraham Moles and Elisabeth Rohmer, *Labyrinthes du vécu: L'Espace, matière d'actions* (Paris: Librairie des Méridiens, 1982).

30. *The New Yorker,* May 26, 1975, p. 117.

31. Eduardo Mallea, *La ciudad junto al río inmóvil* (Buenos Aires: Sudamericana, 1975), p. 17.

32. Burton Pike, *The Image of the City in Modern Literature* (Princeton: Princeton University Press, 1981), p. 139.

33. James Joyce, *Ulysses* (1922; New York: Random House, 1986), p. 47.

34. Peter F. Smith, *The Syntax of Cities* (London: Hutchinson, 1977), p. 171.

35. This is a well-known component of Borges's stories which I will not

investigate here. See the discussion in David I. Grossvogel, *Mystery and Its Fictions: From Oedipus to Agatha Christie* (Baltimore: Johns Hopkins University Press, 1979), pp. 127-46.

36. Gaston Bachelard, *La Terre et les rêveries du repos* (Paris: Corti, 1948), pp. 5-6.

37. Mario Maurin continues this orientation in his article on "Zola's Labyrinths," *Yale French Studies* 42 (1969): 89-104.

38. Hermann von Keyserling, *Méditations sud-américaines*, trans. Albert Béguin (Paris: Stock, Delamain, and Boutelleau 1932), p. 36.

39. Bachelard, *La Terre et les rêveries du repos*, pp. 5-6.

40. Butor, *Répertoire II* (Paris: Editions de Minuit, 1964), p. 94.

41. J. Hillis Miller recognizes the propensity of the labyrinth pattern to expand into the representation of multiple journeys. Miller uses the metaphor of Ariadne's thread to characterize the processes of repetition in narrative; J. Hillis Miller, "Ariadne's Thread: Repetition and the Narrative Line," *Critical Inquiry* 3 (1976): 57-77.

42. Pierre Rosenstiehl, "The *Dodécadédale,* or In Praise of Heuristics," *October* 26 (Fall, 1983): 19.

43. *Science,* March, 1985, pp. 68-69.

44. Pierre Rosenstiehl, "Les mots du labyrinthe," in *Cartes et Figures de la Terre* (Paris: Centre Culturel Georges Pompidou, 1980), p. 99.

45. Another example to confirm that the labyrinth frequently symbolizes the particular complexities of modern thought is a book on contemporary culture by O. B. Hardison entitled *Entering the Maze* and organized into sections called "Taking Bearings," "Past Structures," "Mazes Lost," "Mirrors on the Wall," and "The Thread of Ariadne." In introducing his topic, Hardison maintains that "in the metaphor of the title, contemporary culture is a maze, a tangle of paths that seem to lead everywhere and nowhere at the same time." Hardison also points to the ambiguities I have described between centered and decentered structures of thought in explaining that the self as center of perception seems stable but that that stability is an illusion, and also that a basic problem in modern thought may be the persistence of a belief that at one time there was an exit to the maze; O. B. Hardison, *Entering the Maze: Identity and Change in Modern Culture* (New York: Oxford Univ. Press, 1981).

46. See Allen Weiss's discussion of Nietzsche, Bataille, and Klossowski, "Impossible Sovereignty: Between *The Will to Power* and *The Will to Chance,*" *October* 36 (Spring, 1986): 133.

47. Kristeva, *Desire in Language,* p. 99.

48. We might say of the labyrinth as a structure of thought what Kristeva says of Barthes's critical strategies, which seek "whatever can be mastered and experimented upon in schematic form; whatever is regularity, code,

formality, necessity, and algebra: in short, semiology," and yet "rise up from a base that cannot be made axiomatic and is summarized by desire and history." Thus "the empirical, unmasterable, aleatory, hazardous object appears from beyond the diagram—it supports it, gives it its buoyancy, and engenders it"; ibid., p. 118. This is just the combination of schema and desire, the encoding of rule and chance, or chaos and order, that the labyrinth embodies.

49. For a discussion of this problem of the relations between modern and postmodern literature and the female imagination, see Alice A. Jardine, *Gynesis: Configurations of Woman and Modernity* (Ithaca: Cornell University Press, 1985).

50. Sarah Kofman compares the discovery of the Mycenean civilization that preceded the Greek to the discovery of the pre-Oedipal phase of sexuality before the Oedipal period, but maintains that even though he may have "indeed discovered Mycenean civilization, Freud refuses to be Theseus, refuses to plunge into the labyrinth, into the palace, with a 'double-headed axe,' to rescue Ariadne, the fiancée. Freud's heroic model continues to be Oedipus, and for him woman is never the fiancée but still and always the mother"; Sarah Kofman, *The Enigma of Woman: Woman in Freud's Writings,* trans. Catherine Porter (Ithaca: Cornell University Press, 1985), pp. 34–35.

51. Carolyn Merchant, *The Death of Nature* (San Francisco: Harper and Row, 1980).

52. Marcel Brion, *Léonard de Vinci* (Paris: Gallimard, 1952), p. 201.

53. Hélène Cixoux and Catherine Clément, *The Newly Born Woman,* trans. Betsy Wing (Minneapolis: University of Minnesota Press, 1986), p. 69.

54. Kristeva uses the semiotic to mean "a distinctive mark, trace, index, the premonitory sign, the proof, engraved mark, imprint—in short, a *distinctiveness* admitting of an uncertain and indeterminate articulation because it does not yet refer (for young children) or no longer refers (in psychotic discourse) to a signified object for a thetic consciousness (this side of, or through, both object and consciousness)" (Kristeva, *Desire in Language,* p. 134.)

55. See the historical account of the labyrinth at Versailles, *Le Labyrinthe de Versailles, 1677. Présenté par Charles Perrault avec des gravures de Sébastien Le Clerc,* ed. Michel Conan (Paris: Editions du Moniteur, 1982).

56. Luce Irigaray, *Speculum of the Other Woman,* trans. Gillian C. Gill (Ithaca: Cornell University Press, 1985), p. 346.

57. Weiss, "Impossible Sovereignty," p. 135.

58. Kristeva, *Desire in Language,* p. 136.

59. Jardine, *Gynesis,* pp. 114–15.

60. This same kind of integration is the goal of Jungian therapy, which often uses the image of the labyrinth to picture the path to individual development: "According to analytical psychology, the appearance of Ariadne, the outer woman who lends help to the hero, expresses the possibility of a collaborative relationship between the masculine ego and the inner feminine image, which Jung calls the *anima*. The act of courage, by which the hero penetrates the labyrinth and confronts the Minotaur, transforms the conscious attitude, and this transformation is connected with the encounter with the inner feminine element, that is, with a dimension other than the usual one of consciousness and the ego"; Aldo Carotenuto, *The Vertical Labyrinth: Individuation in Jungian Psychology,* trans. John Shepley (Toronto: Inner City Books, 1985), p. 51.

61. Kristeva, *Desire in Language,* p. 137.

62. Michel Foucault, *Death and the Labyrinth: The World of Raymond Roussel,* trans. Charles Ruas (New York: Doubleday, 1986), pp. 69-70.

63. See David Grossvogel's discussion of these mental processes in his *Mystery and Its Fictions,* pp. 1-2.

64. For more complete discussions of the history of the labyrinth, see W. H. Matthews, *Mazes and Labyrinths* (1922; Detroit: Gale, 1969); W. F. Jackson Knight, *Cumaean Gates,* in *Vergil: Epic and Anthropology* (New York: Barnes and Noble, 1967); and Paolo Santarcangeli, *Le Livre des labyrinthes: Histoire d'un mythe et d'un symbole,* trans. Monique Lacau (Paris: Gallimard, 1974).

65. Francis Thompson, *The Hound of Heaven* (London: Burns and Oates, Ltd., 1917), *p.* 1.

66. María Rosa Lida's discussion of the labyrinth as a symbol for elaborate rhetoric in the late Middle Ages leads me to believe that what I have characterized as the labyrinth's strong metafictional dimension in the modern and contemporary periods may have substantial roots in medieval and Renaissance rhetorical traditions, but the investigation of that possibility is beyond the scope of this study. See María Rosa Lida de Malkiel, *Juan de Mena* (Mexico City: Nueva Revista de Filología Hispánica, 1950), pp. 262-63.

67. Quoted in Weiss, "Impossible Sovereignty," p. 130.

68. Lotman, "On the Metalanguage of a Typological Description of Culture," p. 111.

69. See Layard, "Maze-Dances and the Ritual of the Labyrinth in Malekula," *Folklore* 48 (1937): 144-45.

70. See Santarcangeli, *Le Livre des labyrinthes,* p. 296.

71. Recently, in his *Le Tombeau de Minos* (*The Tomb of Minos*), the French novelist Dor-Rivaux calls on this aspect of the labyrinth design to symbolize the discouragingly regulated nature of contemporary life and

perhaps even of all fiction. After each section of text, he includes a small design of the labyrinth at Chartres, and the book ends with a note to these emblems, concluding that their unicursal path "implies that one essentially requires people who enter the 'maze' to follow a particular trail; to go along one road and not another"; Dor-Rivaux, *Le Tombeau de Minos* (Paris: Albin Michel, 1978), p. 220.

72. See the discussions of liminality by Gustavo Pérez Firmat, in his *Literature and Liminality: Festive Readings in the Hispanic Tradition* (Durham, N.C.: Duke University Press, 1986), and George Yúdice, "Marginality and the Ethics of Survival," a paper presented to the International Association of Philosophy and Literature, Lawrence, Kansas, May 1987.

73. Nicolás Rosa, "Borges o la ficción laberíntica," in *Nueva novela latinoamericana,* ed. Jorge Lafforgue (Buenos Aires: Paidos, 1969), 2:147.

74. Gustav René Hocke, in the chapter of his study on Mannerism entitled "The World as a Labyrinth," suggests that he who constructs labyrinths will always be nostalgic about the pleasure of freedom—of any essentially "simple" experience; see Gustav René Hocke, *Labyrinthe de l'art fantastique: Le maniérisme dans l'art européen,* trans. Cornelius Heim (Paris: Gonthier, 1967), p. 247.

Index

Labyrinths of Language

Designed by Chris L. Smith.
Composed by A. W. Bennett, Inc., in Sabon text and display.
Printed by the Maple Press Company, Inc., on S. D. Warren's 50-lb. Sebago Eggshell
Cream offset paper and bound in GSB and stamped in silver.